TECHNOLOGICAL INNOVATIONS IN PARTICIPATORY HEALTH RESEAR WITH ADOL

This book offers a critical overview of participatory methods in health research with adolescents. It introduces participatory methodology as an ethos and practice, before covering specific paradigms and methods, including participatory action research, community-based participatory research, co-design, co-creation, participatory design, peer research, youth as researchers, integrated knowledge translation and youth–adult partnerships. Specific technologies are also covered, such as mobile apps and video games, sonification, photovoice, visual mapping and internet-based approaches. A guidebook to both theory and methods, it demonstrates technology's potential to drive impactful research and inclusive study design.

LEONOR RODRIGUEZ ESTRADA is a lecturer at the University of Edinburgh in psychological research methods, specialising in mixed methods applied to research with children and adolescents. With a focus on chronic illnesses and family dynamics, her research endeavours are driven by a commitment to advancing innovative, creative methods while upholding scientific rigour and ethical standards.

TECHNOLOGICAL INNOVATIONS IN PARTICIPATORY HEALTH RESEARCH WITH ADOLESCENTS

LEONOR RODRIGUEZ ESTRADA
University of Edinburgh

CAMBRIDGE
UNIVERSITY PRESS

CAMBRIDGE
UNIVERSITY PRESS

Shaftesbury Road, Cambridge CB2 8EA, United Kingdom

One Liberty Plaza, 20th Floor, New York, NY 10006, USA

477 Williamstown Road, Port Melbourne, VIC 3207, Australia

314–321, 3rd Floor, Plot 3, Splendor Forum, Jasola District Centre, New Delhi – 110025, India

103 Penang Road, #05-06/07, Visioncrest Commercial, Singapore 238467

Cambridge University Press is part of Cambridge University Press & Assessment, a department of the University of Cambridge.

We share the University's mission to contribute to society through the pursuit of education, learning and research at the highest international levels of excellence.

www.cambridge.org
Information on this title: www.cambridge.org/9781009450461

DOI: 10.1017/9781009450485

When citing this work, please include a reference to the DOI 10.1017/9781009450485

First published 2025

A catalogue record for this publication is available from the British Library

Library of Congress Cataloging-in-Publication Data
NAMES: Rodriguez-Estrada, Leonor, author.
TITLE: Technological innovations in participatory health research with adolescents / Leonor Rodriguez-Estrada, University of Edinburgh.
DESCRIPTION: Cambridge, United Kingdom ; New York, NY : Cambridge University Press, [2024] | Includes bibliographical references and index.
IDENTIFIERS: LCCN 2024036219 (print) | LCCN 2024036220 (ebook) | ISBN 9781009450461 (hardback) | ISBN 9781009450478 (paperback) | ISBN 9781009450485 (ebook)
SUBJECTS: LCSH: Teenagers–Health and hygiene–Research–Technological innovations.
CLASSIFICATION: LCC RA777 .R638 2024 (print) | LCC RA777 (ebook) | DDC 613/.0433–dc23/eng/20240814
LC record available at https://lccn.loc.gov/2024036219
LC ebook record available at https://lccn.loc.gov/2024036220

ISBN 978-1-009-45046-1 Hardback
ISBN 978-1-009-45047-8 Paperback

What we know about the world is influenced by who gets to ask and who gets to answer questions.

L. Terry and V. Cardwell, Refreshing perspectives: Exploring the application of peer research with populations facing severe and multiple disadvantage

Contents

Figure

Tables

Introduction

The origin of this book comes from my life story. As a child, one of my favourite games was pretending to be a teacher, and I wanted to be one. My sister was usually a pupil, with my two aunties the 'naughty' ones. I had a board and what seemed like loads and loads of stationery. That last bit never changed (and never will!). I was generally always a very good student and I didn't do the adolescence bit very well, to be very honest. I was in therapy for over 10 years, and I loved having an hour of my life where somebody sat down and listened and cared about what I had to say (not that I did not have that in my life; it was just different). Therapy saved me from having a very different story. The time came when I had to decide what I wanted to be 'for real' this time. My auntie (one of the naughty pupils and basically a person who was a significantly positive influence in my life) suggested that if my goal was to help children maybe I could do that if I became a psychologist. So here I am, a psychologist writing about research methods (so that plan did not work out so well either).

Generally, I managed to stay away from the subject of adolescence and anything to do with it for as long as I could (and that was the plan forever and ever). Then I ended up doing my PhD and the topic of illness, cancer and families came up as available to research, which I was very interested in. This project, however, involved adolescents. It was certainly not my first choice. Talking to people or, more probable, talking to myself, I decided to try this adolescence "thing" again; if anything I could learn a thing or two, and I could always rely on the fact that I was not one of them anymore.

To cut a long story very short, I worked with adolescents who were experiencing maternal cancer. I loved it. I got to know some of them and they were smart, resilient, kind, strong and basically just wonderful. Working with them healed a difficult time in my life. I liked them (I still really do!). Some of them only needed somebody to sit and listen to them for an hour, which was not a big ask. They have a lot of interesting things to say, if they are allowed to.

I then worked in the UNESCO Child and Family Research Centre, University of Galway, where children and adolescents were the centre, the ethos, the language spoken, a language that I learnt to speak myself watching them design their own research, present at conferences, film their own dissemination videos, talk to policy makers . . . in fact, just children and adolescents taking over their worlds and making it better for themselves and others. And it was really fascinating to watch them do it!

So, this book comes from my conviction that participatory research with adolescents is interesting, useful and important. The technology aspect is an area I am interested in personally and is one that adolescents are captured and fascinated by (kind of a win-win situation!), and health is my other favourite topic.

As researchers and mostly as human beings we have an ethical duty to make sure the adolescents we work with are better off than they were when we met them. Evidently that means not worse and not the same, but better, stronger, wiser, happier, prouder. . . This is independent of methodology and methods, world views, experiences and beliefs; this is an ethical duty as adults. Actions and changes in policy and practice can take a long time; however, providing feedback and a clear route of how the change will be achieved is fundamental for adolescents involved in research to know.

Stafford et al. (2003) described primary school children as enthusiastic about being consulted about their opinions by adults, while secondary school adolescents were not. The experiences of consultation and participation may not be positive ones, particularly if they are not representative and if they lack any impact. 'A bad experience of consultation can result in cynicism about future attempts, a good experience can lead to more positive attitudes' (Stafford et al., 2003, p. 363). This a book about ensuring that participation and consultation with adolescents is a positive experience for them – not perfect, just positive. You may have one chance; be sure you use it wisely.

This book is focused on participation, which suggests that it is coming from a perspective where participation is considered a 'good thing'; however, I wish to give careful consideration as well to circumstances and situations where participation may not be a good thing. Farthing (2012) described some of the theories and corresponding criticisms of participation. Its limitations are also real, in that it can be unhelpful to individual adolescents and to adolescents as a social group (Farthing, 2012).

Researchers should be very aware that 'consulting poorly is worse than not consulting at all' (Stafford et al., 2003, p. 372).

Participation is supported by a rights-based approach. Participation is good because it is a right of the adolescent, and good societies are those which adhere to international legal obligations that mandate their rights be respected. Participation can also be a form of social control, inviting adolescents to participate to ensure they support specific views, which is a violation of their right to freedom and equality (Farthing, 2012).

Empowerment is another justification for participation, supported within a democratic and inclusive society. According to Esau et al. (2016) empowerment is multifaceted and may have different meanings to different cohorts such as scholars, practitioners and the public. Empowerment in the context of health can be defined as 'an act of granting autonomy, a process of granting power and control over health outcomes, or as psychological state of feeling enabled' (Esau et al., 2016, p. 60). Understanding what adolescents identify as being important to their health is fundamental for health promotion efforts to be successful (Esau et al., 2016). Citizen engagement, public participation and the involvement of people with lived experience to redesign and improve health systems represents the new 'Zeitgeist – the spirit of our times' (Palmer et al., 2019, p. 247), therefore this book comes at a critical time.

The counterargument for empowerment would be that participation can be a way to subjugate adolescents to bring them under more social control. Empowerment may be undesirable in children and adolescents, assuming that there are things they cannot do or cannot understand 'before their time'. There are situations whereby experts or adults may know best and produce better outcomes (Farthing, 2012).

Participatory research can build a sense of trust and collaboration between researchers and participants which enables a more inclusive and equitable research process (Labusch et al., 2024). Participation can also be a way to improve policy, practice and service delivery. This argument, however, is justified by a neoliberal society where citizens are consumers of state services. Both adolescent knowledge and the experience of professionals are needed to achieve efficient outcomes to improve service delivery (Farthing, 2012). Fox (2013) commented that good participatory research should be a 'threat' to the institutions and powerful forces which mediate adolescents' lives and, I would add, participatory research should question the current status quo and ensure the lives of adolescents will be changed for the better as a result of the research at an individual level (at least) and at an institutional level (ideally).

Participation can also be justified from a developmental perspective. The argument in favour is that participation enables adolescent individual and personal development. Radical critiques suggest that this can lead to quietening opposing voices by developing more social citizens (Farthing, 2012).

So overall, beyond debating who is right or wrong, it is more useful for researchers and adolescents to be aware of these arguments (for and against participation) and how they may be relevant or not in a specific context and time. Both adolescents and researchers are entitled to make informed decisions. By no means is it the intention of this book to promote a passive approach to adolescent participation but instead a critical and evidence-based one that will maximise the best possible outcomes for adolescents as individuals and us researchers as part of the same social group. Defining participation is challenging; the book suggests degrees of participation is a better approach and a valid one. Participation happens within a political, social, legislative and specific time as well as between individuals with different beliefs, needs, characteristics, and well ... challenges in this complex scenario are expected. Anticipate challenges but also look forward to overcoming them, making participation part of your world, and enjoying this work as well.

CHAPTER 1

Health Research with Adolescents

> [S]haring power ... is particularly vital in working with youth who are subordinated in multiple realms of their lives.
>
> L. Rodriguez and T. Brown, 'From voice to agency: Guiding principles for participatory action research with youth'

Chapter Highlights

1. Adolescence is a complex and multifaceted concept as biology, age, psychology, culture, content and time have an impact on this definition.
2. Adolescents should be included in health research and service development, but there are still significant barriers to their participation.
3. Participation is a multidimensional concept.
4. Participatory methods is an umbrella term encompassing several epistemological approaches and methods.

This chapter is focused on understanding crucial concepts including adolescents, participatory research and health research and technology, and how and why these concepts can be related to each other. The chapter begins by providing a definition of adolescence. Why? Because depending on your culture and your background, this might mean something different to you. Participatory research is also an umbrella term for a series of methods which share commonalities but also important variations. These methods serve different purposes and uses. Some are more suitable to answer specific research questions than others. Therefore, a guide to this variety of methods – together with examples, facilitators and challenges – is given in this chapter.

1.1 What Is Adolescence?

The term adolescence originated from the Latin term *adolescere* which means 'to grow maturity' (Banati & Lansford, 2018). It is important to acknowledge that adolescence is a social construction, defined by specific communities and cultures (Sawyer & Patton, 2018). Historically, adolescence begins with the onset of puberty (biological) and ends with social role transitions into adulthood (social), for example, employment, financial independence and parenting (Sawyer & Patton, 2018). The definition of adolescence, however, varies by country and cultural context (Patton et al., 2016), as well as historical time and location (Wulf-Andersen et al., 2021a).

Adolescence has been defined as a transitional phase of life between the two more stable stages of childhood and adulthood (Wulf-Andersen et al., 2021a). There are also biological changes that characterise this developmental stage (Patton et al., 2016). Adolescence is characterised by brain development and interaction with the social environment shaping the capabilities adolescents will bring to their adult life (Patton et al., 2016). The physical, psychological and cultural expressions of adolescence can appear at different times in a person's life (Banati & Lansford, 2018). Adolescents should not be understood as a specific age cohort (Wulf-Andersen et al., 2021a). Adolescents in this stage acquire the physical, cognitive, emotional and economic resources that are the foundation for health and well-being later in life (Patton et al., 2016).

Adolescence has also been explained by theories of adolescent development. For example, Erik Erikson proposed an eight-stage model. The identity versus role confusion stage covers 12–18 years of age, with people of this age typically described as adolescents. In this stage adolescents affirm their ideals, values and sense of self, as well as experience rejection, which may lead to insecurity and confusion. Another classical theory of development is that of Jean Piaget. Adolescence corresponds to the fourth and last stage of his theory, the formal operational stage. This is a stage of the establishment of reasoning about tangible, hypothetical and abstract objects and manipulating mental representations. These classic models of development are informative; however, research has identified that not all children and adolescents follow these developmental trends. Determining adult–child communication solely by developmental ages and stages can be misleading, as this may underestimate or overestimate children's and adolescents' abilities (Alderson et al., 2006), particularly those who have experienced illness or disability from a young age.

Wulf-Andersen et al. (2021a) defined adolescence as 'a life stage in which social positions and processes shape young people's ability to make choice, and their life chances, in particular historical and societal contexts' (p. 12). Therefore, research and methods must be capable of dividing up and capturing the commonalities and differences between adolescents. Adolescents and researchers are not a homogeneous group and therefore specific research activities may impact young people and researchers differently (Wulf-Andersen et al., 2021b). Research must not privilege the views and perspectives of specific groups of children and adolescents over others. According to Hampshire et al. (2012) differences in age, gender, class, wealth, disability, family situations and personality are bound up in complex power relations that ultimately shape the research carried out with these children and adolescents.

Even though adolescence should not be defined exclusively by age, sometimes this is needed to define the samples or populations that will be included or excluded from a research study. This has a practical justification; for example, the research resources and capacities for inclusion and other developmental markers of a specific culture or group where there is an agreement of adolescents as a group. Considering the limitations of this generalisation, defining a group by age may be justified. And, if so, the next challenge is to define the age boundaries of adolescence, on which there is no consensus either.

Under the United Nations Convention of the Rights of the Child (UNCRC), a child is defined as anybody under the age of 18. The World Health Organization defines adolescents as aged between 10 and 19 years of age, whereas youth is between 10 and 24 years of age (King et al., 2022). Different definitions can also be found in published research studies; however, these use different groupings and terminology. For example, youth (15–24 years) (Patton et al., 2016), young people (10–24 years) (Patton et al., 2016), youth and teenagers (13–18 years) (Hart, 1992) and young people is the umbrella term to refer to both groups (Hart, 1992). Overall, the terminology used is complex and often differs across countries and social contexts (Gibbs et al., 2020).

Age Categories

For reporting age disaggregated data in adolescent research, Patton et al. (2016) provided the following age categories:

1. Early adolescence: 10–14 years
2. Late adolescence: 15–19 years
3. Young adulthood: 20–24 years

1.2 Participatory Health Research with Adolescents

Investing in adolescent health and well-being is beneficial today but the impact lasts over decades and into the next generation (Patton et al., 2016). Adolescent morbidity has an obvious consequence but also a cost for society. It is necessary to consider public accountability of money invested in adolescent programmes to reduce risk and improve adolescent health if these programmes are ineffective (Rogers et al., 1994). Adolescence is a time when individuals make increasingly complex decisions affecting their health and wellness (Flicker & Guta, 2008). Adolescents' healthy development involves making informed decisions, managing risks and negotiating options regarding their health (Flicker & Guta, 2008). There are major knowledge gaps in adolescent health needs and, therefore, there is a lack of evidence base for action, civil structures for advocacy and the systems to ensure intersectoral action (Patton et al., 2016). Additionally, participation of adolescents in healthcare may be more viable in some countries than others. In some jurisdictions their involvement is compulsory. For example, the Medical Treatment Agreements Act (WGBO, 1995) is a Dutch Act where adolescents between 12 and 15 years can co-decide with their parents about their treatment. Adolescents over 16 years of age can make treatment decisions on their own. According to Van Staa et al. (2009) these opportunities are limited in primary care. Particularly relevant to participatory methods, adolescents are often excluded from research that is necessary to improve their health and inform health policy (Society for Adolescent Medicine, 2003).

Research has a significant role in ensuring healthcare is sustainable, effective, efficient, safe and appropriate; however, society and health systems are not currently getting the maximum benefits from research findings (Jull et al., 2017). Adolescent research is also disproportionately focused on adolescents in high-income Western contexts and is mostly published in English (Banati & Lansford, 2018). Effective adolescent health programmes need adolescents' involvement in designing programme objectives, policy development and allocation of resources (Ballonoff et al., 2006). Health disparities that adolescents experience will continue until they are fully engaged as partners and leaders in addressing social inequalities and health issues as well as planning and evaluating health programmes targeted at them (Ballonoff et al., 2006). Younger adolescents are usually missing from the data, which mostly focuses on those aged 15 years or over (Patton et al., 2016). Effective planning responses require data that is timely, developmentally appropriate and locally relevant. Ideally, data should be longitudinal and global, enabling analysis of differences between countries over time (Patton et al., 2016). Currently, low- and middle-income countries are dependent on global surveys for their own health policy and planning (Patton et al., 2016).

On a positive note, research with children and adolescents is increasingly using participatory approaches to inform health resources and interventions (Freire et al., 2022). Participatory health research is based on the premise that children and adolescents should be involved in decision-making processes about their health as this is a way to enhance and promote their self-esteem and positive self-regard, which can subsequently enhance their well-being (Coyne, 2006). Including adolescents in health-care agendas is an acknowledgement that they are important consumers of healthcare, individually and collectively (Coad & Shaw, 2008). Giving citizens choice about services can improve standards, efficiency and increase patient-centred care (Coad & Shaw, 2008). Children and adolescents can express their views on living with chronic illness and disability, as well as communicate their needs and provide ideas on how to improve the quality of healthcare services (Van Staa et al., 2009). Coyne (2006) asked children about being involved in decision-making and they expressed a need for consultation and information to help them understand their illness, prepare themselves for procedures and take actions towards 'getting well'. The study found, however, that opinions were often underused, with some expressing a lack of consultation about bed allocation, food preferences, waking time and sleeping time.

Adolescence is the developmental stage where specific health problems emerge due to the beginning of sexual activity, emotional control and risky behaviour (Patton et al., 2016). Adolescence is also a time of academic disengagement and emerging psychopathology (Ozer et al., 2010). Globally, adolescents can experience health issues as a consequence of unhealthy lifestyles, unemployment, lack of family stability, environmental issues, armed conflict and mass migration (Patton et al., 2016). Adolescents have several unmet needs in their healthcare, and they may experience barriers due to inexperience and lack of knowledge about how to access it; they can also experience confidentiality breaches (Patton et al., 2016), which could lead to a loss of confidence in the system overall. Adolescents should have accurate knowledge about local services and they should know where to turn to if they need help and advise their peers about where to find the help they need as well (Oppong-Odiseng & Heycock, 1997). Over time, physical health in adolescents has improved; however, mental health issues have increased (Department of Health, 2003). Mental health issues are significant in adolescents as it is the age when mental health outcomes persist and can even worsen over time, even for adolescents in clinical care (Cheng et al., 2018). A significant challenge is that research on adolescent health lacks indicators on topics such as mental health, substance disorders, obesity, physical activity and fruit and vegetable intake (Patton et al., 2016). Adolescence, however, is also the stage where opportunities for good health are created for adulthood (Whitehouse et al., 2013).

Overall, the way to achieve a fairer and healthier society is to improve health and overcome health inequalities early in life (Department of Health, 2003). Almost all the countries in the world have ratified the UN Convention on the Rights of the Child; however, there are vast differences in legal frameworks which underpin adolescent health. Additionally, in some countries customary or religious laws take precedence over adolescent rights (Patton et al., 2016). At a practical level, some hospital policies support child-centred services, for example. This means children and adolescents should be partners in decision-making and exercise choice about their health and care (Coyne, 2008). Despite this, children and young people are rarely involved in consultations and decision-making regarding their healthcare. Coyne (2008) identified some of the reasons for this as:

1. not knowing health professionals
2. not wanting to hear bad news
3. fear of asking questions and causing trouble
4. being ignored
5. not being believed
6. experiencing difficulties contacting health professionals
7. not being listened to
8. difficulty understanding medical terms.

Healthcare professionals and parents have a significant role in enabling adolescent participation (Coyne, 2008). Healthcare professionals usually direct conversations mostly to parents, and children and adolescents become accustomed to playing a passive role or may assume this role to avoid censorship from adults (Coyne, 2008). The situation can be more difficult for specific groups of adolescents, as they experience added exclusion and vulnerability; for example, the needs of ethnic minorities, LGBTQ+ people, those with disabilities and those who are homeless or in juvenile detention are usually invisible (Patton et al., 2016). Seldom are children and adolescents with disability and chronic illnesses involved in health service development (Sloper & Lightfoot, 2003; Watson et al., 2006). Adolescent involvement is possible and can generate benefits for them. There is currently, however, a gap in children's and adolescents' own views of their experiences in service development (Sloper & Lightfoot, 2003). There is a lack of evaluative research to determine if adolescents' decisions and choices are acted upon and if healthcare providers are responsive to their needs (Coad & Shaw, 2008). Hallström and Elander (2004), for example, explored decision-making of parents and children aged 5 months to 18 years during hospitalisation and identified that children and parents made few decisions themselves and, if they disagreed with a decision, on very few occasions was that reconsidered. The authors argue that children and adolescents may not have the knowledge to make decisions about medical interventions but that they can participate when decisions are made.

When including adolescents in research and service development, methodology is fundamental. Stafford et al. (2003) suggested that there is an increasing tendency in research with children and adolescents to use a combination of methods, as this can help overcome the limitations of a single method. It has been established that a single method cannot capture the fullness of the experience of participants and therefore the use of multiple methods can also help active engagement (Stafford et al., 2003). According to Larsson et al. (2018), methodology can convert a traditional top-down research paradigm into a more egalitarian one, increase credibility and reduce biases by triangulating different data sources. Methods that enable participants to actively express themselves – including drawing, painting, storytelling, software, digital tools and mapmaking – achieve higher levels of participation (Larsson et al., 2018). These methods are not a guarantee of a participatory approach, but they can promote a sense of control in participants that may lead to more active participation (Larsson et al., 2018).

Setting is another important element to consider when carrying out participatory health research. For example, Sartain et al. (2000) showed that episodes of illness and unfamiliar environments (e.g. hospital settings) may have an effect on the cognitive and behavioural activities of children. This may also have an impact on research and data collection and the answers participants provide as a result of a crisis or a specific situation, which may not have been their answer in different and more familiar circumstances.

Sommer et al. (2021) suggest that it is essential to use creative approaches that have rigorous designs, capture the richness of the data and empower adolescents to capture their perceptions, desires, experiences and recommendations. Additionally, Sommer et al. (2021) suggest that data triangulation can be very useful to gather in-depth sensitive data such as that regarding adolescent alcohol consumption and sex life. Triangulation can combine, for example, participatory and more traditional methods such as in-depth interviews.

Table 1.1 *Methodologies by research objective*

Research Purpose	Suggested Methodologies
1. You want to understand what adolescents perceive as a problem, the context of adolescents' lives and where there is potential for most impact.	Surveys Co-design workshops Focus groups Interviews Online discussions Facebook polling
2. The area of focus, impact and outcomes are already defined. You want to use these methods to understand how the issues/topics should be positioned in a meaningful and engaging format which will lead to developing concepts and strategies relevant for adolescents.	Focus groups Brand testing Friendship interviews Online discussions Card sorting Co-design workshops Crowdsourcing
3. You have concepts, prototypes, products and services. You want to know if these are engaging for adolescents and how to improve them.	Co-design workshops Prototypes Usability testing Pilot testing Mobile diaries

Hagen et al. (2012) provided useful suggestions for adequate methodologies by research purpose or objective, as shown in Table 1.1.

There is also no 'right method' as different methods will suit different adolescents; every method will suit a different research purpose, so the 'fit' should be carefully considered (Lightfoot & Sloper, 2002). The skills and experience of the research team are therefore crucial to select the most suitable method or combination of methods according to the research aims, objectives and resources available.

Incorporating adolescents with special needs and characteristics is a challenge. Working with adolescents with a chronic illness or disability requires serious consideration regarding their needs. For example, Lightfoot and Sloper (2003) experienced challenges with data collection with adolescents as they wanted to carry out group interviews but participants with cystic fibrosis, for example, were at a high risk of cross-infection in group situations. This shows that researchers should consider the specific diagnoses of potential participants when designing studies. Additionally, children with chronic illnesses should not be treated as a homogenous group, but their abilities, diversities and specific illness needs should be taken into consideration (Sartain et al., 2000). B. Young et al. (2003) identified that managing communication with adolescents who have a life-threatening chronic illness can be complex, as parents have an important role in communication, and they can both facilitate and constrain that communication. Health professionals, as well as researchers, need to be aware of the executive roles parents have when professionals seek a relationship with adolescents (B. Young et al., 2003). This may explain why participation of adolescents with chronic conditions in medical decision-making and service evaluation is limited (Van Staa et al., 2009).

Burstein et al. (2005) carried out a study with adolescents with special health needs using a participatory action research (PAR) approach. Adolescent diagnoses included spina bifida, cerebral palsy, traumatic brain injury, spinal cord injury, epilepsy and errors of metabolism. The research study was carried out by the researchers and three adolescents with special needs themselves. It is important to note that these adolescents had specific characteristics and experiences that made them suitable for this role. Two adolescents had taken part in the pilot study and another adolescent had previous experience working with adults with acquired disability and was a community advocate (Burstein et al., 2005). Burstein et al. (2005) used different technology to support data collection; however, alternative methods were also available to cater for the different needs of participants, therefore maximising active participation. The *Youth Individualized Planner* consisted of emergency medical information, medical records and a daily planner. It also included data collection sheets, weekly and monthly summaries of health status, social events and records of research goals. The *Personal Digital Assistant* recorded participants' personal data digitally and this information could be downloaded for tracking, analysis and graphing. This tool was particularly suitable for those adolescents that struggled to write (Burstein et al., 2005). Burstein et al. (2005) argue that PAR is ideal to work with adolescents with disabilities, as it is empowering and focused on identifying solutions for participant problems.

1.3 Adolescents, Technology and Health

Technology is becoming and will continue to be the driving force of economic growth and social development; however, investment in digital education is low (Banati & Lansford, 2018). Contemporary life is saturated with technology and media and these drive and transform society, culture and individuals (Moyer, 2023). It is therefore important to ask how adolescents navigate their identity and perceptions within this heavily mediated society in which they live (Moyer, 2023).

Technology is a seamless part of how adolescents conduct their lives (Flicker et al., 2008). New media and technology are now a central part of adolescents' lives, resulting in new forms of communication, identity formation and social relations (Mallan & Singh, 2010). Adolescents are having to adopt technologies at a faster rate (Moyer, 2023). Adolescents tend to embrace new technologies, currently representing an estimated one in three users worldwide (Gibbs et al., 2020).

Technology and new digital media provide opportunities for adolescents to nurture skills, connect with others and engage in meaningful play. They also offer skills that can support their future careers, civic engagement and contribute to overall good (James et al., 2009). Adolescents can engage with new digital media in many ways and therefore can assume a variety of different roles (James et al., 2009) including the ones shown in Table 1.2.

One of the challenges of involving technology in research with adolescents is the fact that there is still an uneven access, due to several factors including geographical and economic inequalities. These differences shape the ways in which adolescents use and interact with technology in their daily lives (Mallan & Singh, 2010). It is therefore necessary as researchers to reflect on how your study will approach these inequalities. Will the research continue to reinforce the existing inequalities? For example, by including those who currently have access or to instead take a more democratic approach and include those who have traditionally been excluded or have had limited access. This, of course, is determined by

Table 1.2 *Adolescent roles in digital media*

1.Self-expression and identity experimentation	Adolescents can engage in creative activities such as creating avatars, role playing, games, virtual worlds, creating content, sharing content through blogs, music sharing sites and social media.
2.Social networking	Adolescents can engage with friends, reach out to people with similar interests and find social support.
3.Gaming	Adolescents can engage in single- and multiple-player games and role-playing games.
4.Consumption and entertainment	Adolescents can do online shopping, download music and watch videos.
5.Education	Adolescents can engage in teaching, mentoring and learning from their peers through online communities, programmes and other informal learning environments.
6.Knowledge building	Adolescents can engage in different activities such as research, schoolwork, following news and using other ways of gathering information like Wikipedia, Google and online news.
7.Dialogue and civic engagement	Adolescents can engage in public discourse, promoting social change and political, social and cultural critique.

many factors such as local access to resources such as internet access and funding. How much of the research funding can support democratisation of technology? For example, by providing adolescents with hardware to increase their access or software to be involved in a study. At the very least, research studies should be transparent and explicit about how these inequalities were given careful consideration and a description of the efforts made to reduce them. They should also include the reasons why these inequalities (geographical, economical, structural) were not dealt with if this were the case.

Researchers working with adolescents and technology should not assume that all adolescents are interested in technology, that they are all tech-savvy and have the skills and knowledge to work with technology successfully. The reality is they may not be. Research with technology should also be transparent and admit that studies using technology will probably include a sector of adolescents who are interested and possibly confident in the use of technology. As Mallan and Singh (2010) suggested, the social realities and lived experiences of adolescents are different; there is no 'one best' approach to researching their experiences.

Rapid advances in technology can provide opportunities for adolescents to influence health policy and practice (Gibbs et al., 2020). 'Adolescents are not passive technology users but active agents capable of widespread social change' (Gibbs et al., 2020, p. S15). Technology can be an opportunity to appeal to adolescents and engage them in health promotion (Flicker et al., 2008). For example, health intervention with adolescents has been traditionally delivered face-to-face in individual or group sessions. This means sessions rely on factors such as ability to travel, time commitment and financial capacity of participants (Malloy et al., 2023). The digitalisation of healthcare can contribute to facilitating reach and access to health services (Malloy et al., 2023). Adolescents who are active technology users may be suitable to produce adequate content that is attractive to their peers (Oridota et al., 2023). Social media can provide a 'voice' for adolescents to engage with peers and communities (Patton et al., 2016). Digital media has the potential to improve the sharing and presentation of data, generate new data, improve the quality of data and enable data sharing with a wider audience (Patton et al., 2016). New media is an opportunity to extend adolescents' social networks and engage with new ideas and like-minded peers despite cultural and geographical differences (Patton et al., 2016). Technology, therefore, offers a possibility of having the healthiest generation of adolescents ever (Patton et al., 2016).

Recommendations for Participatory Action Research (PAR) Authors

The following are recommendations for PAR authors on how to report their research (Shamrova & Cummings, 2017):

1. Include participants' age.
2. Describe in depth the involvement of adolescents and their roles in the research.
3. Be explicit about the distribution of power between adults and participants and the nature of the relationship (e.g. who initiated the research, description of the cultural context in which adult–participant relationships take place).
4. Describe the PAR methodology used in detail as well as any challenges experienced.

1.4 Participation

Participation is defined by Hart (1992) as the 'process of sharing decisions which affect one's life and the life of the community in which one lives' (p. 5). It is described as a fundamental right of citizenship; according to Hart (1992) participation is the standard by which democracies should be measured. This definition, however, excludes children and adolescents who do not live in a democratic regime or culture which means their participation is already limited by the context they live in, and research may reinforce this. Participation becomes particularly relevant for children who live in disadvantage, as this is an opportunity to learn about their capacity and ability to fight for their rights in equality and solidarity with others and also to exert their rights (Hart, 1992).

Participation as a democratic exercise requires confidence and competence; according to Hart (1992) these must be acquired gradually through practice. Participation also requires motivation from adolescents. Adolescents can manage complex projects if they have a sense of ownership (Hart, 1992). In research, this means involving adolescents in designing project aims, for example (Hart, 1992).

Participation is a multidimensional concept. According to Sinclair (2004) it is made up of four components:

1. Level of participation. The level of participation can be determined using different models of participation, for example Hart's ladder of participation; however, there are several models that are described in more detail in Chapter 10. The ideal level of participation may be different depending on the activity, the project or the organisation.

2. Focus of the decision-making. The focus of decision-making may vary depending on the target, whether it is service planning, service development, policy, or decisions targeted at a specific organisation only. Private refers to decision-making within the family context or between people. Public refers to public services. Additionally, decisions may also relate to the child individually and others may affect the whole group.
3. Nature of the participatory activity. Participation activities can have many different forms, for example one-off consultations, involvement in governance or adolescent-led initiatives.
4. Children and adolescents involved. Children in this case are defined as those under 18 years of age (UNCRC definition). This, however, includes a very diverse group with different personal circumstances (age, sex, ethnicity, culture, disability, social and economic circumstances), interests and capacities, which also change over time as children grow. Therefore, there should be an array of forms of engagement and dialogue that 'start from the position of the child' (Sinclair, 2004, p. 109), independent of their age or ability.

Specifically, regarding different levels of participation, adolescents may have various roles in research, which are described by Checkoway and Richards-Schuster (2003) in Table 1.3.

Table 1.3 *Adolescent levels of participation*

Adolescents as subjects	Adolescents are observed, tested, measured, enumerated and analysed by researchers. Participants are usually unaware of how the research was designed, how the data was gathered or how the findings were disseminated, even if these are included in subsequent publication that may benefit adolescents.
Adolescents as consultants	A study is initiated by an adult in consultation with adolescents to make the study more effective. This consultation may include advice on the age or cultural appropriateness of interview questions. Adolescents' knowledge about themselves is recognised.
Adolescents as partners	Adults initiate a project and involve adolescents as partners with both an equal and unequal level of participation. For example, young people may be trained in research methods and actively engage in the research, for example involving students in surveys with younger classmates.
Adolescents as directors	Adolescents organise their own research project to work on solutions needed in their communities. The underlying motivation is to take action and not to develop knowledge.

1.4.1 *Theoretical Underpinning of Participation*

Gibbs et al. (2020) provide some of the theoretical underpinnings of participatory research. This includes a rights-based, an instrumental and an empirical approach. Ozer et al. (2018) consider these frameworks should be complementary instead of dichotomous.

1.4.1.1 *Rights-Based Approach*

Adolescent participation in health-related research, specifically in relation to services and systems that affect them, is a fundamental right (Gibbs et al., 2020). International policy has been very significant in the development of participatory research, for example the UNCRC. The United Nations (UN) held a special session at the UN General Assembly on Children in 2002 where the document 'A World Fit for Children' was supported by the UN, UNICEF, UN agencies, governments, civil society organisations and non-governmental organisations. This document states that:

> Children, including adolescents, must be enabled to exercise their right to express their views freely, according to their evolving capacity, and build self-esteem, acquire knowledge and skills, such as those for conflict resolution, decision-making and communication, to meet the challenges of life. The right of children, including adolescents, to express themselves freely must be respected and promoted and their views taken into account in all matters affecting them, the views of the child being given due weight in accordance with the age and maturity of the child. (United Nations General Assembly, 2002, p. 7, cited in Coyne, 2008)

1.4.1.2 *Instrumental and Epistemological*

Adolescents can provide a unique 'insider's' expertise that increases the validity of adolescent-generated research knowledge on health and well-being, which can lead to better and more effective design of service and systems for adolescents (Gibbs et al., 2020).

1.4.1.3 *Impact on Development*

Youth-led participatory action research (YLPAR) can positively impact on adolescents' development by enabling leadership opportunities for them, shifting the perspective of practitioners in recognising the value of adolescent input in key decisions (Gibbs et al., 2020). Involvement in YLPAR can be particularly beneficial for adolescents who experience disadvantages and challenges to their agency (Gibbs et al., 2020).

1.4.1.4 *Empirical Rationales*

Empirical rationales are focused on the potential to enhance the effectiveness and impact of programmes and policies designed with adolescents as 'active partners rather than passive recipients' (Ozer et al., 2018, p. 671). Empirical rationales perceived adolescents as 'experts', therefore capable of generating valid knowledge (Ozer et al., 2018).

1.4.2 *Developmental Considerations of Participation*

Development is one of the underpinning theoretical principles of participation. This section describes in more detail the developmental principles in participation. Development can be defined as a process of 'mutual interaction between the individual and their environment', which, according to de Winter et al. (1999, p. 16), consists of family participation, social and emotional development, perspective of others and gender. These are explained below.

1.4.2.1 *Family Participation*

Adolescents, in most cases, will probably have a family, or a unit they perceive and describe as family. An adolescent's rearing and attitudes towards their participation may not include providing or enabling them to have a voice. According to Hart (1992), this can be particularly relevant for children who live in disadvantaged countries or in low-income contexts, as parents (or the adults who fulfil this role) may perceive that they themselves have no voice or authority. Adolescents' participation may mean and involve whole family participation. Adolescents could be the instigators and their parents/families should at least be aware of the process (Hart, 1992). Working with families may start a move towards creating a more democratic society with equal rights for all (Hart, 1992).

1.4.2.2 *Social and Emotional Development*

According to Hart (1992), self-esteem is a critical variable affecting children's and adolescents' participation. The value judgement children and young people make based on their sense of competence in doing things has an impact on their participation and can also improve their self-esteem (Hart, 1992). Children and adolescents with low self-esteem may have distorted communication and difficulties expressing themselves and this might negatively impact their participation (Hart, 1992).

1.4.2.3 Perspective of Others

The ability to participate also depends on children's and adolescents' capacity to take the perspective of others. This ability develops over time from an early age to adolescence (Hart, 1992). Having the capacity of 'mutual perspective taking' is crucial when being part of democratic groups (Hart, 1992). Adolescents, developmentally, can imagine multiple mutual perspectives including social, legal and moral ones that all individuals can share (Hart, 1992).

1.4.2.4 Gender

Participation opportunities for girls and boys are unequal. Girls and boys are treated differently in different cultures and societies (Hart, 1992). Research studies and programmes should include boys' and girls' participation equally and this can have special significance for girls who can experience barriers to effective participation in family, school and community (Hart, 1992).

There is significant growth in participation activity (Sinclair, 2004); however, the challenge remains around the clarity of who is involved and who is not. Some groups of children are less likely to be included, for example young children, children with communication difficulties and those who in general have limited involvement in local agencies. Information is needed to monitor the extent to which children are being provided opportunities for participation (Sinclair, 2004). According to Stafford et al. (2003), girls are more likely to volunteer for consultative research than boys and they tend to have more verbal skills to express themselves assertively in group discussions. The reasons for these differences were not described; however, it seems to be important to create safe and appropriate environments where adolescents from both genders feel comfortable and happy to express their views.

1.5 Participatory Research

Defining participation is challenging; therefore, defining participatory research is challenging, as different authors have overlapping principles, but add or focus on different aspects. Some authors emphasise participants' creation of knowledge as the ultimate characteristics of participatory methods. For example, Foster-Fishman et al. (2005) highlighted that the role of the researcher is to facilitate knowledge creation and support participants to discover their own understandings to facilitate them in creating change. Participatory methods promote participant control over what knowledge is generated and how it is used, and they foster learning through action and reflection (Foster-Fishman et al., 2005). Participatory research is 'carried out with and by the research subjects rather than on them' (Van Staa et al., 2009, p. 96).

Knowledge produced in participatory research is used to guide and achieve collective change in communities, organisations, programmes and research participant themselves (Powers & Tiffany, 2006). Additionally, knowledge generated through participation is culturally relevant and connected to the lived experience of participants, therefore it is more readily converted into action compared with academic theory and knowledge generated by outsiders (Wridt, 2018).

Participatory research 'can fall between the crack that separates intention from action' (Mallan & Singh, 2010, p. 269). There are several factors that can lead to this fall including institutional, generational and ideological ones. Institutional ones may include funding timelines and expectations. According to Mallan and Singh (2010) there is an inevitable mismatch between the world views of researchers and participants. Practical reasons may include negotiating spaces for adolescents that can meet the ethical expectations from schools, parents and universities (Mallan & Singh, 2010).

Participatory approaches have shown promise in increasing participation with adolescents that have been historically underrepresented in research, for example adolescents of colour and immigrants (Valdez et al., 2021). Geppert (2023) chose a participatory design in a research study with adolescents who were marginalised by race, class, ethnicity, gender and sexuality.

1.6 Adolescent Participation

Adolescent participation approaches is an umbrella term which encompasses a variety of ways in which adolescents can provide their expertise, from informal sharing in adult-led environments to more formal advisory boards and councils, and systematic youth-generated research as well as structured planning and design processes (Ozer et al., 2018). Participatory approaches share the principle that young people have the expertise to address issues that have an impact on them; however, they differ in their emphasis on research and equity (Ozer, 2016).

Adolescent participation is the process of sharing decision-making on issues that affect adolescents and their communities (de Winter & Noom, 2003; Shamrova & Cummings, 2017). Participatory research involves adolescents not as 'the problem' but as 'subjects of knowledge' who can identify, understand and find solutions for social problems (Wulf-Andersen et al., 2021a, p. 6). Not listening to the views of children and young people on matters that affect them is wrong, as it is a breach of their human rights (Lundy, 2018). Also, not seeking their views on the basis that it would be tokenistic is also wrong (Lundy, 2018). This means it is also wrong of adults to encourage participation if adolescent views are not given due weight (Lundy, 2018). Providing participants with the results of the research study is important; however, it is more important to also provide feedback on how their views are taken seriously (Lundy, 2018). This is described by Lundy (2018) as the necessary minimum, but researchers should encourage adults to engage in more meaningful ways.

Adolescent participation is therefore recommended practice; however, this has challenges, both logistical and ethical (Schelbe et al., 2014). Participation requires effort, resources and time, ensuring participants have access to information, understand the research topic and support provision (Lundy, 2018). Adolescent participation is uneven; some participate with fervour and others may express interest but may be unsure about how to deal with the research process (Checkoway & Richards-Schuster, 2003). Others may participate but lack support from adults or face obstacles to their participation (Checkoway & Richards-Schuster, 2003). Participation is always imperfect (Lundy, 2018). This is not bad; this is the validation that 'real world research' is challenging and there is no expectation of perfection, which is not the same as ethical and good practice, which should be the goal.

Participation quality is not measured by the quantity of adolescents who are involved in the research; it is measured by its effectiveness when adolescents influence the process, how they have an impact on decisions or how their involvement leads to a favourable outcome (Checkoway & Richards-Schuster, 2003). Additionally, participants may have not perceived or understood the process as participatory for themselves (Holland et al., 2010), even it was intended as participatory research design.

Adolescent participation can have several benefits and provide significant skills for adolescents. Benefits of participation can have a long-term impact. For example, de Winter and Noom (2003) used the participatory method in their research project as a model that could be adapted and used by agencies and institutions dealing with adolescents to enhance their dialogue and quality of care over time. Some of the benefits of adolescent participation are enumerated below:

1. Social action. Participation can be a way to develop knowledge for social action. Adolescents want to act, improve their communities and

provide credible information for action-taking (Checkoway & Richards-Schuster, 2003).
2. Political rights. Participation can enable adolescents to exercise their political rights (Checkoway & Richards-Schuster, 2003).
3. Democratisation of knowledge. Adolescents can mobilise knowledge to break the monopoly on it and enable youth to have information they need for competent citizenship (Checkoway & Richards-Schuster, 2003).
4. Active participation in democratic society. Participation can activate adolescents' civic engagement and enable reflection about problems in their community as well as acting in civil society (Checkoway & Richards-Schuster, 2003). It can also empower them to create social change (Powers & Tiffany, 2006).
5. Social development. Adolescent participation can encourage social development in adolescents by increasing their involvement, organisational development and their capacity to generate change in their community (Checkoway & Richards-Schuster, 2003). Adolescents can also serve as role models to other youth as experts with local knowledge about issues that affect them (Powers & Tiffany, 2006).
6. New relationships. Adolescents can form new relationships with adults and members of the broader community (Powers & Tiffany, 2006).

Participation can also foster psychological well-being (de Winter & Noom, 2003) and civic engagement as well as increased self-confidence (Van Staa et al., 2009) and an opportunity for meaning-making for research participants. Van Staa et al. (2009) found that taking part in the study turned participants' illness into a positive experience (Van Staa et al., 2009).

Fox et al. (2010) argue that the lack of access to civic engagement is sometimes misinterpreted as a lack of motivation. It should be noted that significant differences in race and social class can lead to uneven opportunities of participation for children and adolescents. M. Fox et al. (2010) identified poor, working-class youth of colour and immigrant adolescents as more likely to have fewer opportunities for meaningful involvement in civic engagements and have too many family responsibilities that hinder their full participation. Fox et al. (2010) enumerated five principles that are crucial for critical adolescent engagement. These principles share many similarities with participatory research principles:

1. Children and adolescents are a source of knowledge and power. Children and adolescents have important knowledge about their social conditions and have ideas about social change, meaning they have political wisdom and an understanding of injustice. Traditional epistemologies where researchers and elders are the ones in possession

of valid knowledge are questioned. Instead, multigenerational collectives of adults and adolescents gather to share their experience, knowledge and ideas about social inquiry. In the research context, research questions, methodological approaches and data analysis are made across the different age groups.

2. A critical analysis to facilitate critical consciousness of history, privilege and power. Adolescents' engagement requires the spaces designated for critical community education where adolescents can develop a systemic perspective of their life circumstances and the impact on their lives of issues like racism, sexism, homophobia and classism which perpetuate inequality. This understanding is the basis of planning, researching, mobilising and campaigning for change.
3. Youth leadership in partnership with adults. At the core of critical youth engagement is adolescent voice and empowerment. The role of adults is to actively guide and educate adolescents with a spirit of mutual inquiry, collaboration and problem-solving. The role of adolescents is to take the lead to generate ideas, facilitate meetings and make decisions. To support adolescents in this role, adults can help them identify relevant information, share knowledge and insights, role play, rehearse, listen and challenge.
4. Intersectionality. Analysing and organising across sectors of everyday life: Critical youth engagement is founded on the idea that different sectors of public life are not separate but are woven into the lives and communities of adolescents. These sectors are health, criminal justice, education, housing, immigration status and economics. Adolescents study and organise within and across all these sectors. Understanding these aspects that shape the lives of adolescents creates the conditions for critically envisioning an alternative future. Cook and Krueger-Henney (2017) additionally consider that unequal structures, such as marginalisation and discrimination, impact adolescents in different ways; every adolescent is implicated as they are bound within the same sociopolitical power dynamics.
5. Collective action for social change. Adults and adolescents can use an intersectional lens to analyse problems in a historical and structural manner to mutually develop strategies for collective action which challenges those same problems. This creates a sense of collective efficacy where everyone must contribute to the effort. This collective efficacy means everyone shares a perception of mutual trust and willingness to help community members in need. This is further supported when it has positive effects on health and student academic achievement.

Participatory research methods are also beneficial for researchers. Sharpe et al. (2022) explained that participatory methods are very suitable for researchers who want to use their creativity to develop inclusive, accessible and adolescent-centred research.

Participatory research also has challenges. It can be more research-intensive, time-consuming, complicated and less efficient than traditional research (Van Staa et al., 2009).

Finally, a concept closely related with participation is co-participation. Although they are presented as separate concepts in research, they have many commonalities. Co-participation, as well as participation, defines children and young people as co-constructors of knowledge as well as co-designers and facilitators of research (Purdy & Spears, 2020). For co-participatory research, the process of research inquiry is as important as the product, findings, outputs and outcomes (Purdy & Spears, 2020).

1.7 Participatory Methods

The following sections of this book explore different methods that share participatory principles but have some epistemological and practical differences. These should not be used interchangeably in research, even if they have shared similarities; these are methods in their own right.

1.7.1 Community-Based Participatory Research

A method included under the participatory research umbrella is community-based participatory research (CBPR), which is a collaborative approach involving all partners equally in the research process and recognising the strengths they bring (Merves et al., 2015). CBPR begins with a research topic relevant to the community which combines knowledge and action for social change (Flicker, 2008). Therefore, the main objective of CBPR is to combine knowledge and action to achieve social change and improvements in the community (Merves et al., 2015), as well as to integrate knowledge gained into policy change to improve health and quality of life of participants (Israel et al., 2005). CBCR is increasingly recognised as a strategy that can lead to eliminate health disparities, achieve community change and improve health indicators (Ballonoff et al., 2006). It has the potential to be transformative and empowering, enabling individuals and communities to achieve sustainable personal and social change (Flicker, 2008). Empowering, however, can go wrong or set up unrealistic expectations for adolescents (Flicker, 2008); this must be prevented by good and ethical practices in research.

Research has identified several benefits of CBPR. Flicker (2008) identified benefits for the research, the researchers and the adolescent participants (Table 1.4). Benefits, however, happen because of substantial investment and may not be equally distributed (Flicker, 2008).

Table 1.4 *Benefits of research for stakeholders*

Research	Stakeholders: Youth	Stakeholders: Academics
Better questions: adolescents helped develop questions that met their needs.	**Heard:** those in a position of authority listened to and acted upon adolescent recommendations.	**Youth:** academics had an opportunity to demonstrate their passion and commitment to work for youth.
Better recruitment: adolescents designed the recruitment materials in youth-friendly formats and placed them where they looked for information themselves.	**Feeling part of:** adolescents thought it was important to be part of a productive and socially respected team.	**Inspiration:** adolescents were inspired by youth talents and imagination.
Better data collection: protocols were revised according to feedback provided by adolescents and considering confidentiality and anonymity.	**Structure:** the project provided structure without school or work, considering their skills and abilities and their barriers including their illness.	**Mentoring:** academics found satisfaction in their roles as mentors for the community and graduate students.
Better analysis: adolescents provided new perspectives and understandings for the data.	**Access:** the project facilitated links to other economic supports and social services.	
Better dissemination: all involved (team, researchers, community providers, adolescents) led dissemination towards their target audiences.	**Confidence:** some adolescents experienced confidence in their education and their analytical and research skills. Some considered going back to education.	
Better action: community-based organisations integrated recommendations in their work immediately.	**Learning:** adolescents learnt several social and practical skills transferable to other settings.	

Researchers may also experience different challenges when using CBPR. It requires a significant amount of time. According to Flicker (2008), the CBPR project that was undertaken took longer than expected and was demanding for the research team workload as well as partner organisations. Difficulties finding sustainable funding were described, as well as the different perspectives of stakeholders when writing applications (Flicker, 2008).

Israel et al. (2005) identified several potential challenges of using CBPR:

1. Costs incurred and lack of resources. There are community and academic partners involved in CBPR. Developing partnerships requires time and infrastructure, remuneration for involvement and cost coverage.
2. Institutional constraints. Institutional requirements may not match the timelines and needs of communities, for example requirements from review boards, overhead issues, long delays due to data analysis, among others.
3. Lack of trust and respect. Maintaining trust between researchers and communities can be challenging, particularly if there are historical challenges.
4. Ensuring community participation and influence. Building relationships in the community is essential for collaborative and equitable partnerships. This requires skill, time and commitment from all partners to ensure participation and shared decision-making. Flicker (2008) also recognises that with certain topics, such as HIV in adolescents, partnering was crucial as this enabled a new and sensitive territory to be entered in a respectful manner.
5. Lack of training and experience in conducting CBPR. Many researchers and community partners may lack training in CBPR.
6. Different emphasis on goals, values, priorities and perspectives. There are no right or wrong ways in which partnerships work; these should instead accommodate diverse perspectives and cultures.
7. Different languages and communication styles. Members of partnerships and researchers may have different styles of communication.

By itself, CBPR cannot create sustainable change (Ballonoff et al., 2006) – a supportive and comprehensive strategy is required. This will involve a cycle of research, evaluation, planning, implementation, youth organising and youth policy development which leads to social action (Ballonoff et al., 2006). Specifically, regarding health, social change requires time to understand the profound causes and implications of health inequalities

Table 1.5 *Wingspread Declaration*

Community-based Participatory Research and Evaluation with Young People Wingspread Declaration (2002) • Youth participation in community research and evaluation transforms its participants. It transforms our ways of knowing, the strategies we devise, the methods we employ and our programme of work. • Youth participation promotes youth empowerment. It recognises the experience and expertise of all young people, and respects their leadership capacities and potential contributions. • Youth participation builds mutually liberatory partnerships. It values the assets of all ages and fosters supportive and respectful youth/youth and youth/adult working relationships. • Youth participation equalises power relationships between youth and adults. It establishes a level playing field clarifying for participants the purpose of the process and the power imbalances between groups. It structures environments that respect the involvement of young people, and trains adults in supporting genuine youth decision-making and leadership development. • Youth participation is an inclusive process that recognises all forms of democratic leadership, young and old. It involves diverse populations and perspectives, especially those who are traditionally underserved and underrepresented. • Youth participation involves young people in meaningful ways. Young people participate in all stages of the process, from defining the problem, to gathering and analysing the information, to making decisions and taking action. • Youth participation is an ongoing process, not a one-time event. Participants continuously clarify and reflect upon its purpose and content. Research and evaluation are viewed as an integral part of knowledge development, programme planning and community improvement.

(Ballonoff et al., 2006). Adolescent involvement in social change can lead to meaningful health reforms and health delivery systems that serve the needs of adolescents (Ballonoff et al., 2006).

The Wingspread Declaration of Principles (Table 1.5) is the outcome of a collaboration between adolescents and adults in the Wingspread Symposium on Youth Participation Community Research in 2002. These are useful principles to ensure researchers are adhering to the principles of CBPR.

1.7.2 Co-design

Co-design is another method that is usually associated with participatory methods. It consists of a space where adults and young people work together in the creation of something new (Bowler et al., 2021). According to Malloy et al. (2023) co-design arose from participatory design, and it consists of several participatory methods which seek to understand and integrate real-life experiences from participants to improve services in an ethical and pragmatic way. Co-design therefore shares some similarities with PAR, as both approaches enact the views of adolescent participants and validate the participants' lived experiences (Bowler et al., 2021). One of the challenges of co-design is the lack of clarity around its definition and there is also a need for evaluative research to determine its impact. These two elements have been described as 'especially unhelpful' for the field (King et al., 2022).

Co-design interventions have the advantage that these will be better used and accepted, if they are co-designed with the target populations, particularly if these are traditionally vulnerable populations. These interventions can be useful to reduce inequality (King et al., 2022). One of the challenges with co-creation is the clarity and transparency of the method and its application. Bowler et al. (2021) consider that co-designing with children and adolescents can seem like a 'black box' as there should be transparency in what happens in the collaborative space, and this is not always the case.

1.7.3 Co-creation

Co-creation is the 'collaborative generation of knowledge by academics working alongside stakeholders from other sectors' (Ito-Jaeger et al., 2022, p. 1634). Fisher and Jensen (2013) defined co-creation as an approach where researchers, users and others work as a team through direct involvement in the design of a product, in this case. The product can be the research study. Leask et al. (2019) defined co-creation as the process where solutions are tailored based on the needs of individuals and circumstances in collaboration with these individuals. Co-creating places with adolescents will enable critical inquiry about their lived experiences towards acting and this can be a healing process (Goessling, 2020). Participatory methods have also been described as a 'co-creation' between researchers and participants (Mallan & Singh, 2010), so both concepts may be closely related yet not equivalent.

From the perspective of co-creation, adults have a duty of self-awareness and self-reflection on the impact they have on the research process. 'Conscious co-design' consists of a self-reflective and deliberate planning from the adults involved in the process, preventing already existing problematic dynamics which may affect less empowered participants; these should not be reinforced in the co-design process (Bowler et al., 2021).

According to Bowler et al. (2021) this represents an 'ethical stance'; the role of all participants should be transparent and demonstrate respect for all participants, independent of their level of involvement.

In terms of suggested sample sizes for co-creation, Leask et al. (2019) recommends having between 6 and 12 participants when using methods such as focus groups. Having the upper range also enables the group to be divided into smaller groups for other types of activities.

1.7.4 Participatory Design

Participatory design is a method in which the end user has an active role in the design process (Bowler et al., 2021). It also shares principles of participatory research. Users and designers engage in a collaborative relationship where users are members of the design team. Children, adolescents and adults actively shape technology development and advancement (Bowler et al., 2021). Including end users does not lead directly to equality; this will only be achieved when adolescents are recognised as partners.

Participatory designs have also been applied in other areas such as healthcare, civic engagement and cultural heritage, moving from focus on a specific product to improving quality of life more generally (Bowler et al., 2021).

1.7.5 Participatory Action Research

Participatory action research (PAR) is an empowerment approach for social change (Flicker et al., 2008) and has a strong social justice orientation (Rodriguez & Brown, 2009). It encourages participation and leadership, as it enables participants to develop autonomy as they are creators of knowledge (Teixeira et al., 2021). It is not a method but an epistemological orientation which emphasises the significance of subjective experiences in knowledge construction (Shamrova & Cummings, 2017). It is a '[c]-ooperative, iterative process of research and action in which non-professional community members are trained as researchers and change agents, and power over decisions [is] shared among the partners in the collaboration' (Ozer & Douglas, 2013, p. 66). Shamrova and Cummings (2017) have defined PAR as a response from academia to ensure the implementation of children's rights to participate and challenge adult centrism.

Under the umbrella of PAR there are various approaches including community-based participatory research, collaborative research and community-centred research, among others (Shamrova & Cummings,

2017). These approaches have different components in common which are: participation, engagement, empowerment, mutual learning, capacity building and fulfilment of research and action agendas (Shamrova & Cummings, 2017). E-PAR is the online version of PAR which encourages youth to carry out research using media methods they are familiar with and to develop strategies for change (Flicker et al., 2008).

Hart (1992) described the essential features of PAR:

1. Research is carried out by or with the people concerned.
2. Researchers have a commitment to the participants and to their control of the research analysis.
3. Participants themselves identified the concrete problem which initiates the research.
4. PAR proceeds to investigate the underlying causes of the problem so that participants can address them.
5. The researcher has the role of providing technical assistance in the research process.

PAR assumes that communities have local knowledge, which is crucial in understanding and addressing their own problems and issues (Flicker et al., 2008). Therefore, it is vital for researchers to be clear about their theory of social change and this must be shared with participants in a democratic way early in the research process (Hart, 1992). The validity of the knowledge generated by PAR does not depend on the objectivity of an outsider, rather on the closeness of the participant to the issues (Chen et al., 2010). One very important issue that Chen et al. (2010) added is that validity of the knowledge is also determined by the degree to which the knowledge is translated into actions to address the issues.

Rodriguez and Brown (2009) developed a set of guiding principles to work with PAR and marginalised adolescents. These principles are intended to improve adolescent well-being and development, creating a more democratic society. The authors do not provide a specific definition of marginalised youth in their research, but they refer, for example, to adolescents of colour who are being systematically removed from their schools and their communities. These principles are useful, however, when working with adolescents in PAR, not only for a specific group.

1.7.5.1 Situated and Inquiry Based

This principle is based on research and learning that reflects on and addresses adolescents' real-life issues, desires and experiences. This guides the creation of policies and practices which are meaningful and relevant to their participation. Social researchers help adolescents to theoretically situate their lived experiences within broader structural and cultural contexts. Adolescents, therefore, see their own experiences as worthy of investigation and their knowledge validated. These frameworks are crucial to validate the research and inform the subsequent data analyses (Rodriguez & Brown, 2009).

1.7.5.2 Participatory

This principle consists of the commitment to collaborative methodological and pedagogical processes which validate the skills of adolescents as researchers and support critical and creative engagement. Adolescents are invited to draw on personal experiences and connect them to those of others and to broader theories.

1.7.5.3 Transformative and Activist

This third principle is a commitment to research and learning that actively seeks to transform knowledge and practices to improve the lives of adolescent participants. Adolescents are intentionally engaged in a critical analysis of their worlds. In the specific case of marginalised adolescents, for example, Rodriguez and Brown (2009) encouraged them to connect their daily experiences to broader systems of oppression in society, for example being silenced in school and experiences of political suppression.

1.7.6 Youth-Led Participatory Action Research

Youth-led participatory action research (YPAR) is a form of participatory research whereby adolescents are trained and supported to conduct research on topics that they have identified as affecting their lives (Bautista et al., 2013; Gibbs et al., 2020; Ozer & Wright, 2012). It is guided by issues of interest and importance for adolescents' lives, communities and institutions (Cook & Krueger-Henney, 2017). Overall, an emphasis is placed on uncovering the power structures and inequities that are limiting adolescents' wellness, mental health and positive educational outcomes by acting and eliminating those oppressive systems in their lives (Cook & Krueger-Henney, 2017). YPAR is advocating for changes based on research evidence and is grounded in principles of equity (Ozer, 2016).

YPAR is not a method but an epistemological challenge to dominant social science and educational research (Aldana & Richards-Schuster, 2021). YPAR as an epistemology represents a stand against the dominant research ideology, as it privileges adolescents' capacity and power to conduct research (Cook & Krueger-Henney, 2017). It provides a systemic and ecological view of a problem, weighing evidence, communication, teamwork and advocacy (Ozer, 2017). It is not an intervention but a process (Ozer & Douglas, 2015), which means that YPAR as an iterative process will unfold differently in a specific context as well as vary between research and action.

Although YPAR has similarities to other participatory approaches, it is different because it places more emphasis on research coupled with action (Ozer & Piatt, 2017). The core epistemological assertion of YPAR is that adolescents have the capacity to create expert knowledge and to understand and address their development and well-being (Ozer, 2016). It is a youth-centred form of CBPR, which is targeted at reducing health disparities engaging communities and organisations (Oridota et al., 2023). YPAR can be used for adolescents to conduct research on how to improve issues that affect their lives (Gibbs et al., 2020). It is focused on achieving sustainable changes in settings, services, programmes or policies (Gibbs et al., 2020).

The approach of YPAR is well suited to address inequalities in adolescents' health and education by creating opportunities to enhance their own knowledge, skills and motivation, have a meaningful influence and voice issues that affect them (Ozer, 2016). Adolescents may be motivated to get involved to increase their sociopolitical skills, influence their schools and communities and raise their participatory behaviour (Ozer & Douglas, 2013). This can enhance their identity formation and sense of purpose (Ozer & Douglas, 2013). The process of YPAR can be used to understand the lives and priorities of adolescents as part of needs assessments and evaluation of services or to design, monitor and adapt programmes and initiatives targeted at them (Ozer & Piatt, 2017).

Adolescents lead YPAR themselves and it is intended at promoting social change and improving healthy development in the community (Ozer & Piatt, 2017). It can foster positive development and civic participation among economically disadvantaged adolescents, for example (Ozer & Douglas, 2013). Adolescents can be 'collaborators' and 'change agents' not just research participants (Ozer, 2016). YPAR repositions adolescents as co-creators, co-leaders, co-visionaries, co-authors and co-owners of their own and group goals (Cook & Krueger-Henney, 2017). It promotes critical reflection, motivation and action that pushes youth beyond individual-level explanations to broader factors in the community and society (Ozer, 2016).

'YPAR aims to shift power over to one of power with research participants' (Aldana & Richards-Schuster, 2021, p. 657). Adolescents are trained to identify major concerns in their communities, carry out research on these issues and take a leadership role to influence policy and decisions that have an impact on them and their peers (Ozer & Douglas, 2013). Therefore, YPAR can be beneficial for communities and local organisations, as actions initiated and led by youth are aligned to the needs of their communities (Anselma et al., 2020). Research has identified other benefits of YPAR for adolescents including increased psychological autonomy, collective sense of identity and purpose, responsibility, positive ethnic identity, more academic skills, increased sense of community, improved communication skills, psychological empowerment, strategic thinking, more perceived control and a sense of moral identity (Ozer, 2017). It enables adolescents to see themselves as leaders with a vision and direction (Cook & Krueger-Henney, 2017).

YPAR is suitable:

1. to develop supportive, cooperative relationships between adolescents and adults
2. to give opportunities to build skills in communication, inquiry and group work
3. for belonging opportunities
4. for meaningful participation and roles.

Adults also have an important role in YPAR. Adults engaged in YPAR need constant reflection on what it means to be an adult working with adolescents (Texeira et al., 2021). Texeira et al. (2021) described the role of adults in YPAR as a 'dance', as they need to take the lead at times but should step back and enable young people to lead at other times. This process is not linear; it is 'back and forth' (Teixeira et al., 2021). Adults interested in engaging adolescents in YPAR research should begin by 'preparing the ground' through activities that build trust and communication skills both between adolescents and between adults and adolescents (Ozer & Piatt, 2017). R. Fox (2013) explains some of the strategies that can be used to support critical reflection. For example, the author kept a fieldwork diary with a record of the sessions, how to improve them in the future, identification of topics which may interest the adolescents more and improvements the facilitator can do in future sessions.

Adults in YPAR should ensure adolescents keep the control when it comes to choosing a topic and design and interpretation of the data. Adults are also in charge of providing a helpful structure to enable adolescent participation, breaking down tasks and keeping timelines (Ozer & Piatt, 2017). Timelines are fundamental in YPAR as taking too long may delay or impede the time needed for change; however, jumping too fast into a solution may lead to a lack of depth and understanding of the issues which can also impede the change (Ozer & Piatt,2017). Adults can also act as problem-solvers, supporting adolescents to deal with personal conflicts as well as navigating institutional and policy change (Ozer & Piatt, 2017).

Researchers can evaluate if they are respecting and following YPAR principles. Ozer and Douglas (2015) created a scale (the YPAR process template) to determine if the YPAR implementation is carried out to a 'good enough' standard. Due to the nature of YPAR not being a structured intervention, the purpose of this measure is to inform a continuous improvement of practice and more effective YPAR approaches.

Ozer and Piatt (2017) provided a phase-based approach of how to apply YPAR in a research study (Table 1.6).

Table 1.6 *Phases of a YPAR study*

Phase	Description
1.Issue selection	The adolescent-led research group reflects on their authentic concerns, which they care about and want to influence. These concerns should not be influenced by adult facilitators. Strategies like anonymous votes can be used to stop social desirability. Once an agreement is reached on the research topic, adolescents can define their research questions, hypotheses and methods.
2.Research design and methods	Adolescents engage in decision-making about the research design, methods and interpretation of the data collected. Some commonly used methods in YPAR are focus groups, interviews, mapping, observations, photovoice and surveys.
3.Data analysis and interpretation	Data should lead to high-quality evidence appropriate to the developmental and literacy levels of the adolescents as well as being in line with time, ethical and financial constraints. Data analysis should be fun and user-friendly with no expectations of adolescents having experience in working with numbers or any science background. Analysis can be carried out low tech or with software available online.
4.Reporting back and taking action for change	Adolescents and adult facilitators can identify the actions that will be carried out to tackle the problem as well as report back the findings to all relevant stakeholders to work towards change. Dissemination of results can be more credible if other adolescents have been involved in the analysis and generation of the evidence.

1.7.7 YPAR 2.0

YPAR 2.0 is the technological application of YPAR. Technology can support the scaling of YPAR (Gibbs et al., 2020). This is confirmed by Akom et al. (2016) who coined the term YPAR 2.0 to refer to the incorporation of technology and digital platforms to extend the traditional forms of YPAR. Technology should not be perceived as a 'panacea'; according to Akom et al. (2016), nothing can replace people's own power and ability to transform the social and material conditions that oppress them. Technology and digital platforms can help by democratising decision-making by amplifying the narratives that question the mainstream narratives, particularly in low-income and marginalised communities (Akom et al., 2016).

1.7.8 Youth as Researchers

Youth-led research builds youth capacities and engages youth to produce evidence for research, but it also contributes to real-life issues (UNESCO, 2022). It is based on the premise that young people are the ones who know their problems better but also know the best solutions for their generation (UNESCO, 2022). Youth research avoids describing adolescents as 'disempowered, disinterested or at risk' as there is instead an awareness that participants have a motivation for their participation (Lohmeyer, 2019). Motivation is crucial to understand how the project may appeal to adolescents (Lightfoot & Sloper, 2002) and, therefore, how to engage them in the study. Having youth as researchers can be very powerful: 'Despite who is listening to the story, the act of telling changes the young person's world' (Lohmeyer, 2019, p. 47).

1.7.9 Peer Research

Peer research consists of creating knowledge collaboratively, challenging dominant discourses, reversing exclusion and amplifying the voices of those who have been denied the right to be experts in their own lives (Terry & Cardwell, 2016). It is for this reason that it has been described as 'ethically imperative', and Terry and Cardwell (2016) argue that naming peer researchers as co-authors is fundamental. Peer research is based on the premise that shared experiences add the qualities of understanding and empathy to research, which enables it to be more meaningful and higher quality (Terry & Cardwell, 2016). Peers, therefore, are qualified based on their lived experience. Peers have also been defined as having similarities like age rather than being due to a shared lived experience (Terry & Cardwell, 2016). Peer research is linked to 'action research'; therefore it should be driven by community needs and achieving positive change for that community (Terry & Cardwell, 2016). Dissemination is a crucial part of peer research as it will enable action.

Peer research can make a study more relevant and effective. According to Terry and Cardwell (2016), it has other benefits such as changing traditional hierarchical practice, promoting personal development for participants, increasing confidence, reversing marginalisation and objectification, and promoting community activism. Other benefits of peer research include participation in civil society, critical thinking and social responsibility, teamwork, knowledge of services and improved employability, for example developing skills such as how to write a CV or obtaining a professional reference (Terry & Cardwell, 2016).

Peer research can be a relaxing experience for participants, as this is a reassurance that the interviewer understands their views, improving the reliability and honesty of data (Terry & Cardwell, 2016). Peers can have 'insider knowledge' that enables them to ask questions and understand the language (slang) and terminology used by the participants (Terry & Cardwell, 2016). This knowledge can also be used in the design phase, selecting the topic and designing the research materials (Terry & Cardwell, 2016). This can also be relevant in the analysis of the data (Terry & Cardwell, 2016). Peer research, therefore, increases the external validity of the research by involving new, unheard perspectives which widen the focus and include issues that may be underexamined (Terry & Cardwell, 2016).

Another important aspect of peer research is training. Peer researchers need to have the tools, knowledge and language to actively participate in the research as 'equals'. This may require training in research methods as well as understanding the policy and social context surrounding the research topic (Terry & Cardwell, 2016). Peers need appropriate training to avoid issues in the research such as unintentionally biasing interviews, using leading questions or focusing on their own interests and priorities (Terry & Cardwell, 2016).

Training for peer researchers should include techniques that cater to lower levels of education and literacy rates. Terry and Cardwell (2016) argue that this should not be perceived as a 'deficit model' but as a model to cater to the natural strengths and interests of these groups. Additional and ongoing support should also be provided for peers if upsetting or sensitive disclosures trigger traumatic or upsetting memories in their own lives (Terry & Cardwell, 2016). Another option is to provide debriefings or have a named worker who could provide support for peer researchers after each interview (Terry & Cardwell, 2016). Researching sensitive topics can be demoralising, depressing or shocking for peer researchers and it can be frustrating if research projects do not lead to policy changes (Terry & Cardwell, 2016). The authors argue that having the experience does not necessarily mean participants are ready to take the role of peer researchers. Some groups may be particularly 'chaotic', and some researchers may have limited patience to accommodate the needs of these populations in their projects. Terry and Cardwell (2016) suggest, for example, that peer research should overrecruit participants to plan for dropouts.

Terry and Cardwell (2016) also criticise the role that peer researchers are given in the research, for example commenting on topic guides or carrying out supervised interviews. It is rare to find research projects where peer researchers are involved in the overall research topic and ethical frameworks. Training programmes for researchers rarely include input from them and their lived experiences (Terry & Cardwell, 2016).

Chapter 3 of this book is focused on ethical considerations of participation research with adolescents in general. There are, however, ethical considerations specific to peer research that should be considered specifically when researchers are working from this perspective.

1. Safety. Peer researchers need to keep their participants and peers safe.
2. Privacy. Privacy is an important consideration in peer research as peers are often working with members of their community where they live and socialise. These spaces can be very small, for example a prison. This can have a negative impact on confidentiality as personal data and interview transcripts may not be kept in a secure environment (Terry & Cardwell, 2016).
3. Consent. Peers should provide consent before taking part in the research (Terry & Cardwell, 2016). It is also crucial to disclose any potential breaches to privacy and confidentiality.
4. Payment. Compensations and payment should be given serious consideration as payment may result in a potential disruption for anyone receiving welfare benefits. Money may be dangerous for anyone at risk of robbery or relapse. Payment, however, may be necessary to compensate for peers' time, skills, effort (Terry & Cardwell, 2016) and their knowledge and expertise.

1.7.10 Integrated Knowledge Translation

Integrated knowledge translation (IKT) emerged as a funder innovation, initially developed by the Canadian Health Services Research Foundation. It shares principles with CBPR which emphasise the need to create partnerships between researchers and knowledge end users (Jull et al., 2017). It also shares a user–researcher knowledge exchange in every stage of the research process: develop research questions, methodology, data collection, tool development, understanding findings and dissemination. IKT emerged to bridge the gap between health researchers and knowledge users (Jull et al., 2017). It tailors knowledge to specific contexts to generate evidence-based decisions to improve healthcare delivery systems and health outcomes.

1.7.11 Youth–Adult Partnerships

Youth–adult partnerships (YAP) have been recently used, particularly in the United States, for organisational and community change, by engaging adults and adolescents in shared decision-making (Zeldin et al., 2006). One of the advantages of YAP is maximising a sense of community in adolescents while ensuring they are active agents in their development and the social organisations where they live (Zeldin et al., 2006). According to Zeldin et al. (2006) YAP has been adopted by public agencies, foundations and non-profit organisations; however, cultural and organisational barriers remain, for example there may be resistance from stakeholders or a lack of understanding about the purpose of involving adolescents in a process of change. There may also be issues of power in organisations, as adults usually have the fiduciary and fiscal responsibility; however, these issues can be dissipated through role clarification (Zeldin et al., 2006). Sustainability may be an issue as well, as organisations need to build infrastructure that formally holds new roles, expectations and boundaries of change and innovation over time (Zeldin et al., 2006).

Diamond Ranking

Diamond ranking (Fallon et al., 2008) is an activity which can be used to help adolescents identify relevant research topics:

1. Discuss and negotiate in the group to identify the importance of each topic.
2. The most important topic is placed at the top of the diamond.

CHAPTER 2

Methodological Considerations in Participatory Research with Adolescents

Frequently, there is insufficient guidance, or practical and effective solutions, to safely collect data directly or indirectly from children within a digital world.

G. Berman and K. Albright, *Children and the Data Cycle: Rights and Ethics in a Big Data World*

Chapter Highlights

1. The issue of power between researchers and adolescents should be given careful consideration.
2. The use of language will have an impact on adolescent recruitment and on every part of the research process up to dissemination.
3. Strategies to ensure participants' engagement over time are necessary.
4. Adolescents can be involved in different parts of the research.
5. Successful participatory research requires a suitable setting and a research team sensitive enough to the needs and lives of adolescents.

This chapter is focused on challenges that researchers may face when adopting a participatory approach as an epistemological stance and working with participatory research methods. These potential issues are presented with the objective of enabling early reflection and stopping these issues from ending up as real ones during a research study. The potential issues are taken from empirical research and solutions or alternatives are provided so that research protocols and proposals already include plans to mitigate and prevent these issues from emerging and affecting the research process but, most importantly, to safeguard research participants and researchers themselves.

2.1 The Issue of Power

I have named this section the 'issue of power' as I think it is a complex and ongoing aspect of participatory research with adolescents. The limits of power sharing with adolescents is controversial in participatory research. Participatory research in general means adults hand over power to adolescents to make decisions in the research study. How much power to give and in which circumstances should it be given requires careful thought.

Rodriguez and Brown (2009) believe power is not always oppressive, that power can be *used with* rather than *over* adolescents by building collaboration between participants and researchers in rigorous, engaging and inquiry-based learning. This use of power, according to Rodriguez and Brown (2009), is necessary and educational in the context of research with adolescents.

Mitra and McCormick (2017) state that there is often an assumption that giving adolescents power means adults lose it. Instead, it has been found that empowerment should be viewed from a perspective of abundance, not scarcity: the more empowered adults are, the more they will enable power in others, adolescents in this case. Adolescents' empowerment can strengthen the agency and empowerment of adults (Mitra & McCormick, 2017). Strong collaboration between researchers and adolescents enables both to achieve their goals and purposes (Vyas et al., 2022). Researchers can deliver more accurate research findings which can impact positively on future change in policy. Changes in policy can also have a positive impact on the lives of adolescents (Vyas et al., 2022). According to Chen et al. (2010), adults have roles and responsibilities in youth-led research and 'it is not about getting out of the way or giving up their power, rather it is about balancing and negotiating multiple roles and constantly adapting them to new situations' (p. 235). Adolescents benefit from participating in the design and critique of policies and interventions that affect their lives. At the same time, adults benefit by recognising the skills and expertise of adolescents in creating policies and interventions that are relevant and appropriate for youth (Wang, 2006) and therefore more successful, beneficial and cost effective.

Holland et al. (2010) defined power as 'dynamic and relational', beyond the dichotomy of researcher as the powerful one and participant as powerless. Participation is not static. As the research develops, Flicker et al. (2008) suggested that adolescents may demand more control and participation as they develop trust with the researchers as well as in their own skills and abilities. Power relations in research are shaped by the status of both the researcher and the adolescents (Healy, 2021). Power relations can be reinforced by institutional constraints regarding for example funding and publication of findings which might be very specific or restrictive for a specific age or social class (Wrede-Jäntti et al., 2021).

Theorists such as Olesen (2021), however, consider that data production will never be unaffected by power relationships, as the responsibility for analysis and interpretation of results falls on the researchers, independent of how close researchers and participants worked in producing the data. There is a fundamental imbalance between researchers and participants (Olesen, 2021), they are not equal. According to Aldana and Richards-Schuster (2021) there is a need to recognise power, bias and privilege within collaborative research.

According to Ozer (2016), youth-led participatory action research (YPAR) is an approach where power and equity are considered with intention regarding processes and outcomes. Power sharing is essential in the definition of the problem, research design, interpretation of data and actions. High-quality implementation of YPAR requires ongoing and intentional processes to build trust and balance power sharing in decision-making between adolescents and adult facilitators in different phases of the project (Gibbs et al., 2020). Youth researchers should share ownership over key aspects of the research design, data interpretation and the strategies to address the problem (Ozer, 2016).

Ethics is another important element interrelated with power. Ethical practices require constant attention and reflection to handle the inevitable power dynamics (Wulf-Andersen et al., 2021b). Sharing information and regular dialogue is essential to make the needed adjustments during the research process. It is a dynamic process (Krane et al., 2021). Power, therefore, is dynamic; involving adolescents in research is a complex, diverse and non-static process that fluctuates between different levels of power (Krane et al., 2021).

The reflexive approach (Healy, 2021) enables researchers to actively seek more inclusive research practices while recognising how the researcher influences who and what is included in the research. Anselma et al. (2020) suggest it is important to reflect constantly with participants on the aims of the study and together create a mutual understanding of its responsibilities and rationale.

There is a need to extend the definitions and boundaries of what research is, in order to include the wide diversity of adolescents and the contexts in which research currently takes place (Healy, 2021). According to Anselma et al. (2020), sharing power may not be possible for every research decision. On occasions, researchers must follow guidelines to ensure scientific integrity and methodological quality as well as follow the principles of any theoretical principles underpinning the study (Anselma et al., 2020).

2.2 Diversity and Inclusion

Providing equal opportunities for all adolescents who want to engage should be part of good practice in participatory research. This, however, is not always achieved. The participation approach is generally practised by adolescents who have volunteered or been selected by adult facilitators (Ozer & Douglas, 2013). These adolescents probably have an existing interest and the potential to become researchers (Krane et al., 2021; Ozer & Douglas, 2013). Involving a wide variety of adolescents can be time-consuming, challenging to manage and requires resources (Krane et al., 2021). Understanding, therefore, that you will never be able to capture all perspectives, the goal should be to include some adolescent voices that can help to contextualise and generate knowledge in a co-creational process (Krane et al., 2021).

Diversity in research is very important. Oridota et al. (2023) found in their systematic review on participatory action research with children and adolescents that only 27 per cent of studies included participants from developing countries. Shortt and Ross (2021) recruited participants from their schools but explicitly requested that these were:

1. students who do not get the opportunity to become involved in projects
2. young people with additional support needs
3. from different genders
4. from different ethnic groups.

Researchers should think about how best to include those adolescents who may struggle to join a group via means of an advocate or using video conference (Lightfoot & Sloper, 2002). Petrie et al. (2006) consider that involving a wide spectrum of adolescents in an effective manner can be difficult, particularly those who may have communication impairments, whose first language is not English (or the research language), whose legal status is in process and those who may be vulnerable and unsettled due to their ethnic background, for example. Responding to these issues means that the most effective methodologies may be developed together with participants while the research is in progress, meaning the study will not be defined at the outset and requires resources and willingness from researchers (Petrie et al., 2006).

Harper and Carver (1999) identified some recommendations provided by adolescents themselves on how to engage adolescents with high-risk behaviours such as injection and drug use in research and programme activities. These recommendations are:

1. Programme activities should be easily accessible to out of school adolescents and those experiencing high-risk living conditions and behaviours.
2. Activities should be carried out away from schools.
3. All aspects of the research and programmes should be confidential.
4. Programme and research communications should be delivered in the 'language' (street talk) of adolescents themselves.
5. Research and programme activities should be culturally sensitive.
6. All materials must be presented in a 'gang-neutral' manner.

Being fair and representative is important for adolescents. Stafford et al. (2003) consulted children and adolescents who said they wished consultations were fair, representative and inclusive. This meant consulting with large numbers of different kinds of adolescents, being picked randomly instead of at the discretion of adults, involving whole schools in consultation, publicly recruiting adolescents to encourage participation (Stafford et al., 2003). Adolescents highlighted the need to be consulted by those who genuinely wanted to hear all their views and take them on board and not just those that fit their agendas. Listening to their views should also include acting on them and they regarded participation as their right and were willing to engage, if it served a useful purpose (Stafford et al., 2003).

Even though researchers wish to be inclusive, recruitment of adolescent research participants can be challenging. According to Van Staa et al. (2009), participatory approaches do not necessarily facilitate recruitment. Adolescents should be given a choice about their level of participation as it should not be assumed that 'more is always better' (Van Staa et al., 2009). Recruitment can be challenging as well due to busy school schedules, exams, geographical location and transportation needs of adolescents with disabilities (Van Staa et al., 2009).

Recruitment can be supported by familiar care providers, for example nurses (Van Staa et al., 2009) and hospital consultants (Beresford & Sloper, 2003), or carried out by investigators (Grady et al., 2014) in a snowballing manner. Beresford and Sloper (2003) also used leaflets for recruitment but had different versions for adults and older and younger adolescents. Leaflets can be distributed, for example, via mental health organisations, high schools, colleges and universities (Ito-Jaeger et al., 2022). Due to the design of their study, Bidargaddi et al. (2017) also advertised the study through a recruitment agency of clinical trials, schools, youth organisations, community-based organisations, local councils. Other methods used to recruit participants have been websites (Van Staa et al. 2009) and paid advertising on social media such as Twitter, YouTube and Google Ads (Bidargaddi et al., 2017). The keywords for these advertisements were selected by adolescent participants themselves. Using a variety of methods may help to target and include a wider variety of adolescents into the study.

2.2.1 *Language*

Language is important in research, as the selection of it can have a different impact on the potential participants throughout the research, from participant recruitment to dissemination. The way participants are defined, described and labelled will resonate, or not, with who they are and how they perceive and describe themselves. It may provide a sense of belonging that interested them to be involved in your research, instead of exclusion and lack of identification where they decide not to engage because it is not relevant or interesting to them. Mallan and Singh (2010) described adolescents as 'tech-savvy'; however, this assumption did not necessarily mean that they were interested in participating in the online research. To support participant recruitment, Mallan and Singh (2010) produced a video which explored the concept of tech-savvy by incorporating different media such as images, song lyrics, videos, articles and characters from adolescent fiction. The video also had a fast pace, a strong musical score and quickly changing imagery (Mallan & Singh, 2010). The video, however, even if it appealed to adolescents, did not mean adolescents understood or perceived themselves as tech-savvy. This was confirmed by the research findings where participants reported that their knowledge of the term was low, and 60 per cent of the 57 participants who took part in the research did not consider the term appropriate to describe themselves (Mallan & Singh, 2010). The researchers interpreted this as participants' reluctance to see themselves in 'adult society's terms' (Mallan & Singh, 2010). Adolescents should probably be consulted on the adequacy of terminology and what language would be more appropriate to use to refer to them. More than adolescent reluctance, researchers should respect adolescents and spend time, energy and resources getting to know them before attempting to engage them in a research study.

Academic language has been described as an obstacle to authentic partnership and collaboration (Krane et al., 2021). Academic language and complex terminology may be difficult for adolescents, and for anyone outside the specific discipline, to understand. Consequently, adolescents may lose interest or decide to not engage at all.

2.2.2 *Acknowledge the Developmental Needs and Capabilities of Adolescents*

Researchers should be aware and consider that adolescents (depending on their age and other factors) will have limited autonomy, which will affect their capacity to attend research-related activities (Merves et al., 2015). Adolescents may have limited control over their own time and schedule (Merves et al., 2015). One strategy used by Chen et al. (2010) in their study involving adolescent girls was to engage them according to their interest and expertise. Participants interested in data oversaw creating charts in Excel. Those girls who enjoyed writing completed the introduction and the overview of the project. There was a section on photography findings, so adolescents interested in editing photos and writing captions oversaw that (Chen et al., 2010). Overall, research with adolescents should focus on creating an environment where participants can develop their current abilities and continue to grow (Chen et al., 2010) and develop their skills.

Studies have identified the need to have a combination of ages in adolescent advisory boards as this can lead to a variety of opinions and strong ties with different groups (Oridota et al., 2023). Participation of younger groups is limited. This age group is underrepresented in research (Shamrova & Cummings, 2017). Including younger adolescents can make them feel appreciated when their input is genuinely valued and they are treated as equals (Oridota et al., 2023).

2.3 Participant Retention

Keeping participants engaged in a research study can be challenging. Age-appropriate designs and topics can be key for ensuring permanence but also giving feedback and continuing to provide activities and ways for them to engage throughout the research process can be useful strategies. Trained participants may outgrow the study and new participants may need to be recruited and trained (Anselma et al., 2020). This may require additional money and time to be invested, which should be included in the research plan otherwise it may mean delays in the overall research process.

Research studies may be subject to funding applications. According to Anselma et al. (2020), these processes can be lengthy and uncertain.

For this reason, engaging participants in the initial design of the study may be challenging when there is no certainty of the funding outcome. There is a risk, therefore, of losing an opportunity of mutual understanding between the researchers and participants early on about possibilities and boundaries (Anselma et al., 2020). Ballonoff et al. (2006) provided some ideas on how to support continued adolescent engagement:

1. Have a clear vision and a timeline of the full scope of the project.
2. Provide opportunities for adolescents to present their ideas and get feedback and encouragement of their content and process.
3. Provide opportunities for adolescents to reflect, initiate and engage in social action.
4. Network with larger social actions and movement organisations to provide support for action and enable adolescents to focus on the 'bigger picture'.

2.3.1 *Facilitating Engagement and Research Retention*

Training can be a way to support retention. Participants may benefit from developing their capacity for participation through training (Shamrova & Cummings, 2017) and these skills may be transferable to other aspects of their lives. Adolescents should be trained if the research involves equipment of any kind (e.g. photo and video cameras) as this will enable them to capture and express their voice in their own terms. Adolescents need to be trained in and informed about the rights and responsibilities of research involving human subjects, particularly the importance of confidentiality (Powers & Tiffany, 2006).

Shortt and Ross (2021) first worked with adolescent researchers to understand their base knowledge of the research topic, for example their ideas about health and well-being. One of the potential limitations of this method is that researchers used flash cards with determinants of health identified by researchers from topics from the literature and not from the adolescents themselves. Even though the adolescents were encouraged to bring their own concepts to the discussion, this did not happen (Shortt & Ross, 2021). Even though they stratified the concepts according to how important these were to them, the set of determinants may not have captured adolescents' views comprehensively. Some studies, such as TEEN HEED (Oridota et al., 2023), included training for adolescents before their involvement in the studies. Components of this training included:

1. team building
2. group facilitation skills
3. reviewing the workshop/intervention curriculum
4. skills for asking questions: ensuring participants provided open responses and knew how to avoid leading questions
5. skills to identify analytical skills
6. identifying and reducing bias in analysis and data collection.

Different strategies and activities were used with adolescents in training which were games, play and mix-match activities (Shortt & Ross, 2021). Chen et al. (2010) used interactive and hands-on activities, practical exercises, discussions and role play to train their research participants in research, training and photography skills as well as research ethics and protecting participant confidentiality. Van Staa et al. (2009) organised interview technique training with a national newspaper. Adolescents were trained for three hours on sample questions. They also carried out role play with hospital staff to evaluate their interviewing technique (Van Staa et al., 2009).

Training, until now, has been described as delivered from adults to adolescents. However, adolescents can also be involved in training adults on how to successfully engage adolescents in participatory research. Chen et al. (2010) described how girls, because of their involvement in the study, taught adult staff in the organisation involved in the research how to engage girls in participatory evaluation.

Training, however, may not be enough. Dunn and Mellor (2017), for example, trained adolescents to carry out literature reviews; however, this training was never put in practice. According to Dunn and Mellor (2017), smaller group sessions, extra time and extra budget were needed to turn this training into practice but there was no capacity for the research to achieve this.

Another way to engage adolescents in research is by having different roles for them. Involving adolescents in varying roles and stages of a research process is a crucial component of participatory approaches (Oridota et al., 2023; Winton, 2007), particularly the inclusion of adolescents in conducting the research and analysing results. Participation must be sustained throughout the research process for the research to be considered truly participatory (Winton, 2007). The challenge is, however, that adolescents and younger research participants tend to be involved at later stages of research and are underrepresented in the early stages of design and data analysis (Freire et al., 2022; Shamrova & Cummings, 2017).

Shortt and Ross (2021) carried out a study where young people ranging from 10 to 18 years of age were the researchers who designed the themes, methods and conducted the research. According to Powers and Tiffany (2006), adolescents may gain the trust of other adolescents more easily than adults and may gather data that is valid and reliable.

Valdez et al. (2021) had an adolescent coalition group. This group approved the questions of the survey used in the study. Adolescents contributed to the regional, cultural and linguistic expertise to develop a community- and adolescent-informed instrument. Coad and Coad (2008) included an advisory board of 12 participants with diverse ethnic origins. The researchers met with the group and explained the need for the study, the roles for adults and children, time commitment, foreseen benefits and recognition for participation (vouchers). Participants were trained at a time convenient for them (e.g. after school or college for six weeks) and at a location and pace suitable for the needs and abilities of young people. The advisory group supported the design, pilot and verification of the interview schedule. Then it contributed to developing the questionnaire used in the study. A pilot study was carried out to validate the scale. Livingood et al. (2017) engaged adolescents through participatory research methods to develop a digital communication intervention to reduce adolescent obesity. As part of their methodology, they included an adolescent advisory board over the three years of the research. Adolescents were asked to attend a two-hour-long meeting bimonthly. One of the challenges, however, is adolescents ageing out or dropping out of a longitudinal project. Adolescents developed questions and probes together with the research team and led the focus groups themselves.

Petrie et al. (2006) also had an advisory board that had specific roles including:

1. sensitising the research team of local youth cultures
2. providing advice on local conditions and where to select research participants
3. drafting information leaflets
4. testing the interview schedule
5. supporting the development of interview schedules
6. acting as co-researchers
7. carrying out data validation and analysis
8. disseminating findings.

All these roles were on a voluntary basis; adolescents could take part in one or several of these roles if they wished to do so.

Maglajlic and RTK PAR UNICEF BiH Team (2004) had a research group in each country where the research study was conducted. The adolescent

Table 2.1 *Participant roles*

YPAR group	Children researchers and academic researchers
Action group	Consisted of the YPAR groups of children recruited in every school 6–8 children Met weekly or every two weeks, for 45–60 minutes
Planning group	Researchers, local government managers and members of the YPAR group
Youth Council	This group started in year 3 and consisted of representatives of three schools; it was more focused on community actions than school-based actions

members decided in conjunction with the research team the research topic, how to carry out the research, when and with whom was the research going to be conducted and the data analysis. They also worked on proposals to develop the strategy which was the main objective of the study.

Anselma et al. (2020) included children, in this case, through several stages of the study, in a longitudinal evaluation; however, the involvement of participants can work for adolescents as well. Participants were involved as partners from the research design stage, for example carrying out a needs assessment to identify two needs they had, which became the research aims (Anselma et al., 2020). Participants were engaged in different roles (Table 2.1).

One important consideration by Anselma et al. (2020) was to allow schools to make their own decisions about engaging participants. Some schools allowed all participants to engage in the research, whereas others selected those who could miss academic time without having a negative impact on their studies. Other schools allowed members of the student council to join. This selection process has implications for participation and may introduce bias in the participants; however, it also engaged schools that may have otherwise not engaged at all and the views of all these participants would have been excluded from the beginning.

Participants in this study were trained in research skills that they used to develop, implement and evaluate throughout the research process.

1. Action teams conducted research to validate the findings of the needs assessment.
2. Programme goals and research objectives were developed.
3. Participants selected the best ideas by voting and were involved in implementation plans.
4. At the end of the first year, these implementation plans were pilot tested.

Participant-driven recruitment is a peer-based method to recruit members of hidden and marginalised populations (Powers & Tiffany, 2006). Valdez et al. (2021) included an adolescent-led recruitment strategy. Adolescents recommended that the recruitment messages should be very clear about the benefits of adolescent participation. The youth coalition also provided insights into the general culture of the research participants, who to partner with and how to incentivise participation. Adolescents emphasised the need for participant confidentiality and safety (Valdez et al., 2021). Merves et al. (2015) consider the importance of placing the responsibility of engagement in the study on the adolescents. They put study information in youth-friendly spaces, but the adolescents had to contact the research team themselves. This exercise was done purposefully to build competency, and it increased the likelihood of engagement and commitment to the study.

De Winter and Noom (2003) involved adolescents in the design of a draft interview and they provided feedback on content and wording. The research team presented a draft protocol of the questions and adolescents provided feedback through in small groups; after that, the group provided additional feedback through email.

Studies need to ensure that they have age-appropriate data collection tools; however, this should be rigorous as well to ensure that the research findings are reliable (Shamrova & Cummings, 2017). For example, Chen et al. (2010) carried out data collection using adolescents themselves working together, in pairs, to support each other during the process. The research team met regularly with participants to evaluate their progress and share any experiences. The research team was still in charge of organising day-to-day activities, administration and coordination of research activities, for example coordinating data collection. Adolescents wanted to be involved in the design and wording of research questionnaires (Stafford et al., 2003; Van Staa et al., 2009).

Not involving adolescents in data analysis is a way to disregard adolescents' knowledge and meaning-making, replacing them with an adult interpretation which may not be accurate (Shamrova & Cummings, 2017). Involving adolescents in data collection, however, needs to be carefully considered. Very sensitive issues may not be suitable for certain ages, and, in some cases, these might negatively impact the data collection. To ensure the quality and validity of the data, adolescents should be involved in data collection training before carrying out the fieldwork. In some cases, data collected from adolescents by other adolescents may reduce anxiety and increase accuracy of results. Oridota et al. (2023), for example, collected data on blood pressure which can be affected by participant stress; it may be more accurate when these external factors are controlled and reduced (Oridota et al., 2023).

To ensure the meaningfulness of participation, adolescents should be included in data analysis. This can be done with different techniques, for example reflection workshops that provide a space for children to voice their opinions on the findings (Shamrova & Cummings, 2017). Involvement in data analysis prevents researchers from drawing quick, shallow and naïve conclusions from the data (Krane et al., 2021). Holland et al. (2010) shared key themes with adolescents after a first level of analysis was carried out. They used photographs and diagrams as well as verbal or written media depending on the needs of each participant. It is important to consider that not all the adolescents will have the same reaction and interaction with the data. Holland et al. (2010) described that some adolescents were interested and engaged in discussion, but some had a passive response and no engagement. Some adolescents were also bored when reading texts. Alternatively, Holland et al. (2010) provided recorded transcripts that adolescents could listen to.

Adolescents were invited to comment on draft versions of the analysis of the research transcripts (Van Staa et al., 2009). This was done through email (Van Staa et al., 2009). Flicker (2008) engaged adolescents who were part of the research working group in the analysis. All identifiers were removed from the transcripts and a coding scheme was designed collaboratively. Adolescents were trained in Nud*ist, a qualitative data management software. The group met once a week over four months. In these meetings, the group reviewed worksheets and discussed main themes, and the collective notes were recorded in summary tables (Flicker, 2008).

Coad and Coad (2008) provided adolescents with an anonymous sample of interview for analysis. The participant advisory group read and coded the information on the margin using words and numerical codes. The group used arts-based techniques to agree on a range of key themes. The researchers supported the analysis by providing sections of published work; however, the coding was agreed by the group. This process was innovative but also described as time-consuming and required flexibility from researchers (Coad & Coad, 2008).

Livingood et al. (2017) also included adolescents in data analysis. They were trained on analysing focus groups notes using content analysis. This enabled them to identify themes. In a second session, adolescents completed a matrix for each theme identified and displayed it on a poster that included notes and quotes under each theme, and these were displayed around the room.

Overall, the inclusion of adolescents in data analysis can be sensitive as this may compromise confidentiality. Data may have been shared with a single researcher based on a relationship of trust and participants may not want to share their experiences with others. Considering this issue, Holland et al. (2010) asked adolescents to look at their own data only. This, however, meant that young people were not able to identify any similarities to, differences with or connections between the data from all participants.

Involving adolescents in data dissemination will enable the inclusion of adolescents' voices in conferences or publications such as supplementary presentations, panel discussion and texts (Wulf-Andersen et al., 2021b). Petrie et al. (2006) facilitated the involvement of adolescents in data dissemination. Members of the Advisory Group carried out a presentation at local conferences and universities. Flicker (2008) had an adolescent intensive dissemination strategy. For a peer research audience, three scholarly papers were written. Adolescents designed zines for community distribution. Zines are self-published, non-commercial magazines using, for example, collage techniques and with original text and images. The team were also involved in developing three community newsletter articles and 21 conference presentations. Flicker (2008) also organised a community-wide forum for youth and service providers. The findings of the work were used to inform practice across sectors. Service providers were advocating more effectively for adolescents. A website was also created to provide youth treatment information needs (Flicker, 2008).

Participatory Data Analysis

Chen et al. (2010) show an example of participatory data analysis, which was carried out in a group workshop.

This study used an inductive qualitative analysis method to analyse participants' responses:

1. Read participant responses. Participants try to identify patterns in the responses and discuss ways to group similar responses into categories.
2. Identify key themes and patterns. Pairs presented their categories on chart paper to the larger group where they received feedback from their peers, adult staff and other team members.
3. Tally responses and calculate percentages. Select quotes to illustrate the themes. Participants presented their findings to the group as a final report using PowerPoint.

Creating the infrastructure and the positive environment to enable interaction between stakeholders, adults and adolescents is another way to promote engagement and retention. The space can induce feelings of safety and or belonging, feeling recognised and able to contribute, or completely the opposite (Wulf-Andersen et al., 2021b). Researchers can ask adolescents themselves to suggest spaces where they would feel comfortable to meet (Wulf-Andersen et al., 2021b).

Adolescents are more likely to open up about their experiences in a supportive environment which enables a meaningful contribution from them (Vyas et al., 2022). The regional context in which research takes place, including the youth culture, research practices and politics of participation, shape the discussion of adolescent participation (Wulf-Andersen et al., 2021a). The setting can have an important influence on the dynamics of a consultation with adolescents. For example, Stafford et al. (2003) suggest that school settings can inhibit adolescents from expressing themselves, so there should at least be a guarantee of anonymity and a choice of non-classroom spaces. The context in which adolescents and researchers meet for the research is a determinant in the involvement that will take place (Wulf-Andersen et al., 2021a).

Group meetings with adolescents can be held in venues that are geographically close, as this can facilitate access to adolescents with physical impairments (Beresford & Sloper, 2003). Meeting spaces and activities must be purposefully youth friendly (Merves et al., 2015). For example, round tables or board rooms may not facilitate interaction and engagement (Merves et al., 2015). In their research study, Merves et al. (2015) provided office spaces for adolescents with cubicles, computers, access to internet, printers and mailboxes for each one.

Creating a suitable environment requires time (Oridota et al., 2023). Lightfoot and Sloper (2002) described that time is needed to carry out social exercises at the beginning of group activities to enable participants to get to know each other and feel comfortable with each other. Activities should also include a balance between serious work and fun (Lightfoot & Sloper, 2002). Other recommendations are to avoid sitting in chairs, use a semicircle and to have drinks, snacks and music (Lightfoot & Sloper, 2002). Research has found that the way the content is presented is important. Workshops, for example, should seem more like a conversation than a lecture (Oridota et al., 2023).

The way in which activities are conducted with adolescents has an impact on their motivation to attend (Petrie et al., 2006). For example, Petrie et al. (2006) summarised past sessions, set the agenda and planned actions at every meeting. This enabled all adolescents to engage even if they had missed previous sessions. Meeting material was circulated in written form (which was ineffective), so other methods were used such as texting (Petrie et al., 2006) as well. Therefore, adolescents could be kept up to date and interested in what was happening in the group. This, however, may not be ethical. Researchers should think about recommendations and restrictions about data keeping and sharing before circulating group information.

Like any other type of research, adolescent participatory health research takes place within an institutional, legal and policy context (Healy, 2021), which will have an impact on the overall process. According to Van Staa et al. (2009) a hospital is not an ideal setting to carry out community-based research. Van Staa et al. (2009) carried out a study with adolescents with chronic conditions in a discotheque. The disco had a radio DJ, graffiti and a breakdance artist. Interviews were held in a discotheque café.

Adolescents' homes can be safe spaces to carry out data collection (Beresford & Sloper, 2003) and it may be suitable for adolescents experiencing an illness or impairment (Birks et al., 2007). Birks et al. (2007) suggest that interviews should be carried out in a room where the child and interviewer are alone; however, due to child protection issues, doors and windows should be open and the child should be visible to other adults in the house. In line with new child protection guidelines, researchers should avoid being alone or behind closed doors with children and adolescents during interviews; however, this can be overwhelming for participants. Small purposeful actions, such as allowing participants to control the recording equipment themselves, can give adolescents a sense of control.

Having an appropriate research team is fundamental (Flicker & Guta, 2008). The team, ideally, should have research, community and clinical experience to meet the professional and ethical standards of research. It is also important to deal with emerging issues with adolescents in a sensitive and responsive way (Flicker & Guta, 2008). Researchers and facilitators should have experience of working with adolescents or, if starting in the field, they should have a commitment, interest and training in the field (Merves et al., 2015). Harper and Carver (1999) highlighted that establishing the initial cohesion with participants was facilitated by a project coordinator and researcher with extensive experience in working with high-risk adolescents who were, therefore, familiar with the norms and 'language' of research participants.

Similarities with peers can also contribute to engagement and retention. Studies should ensure that adolescents who are part of the research team closely resemble study participants to create a sense of comfort and trust (Oridota et al., 2023). Adolescent researchers should be of similar ages to research participants (Shortt & Ross, 2021), have similar ethnic backgrounds and share other similarities with the population targeted by the programme and research studies (Harper & Carver, 1999). In the specific case of Harper and Carver (1999), due to the nature of their study and population, adolescent researchers had to feel confident working on the streets with other adolescents and not be involved in situations where encountering other adolescents may lead to conflict or danger.

Similarities with peers can have a very significant impact on participant recruitment and retention. Harper and Carver (1999) hired adolescents to carry out phone calls to research participants to recruit them for the study follow-up. According to the authors, the adolescents were especially skilled in finding hard-to-reach participants. Having a sense of identification is also important in other aspects of the research. For example, an adolescent designed a logo for the study, and this logo was printed on t-shirts and all materials used in the programme (Harper & Carver, 1999).

2.4 Setting Realistic Expectations

Adolescents may have a variety of reasons for joining a study (Oridota et al., 2023). Maglajlic and RTK PAR UNICEF BiH Team (2004) found adolescents joined to do something useful for their communities, learn something new, become more confident, develop work habits, meet new friends and spend time with them, as well as earn money. Understanding the motivation can contribute to retention: adolescents would be eager to engage in the study if it meets their interests.

It is important to set realistic boundaries in the research study from the start, based on the resources, data and time available, and even on the researchers' skills and capacities; otherwise adolescents may feel let down or betrayed by the researchers. It would be ideal if research could give adolescents exactly what they want or imagine, but this is not always possible. Research, therefore, needs to set some realistic boundaries to avoid disappointment or upset from everyone involved. Shortt and Ross (2021), for example, proposed a qualitative research approach from the outset and then enabled adolescents to select from a variety of qualitative methods.

Merves et al. (2015) developed ground rules in partnership with the adolescents, for example including attendance policies and the consequences of or exceptions to these rules. Additionally, these guidelines included: the role of respect, personal responsibility, responsibility to the research team and accountability. Rules were also agreed upon through a voting process with a two-thirds majority agreement (Merves et al., 2015).

Boundaries should also include ethical and appropriate limits for adolescents involved in the research and research participants (Harper & Carver, 1999). Adolescent researchers should not get involved with co-researchers or other adolescents as this may have a negative impact on research objectivity; for example, participants should not be recruited for inappropriate reasons such as a sentimental interest or attraction (Harper & Carver, 1999). Adolescents should also separate their work life from their social life; no research information should be shared with their friends (Harper & Carver, 1999).

Research that includes adolescents as part of the research team should be flexible. Harper and Carver (1999) worked with adolescents experiencing high risk; this meant there were circumstances where they may not be able to engage in the research, for example due to incarceration, pregnancy, homelessness, depression, substance abuse or trauma. It is important not to exclude adolescents immediately; their circumstances should be evaluated and the necessary changes should be made to accommodate them if possible (Harper & Carver, 1999).

Researchers must set realistic expectations regarding the capacity of the research to generate change and the speed at which this may happen. Aldana and Richards-Schuster (2021) described adolescents getting frustrated with the slow pace of change. Adults must help adolescents to recognise the efforts they are making, visualise the 'big picture' and celebrate small victories along the research process (Aldana & Richards-Schuster, 2021), as well as after it. This means dissemination of findings and the impact of these should be followed up over time and provided for adolescent participants, even if the research process has ended. This, of course, requires resources in terms of time and money and ways to keep engagement over time. Since changes do not happen immediately, this is a crucial component of the research.

2.5 Selecting the Most Suitable Research Method

Stafford et al. (2003) consulted participants themselves about their thoughts about different research methods. These small group discussions were described as positive because adolescents felt less shy around other adolescents, and as a space to share ideas, it was described as fun, quick and convenient. These groups would work better if carried out in privacy, away from teachers and led ideally by an outsider. Adolescents liked having their friends but, importantly, thought sensitive topics would be easier to discuss with other adolescents who they knew they would never see again.

Individual interviews were described by adolescents as a very personal method, which made them feel listened to and they were an opportunity to express themselves in more detail (Lightfoot & Sloper, 2002). This method was described as time-consuming for researchers. Additionally, adolescents recommend that these interviews and group discussions should be carried out by external personnel so that they could express themselves more freely, particularly if they had a criticism or a negative idea to express (Lightfoot & Sloper, 2002).

Questionnaires were perceived as good because many adolescents can take part from different schools and geographical areas. These are also confidential and anonymous, easy and convenient. Questionnaires, however, can be limited in presenting an accurate picture of people's views and some participants can struggle to write about their personal experiences. Questions should not be boring but easy to understand (Stafford et al., 2003). Written methods are a quick and easy way to obtain information; however, the response rate can be poor. Participants are usually limited in the amount of information they can provide and their capacity to accurately express their ideas and feelings in written form. Asking for follow-up clarification from adolescents may not be possible (Lightfoot & Sloper, 2002).

Adolescents suggested that questionnaires must be short, taking no more than 10 minutes to complete (Lightfoot & Sloper, 2002). This, however, may be an unrealistic task as certain research questions and methodologies may require more information and therefore more and longer questionnaires must be designed. Time should be carefully considered; questionaires can't be too long as to avoid causing fatigue; however, making them too short may result in poor quality produced or incomplete data which may be detrimental for the quality of the study and its capacity to respond appropriately to the research question. In this case, it would be beneficial, for example, to have a pilot questionnaire completed by participants like those targeted by the research to determine how long they take to complete the questionnaires, then shorten them if needed or even divide data collection into different sessions.

The Society for Adolescent Medicine (2003) described that parents may have an underlying fear of questionnaires harming adolescents by promoting or inducing unhealthy behaviours. The authors, on the contrary, explained that completing surveys can increase understanding of adolescents' behaviour and facilitate care seeking (Society for Adolescent Medicine, 2003).

Other writing methods, such as writing a letter, can be more suitable for adolescents who like writing and wish to express their feelings and thoughts in more detail (Lightfoot & Sloper, 2002).

Youth forums and councils are perceived as positive because adolescents can express their views in a space where adults are encouraging them to speak, and they feel listened to. Participants, however, perceived a lack of achievements and changes due to inflexible institutional policies (Stafford et al., 2003).

Role play can be used to explore participant experiences of doctors, healthcare settings and healthcare experiences. Beresford and Sloper (2003) asked adolescents to act out a 'nightmare outpatient appointment' and an 'ideal outpatient appointment'. The content of the role play was not analysed, instead the debriefing of the role play and a subsequent discussion and brainstorm were used to achieve the research objectives.

2.5.1 Selecting the Most Appropriate Technology

Researchers need to appropriately select the best technological platform to match the outcome expected and the best suited for their research objectives and design. For example, platforms such as Zoom may be useful for real-time discussions about data analysis (Gibbs et al., 2020). Adolescents may benefit from in-person meetings to develop group norms and upcoming scenarios surrounding decisions within online environments (Gibbs et al., 2020).

Researchers need to identify the most suitable technology for their study before making a purchase. They should consider price, functions and user friendliness, as well as that these are compatible with the software and hardware available for the subsequent analysis and dissemination of the data (Chen et al., 2010). Both researchers and adolescents should be familiar with the equipment before initiating data collection (Chen et al., 2010).

Letter Writing (Lightfoot & Sloper, 2002)

The researcher asked adolescent participants (in-patients) to write her a letter about their experience in the ward and what changes they would make. The contents of these letters helped to identify participant concerns and supported the creation of an adolescent unit in the ward.

CHAPTER 3

Safety and Ethics in Technological Participatory Health Research with Adolescents

Children have participated in design processes for a long time, and as techniques have evolved their voices have been better heard thanks to participatory design.

T. Ugras et al., 'New co-design techniques for digital game narrative design'

Chapter Highlights

1. The existing evidence about the impact of technology on children and adolescents is conflictive.
2. Ethical principles of offline research may not be applicable to online and technologically mediated research.
3. The development of ethical guidelines is not happening as fast as technological changes are and therefore there may be a delay or gap between both.
4. Respecting the autonomy of adolescent participants and balancing these with the policies, guidelines and demands of different stakeholders (adults, legislations, jurisdictions) is still a huge challenge.
5. Ethics is not static. It should be adapted to the ethical, cultural, social and developmental abilities of every participant. Special consideration should be given to vulnerable populations and those with complex needs.

Involving children and adolescents in research requires a reflexive, responsible and ethical commitment. I am an advocate of including adolescents in research that is about them; however, researchers have a duty to carefully assess the purpose of their involvement and the possible harm and benefits of doing so. This exercise needs to happen very early on, as it will determine many of the following decisions that will guide the study design and subsequent execution and dissemination. Ethics is also fundamental in technological, participatory health research with adolescents.

Kennan and Dolan (2017) believe that involvement of children and young people should not be the outcome of arbitrary decisions; careful consideration should be given to what constitutes harm and benefit and that it does not lead to exposing participants to exploitation and harm (Society for Adolescent Medicine, 2003). On the other hand, being extremely concerned about protection can instead 'silence' the voices of adolescents and deny society the possibility of generating knowledge informed by the experiences and perspectives of adolescents (Kennan & Dolan, 2017). Finding the perfect balance is, therefore, challenging.

Determining benefit and harm may also not be an easy task. According to Kennan and Dolan (2017), the lines between the likelihood of achieving benefit versus harm are usually blurred. This is particularly the case with social research, as the damage may not be immediately visible as it would with medical research. Emotional distress may happen because of intruding in people's lives or if the participant did not enjoy the research experience, particularly if the outcome was opposite to their wishes and views (Kennan & Dolan, 2017).

Expectations for participants (and their families or carers) must be managed; this means being transparent about study limitations which are beyond the control of a researcher (Kennan & Dolan, 2017). The research can change over time; however, researchers have an obligation to be open and transparent. If, for example, the purpose of the research is purely to enhance adult understanding, this needs to be explicit from the start (Stafford et al., 2003).

In most cases, parents have the best interest of their children at heart and are concerned with their physical, psychological and economic well-being (Rogers et al., 1994). In some circumstances, however, this might not be the case. Adults are usually the gatekeepers of adolescents' lives and, as such, researchers must respect this and work in collaboration with them to gain access to their population of interest but also understand the parental wider social context and their own views of safety and ethics. The Society for Adolescent Medicine (2003) considers that parents and communities are the entities in charge of protecting adolescents, therefore they should be respected, as well as included and informed, while acknowledging and respecting adolescent autonomy. All stakeholders should agree and accept the ethical measures in place.

Due to these clear challenges of balancing and getting it 'right' and setting adequate ethical boundaries, a chapter on the ethics of adolescent health research using technology is pertinent as there are few direct provisions, regulatory frameworks and data protection guidelines for children and adolescents. Those available rely heavily on parental consent and make no distinction between adolescents and children (Berman & Albright, 2017).

3.1 Ethical Principles

Ethical behaviour could be slightly subjective and dependent on several factors such as context, culture, religion and historical time. There are several ethical guidelines available; for example, the American Psychological Association recommends that, as a minimum, psychologists who conduct research should inform participants about 1) the purpose of the research, expected duration and procedures; 2) participants' rights to decline participation and to withdraw from a study; 3) factors such as potential risks, discomfort or adverse effects; 4) limits of confidentiality (data coding, sharing, archiving); 5) incentives for participation; and 6) contact details. The British Psychological Society also has a code of human research ethics. Academic institutions and professional colleges also have their own ethics committees and ethical guidelines that researchers and professionals must adhere to. There are some ethical principles which are applied to research almost globally and it is good practice for researchers to adhere to them, for example the Belmont Principles.

3.1.1 Belmont Principles

The Belmont Report consist of three ethical principles (The National Commission for the Protection of Human Subjects of Biomedical and Behavioural Research, 1978; hereafter 'The National Commission', 1978) that were submitted in a report known as 'Research Involving Children' which was submitted to the US president in September 1977. At the time, these principles were applied to gene therapy clinical trials with children but have permeated almost all contexts of ethical considerations applied to research studies (Nagai et al., 2022).

3.1.1.1 Respect for Persons

The principle of respect entails treating a person as a person (Hodges et al., 2023). It includes two ethical convictions. The first one is that all individuals should be treated as autonomous agents and the second is that any individual who experiences diminished autonomy is entitled to protection (The National Commission, 1978). This principle requires that individuals enter research voluntarily and with adequate information (The National Commission, 1978).

3.1.1.2 *Beneficence*

Beneficence states that research participants must be safe from harm and enjoy benefits from involvement and a reasonable balance between both (Hodges et al., 2023). This principle also means securing participants' well-being (The National Commission, 1978).

3.1.1.3 *Justice*

Justice entails the risks and benefits of research in the general population to consider the inclusion and exclusion criteria of research subjects (Hodges et al., 2023). An injustice occurs when a person is entitled to a specific benefit and is denied it, or a burden is imposed unduly (The National Commission, 1978). To support beneficence and justice, research questions must matter to participants and benefit their communities (Hodges et al., 2023).

According to the Belmont Report, informed consent is required to ensure individuals are fully informed to decide what happens, or not, to them. Information should be presented in an organised manner considering the individual's level of intelligence, rationality, maturity, language and capacities (The National Commission, 1978).

Incomplete disclosure is only acceptable if it is necessary to accomplish research goals, there are no undisclosed risks that are more than minimal and there are suitable plans in place for debriefing participants. A clear difference should be defined between when disclosure may destroy or invalidate the research and when it is simply an inconvenience for the researcher (The National Commission, 1978).

3.1.2 *Declaration of Helsinki*

The World Medical Association (WMA) developed the Declaration of Helsinki as a statement of ethical principles for medical research involving human subjects and identifiable human material and data from June 1964. The Declaration is clearly targeted at medical research; however, the ethical principles can be useful and applicable to research in other fields. It states, for example, that the researcher has the duty to protect life, health, dignity, integrity, right to self-determination, privacy and confidentiality of personal information belonging to the research participants (WMA, 2008). The Declaration also states that research should conform with scientific principles and have a guiding research protocol submitted to a research ethics committee. Research must avoid harm to the environment. Potential risk and burden to participants should be assessed and justified if included in research. The benefits should outweigh the risks. Researchers must give consent to provide their data and data management procedures should be in place (WMA, 2008).

3.1.3 Gillick Competence and Fraser Guidelines

Other examples of ethical guidelines, which are very applicable to research in health, are the Gillick competence and Fraser guidelines. The Gillick ruling informs English law regarding children's competence. It does not state an age, but it defines a competent child as one who 'achieves a sufficient understanding and intelligence to enable him or her to understand fully what is proposed' and has 'sufficient discretion to enable him or her to make a wise choice in his or her own interest' (Gillick, 1985, cited by Alderson, 2007, p. 2273). The Society for Adolescent Medicine (2003) emphasised that adolescents who experience chronic illness have been through choices and experiences which have challenged them to have increased capacities.

The Gillick competence and Fraser guidelines consist of a legal case about whether doctors should be allowed to give contraceptive advice or treatment to girls under 16 years of age without parental consent (NSPCC, 2018). Specifically, in 1982, Victoria Gillick used the services of her local health authority and the Department of Health and Social Security to stop doctors providing contraceptive advice to girls under the age of 16 without parental consent. The claims were dismissed but the Court of Appeal reversed the decision. In 1985, this was taken to the House of Lords and Law Lords which supported the original judgement. This indicated that the capability of an adolescent to provide consent depends on their maturity and the nature of the consent (NSPCC, 2018). The adolescent should have the maturity to understand what is involved and have the capacity of making their own decisions (NSPCC, 2018).

3.2 Evaluating and Determining Participant Competence

One of the challenges researchers have is identifying the level of 'competency' in research participants. This is usually determined informally (Schelbe et al., 2014). Competency is a multifaceted concept consisting of the interaction between age, maturity, cognitive ability, moral development, psychological state and social environment (Schelbe et al., 2014).

Competence is a fundamental construct that needs to be explored when considering seeking consent in children and adolescents. According to Alderson (2007), researchers have an initial presumption of children as incompetent. It is challenging for children to question those views from adults, and demonstrating competence over incompetence can be even more challenging (Alderson, 2007).

Competence in health research can have very specific characteristics. As Alderson (2007) argues, children and adolescents who have experienced adversity may have more knowledge, skills and courage than their peers or even adults who may have not experienced serious disability or illness in their lives. Children's competence and autonomy develop through personal experiences and not as a direct consequence of age or physical growth (Alderson, 2007). Alderson et al. (2006) described how children with diabetes, for example, were more advanced than their peers in terms of child development theories. Four-year-old children with diabetes were able to understand the importance of controlling their illness and made decisions towards their best interest. These children were aware that their health depended on their informed commitment (Alderson et al., 2006). Children and adolescents need to be fully informed about procedures, particularly the ones that may be painful or frustrating; otherwise, they may be overwhelmed with fear or anger (Alderson, 2007). This 'sense-making' process should be mandatory, whether consent is being requested or not. Children and adolescents should be informed about the nature, purpose and possible effects of the intervention, as this may reduce misunderstandings and fear.

Alderson (2007) described some of the standards to evaluate competence in a person giving consent:

1. Capacity to understand the relevant information.
2. Ability to retain the information.
3. Capacity to weigh the information to make a reasonable choice.
4. Possibility of making voluntary and autonomous decisions.
5. Ability to communicate the decision.
6. Ability to believe the information.

These criteria are useful; however, they may need to be considered carefully with children and adolescents. For example, for information to be understood, it needs to be explained in an age-appropriate manner. Some children and adolescents may be better with their communication skills, and this may mean they are better at explaining their thoughts and emotions. Others may struggle more to communicate but this does not mean they do not understand the information to make informed decisions.

Chapter 2 described the need to train adolescents in research skills so that they could effectively engage in the research study. Kennan and Dolan (2017) added the need for ethics training, whereby adolescents involved as researchers can learn about their responsibilities towards keeping research participants safe from harm.

Another important component of assessing competence is evaluating the skills and competences of practitioners and researchers who are requesting consent. For example, are they themselves sufficiently able to work with children, adolescents and their parents? This entails being able to help them understand relevant information, resolve misunderstandings and assist them in making informed and reasoned decisions, without putting pressure on them (Alderson, 2007).

3.3 Informed Consent in Health Research

Participant information sheets and consent forms are the most basic and widely used tools of applied ethical principles. These documents are summaries of the research in lay language, which include details about 'the ask' of participants, potential risks of participation, as well as possible sources of support and contact details if they experience distress because of participating in the study. These forms are usually compulsory for academic and clinical research and are widely used. An age-friendly version of these documents can be adapted to the needs and comprehension levels of different ages of children and adolescents. Assent instead of consent is usually sought for those participants under the legal adult age. Seeking children and adolescents' assent to participation in research is valid and important as it has been demonstrated that even young children are able to understand the basic components of research (Crane & Broome, 2017). Including adolescents in the consent process can have benefits for them, for example increased self-control and a higher capacity for decision-making (Society for Adolescent Medicine, 2003).

Informed consent is not a one-time decision participants make; it is an ongoing process that reflects participants' potentially changing perceptions of the study's risks and benefits of the research (Hodges et al., 2023). Adolescents may have limited experience to be able to anticipate the nature and type of questions they will be asked as well as their reaction to these. Schelbe et al. (2014) therefore suggest that researchers should provide written examples of the type of questions participants will be asked in the interview. Parents and adolescents should be communicated with about consent both verbally and in writing (Cook & Krueger-Henney,

2017). The research paradigm and methods should be made explicit as well as their potential benefits and limitations, particularly those local and structural issues which may impede change.

Age-friendly material should be provided but in different formats as well to cater to a variety of reading and comprehension competencies in adolescents (Schelbe et al., 2014). Language is another important aspect that should be considered. Birks et al. (2006) highlighted the need to include information sheets in other languages, which is particularly relevant in pluralistic communities and settings. In some cases, children and adolescents may speak the language of the research but their parents, still in charge of parental consent, may not. Parents are entitled to receive information in the language which they can comprehend and make informed decisions with (Birks et al., 2006).

Crane and Broome (2017) recommend the input of children development specialists in the design of scales for children and adolescents. At the least, scales should be piloted before the study. Quizzes can also be used to determine the level of understanding children and adolescents have of the information provided and they can also be an opportunity to talk more about consent (Crane & Broome, 2017). An interest topic introduced by Hampshire et al. (2012) is participatory ethics. This approach consisted of child and adolescent participants working together with adult researchers to develop guidelines, for example the 12-point Code of Practice which stated, for example, that 'children should benefit from being researchers'.

Sharpe et al. (2021) worked with adolescents with disabilities and used alternative methods to communicate, instead of written consent forms:

1. An accessible information pack;
2. Visual timetables;
3. Image-based emotion card to support their understanding of and how to convey feelings;
4. Visual aids to support written language;
5. A video information sheet, which could overlay a sheet or be saved on a device, using an augmented reality smart device.

Alderson (2007) argues that consent should not be based on an arbitrary age but should instead consider every individual's abilities. The statutory age of consent to treatment varies significantly between countries. Some countries consider it to be at 12, whereas others have identified it to be at 19, which suggests a potentially arbitrary approach (Alderson, 2007).

Adolescents themselves should actively inform the process of adolescents' assent; this must be a regulatory requirement and a critical art of demonstrating respect for adolescents enrolling in health research (Grady et al., 2014). Participation in health research needs to be very explicit that agreeing or refusing to participate will not affect the adolescents' care or service provision (Grady et al., 2014). In some countries, such as Britain, doctors are protected from prosecution when they treat children under 16 years of age without having parental consent if they claim that the child is competent to consent themselves (Alderson, 2007). The Childcare Act (1989, 1991) states that a competent child and anyone with parental responsibility for the child can provide valid consent. This means treatment can be enforced on a child resisting treatment if it is considered that this is in their best interest (Alderson, 2007). In other countries, such as the United States, adolescents are not legally permitted to consent to specific health procedures such as clinical research (Grady et al., 2014).

The Society for Adolescent Medicine (2003) suggested that researchers should evaluate their own state (country) laws to determine if adolescents should or should not be considered as children under federal regulations. If they are not considered children, then parental consent is not needed. If adolescents are considered children, the researchers and research ethics groups and organisations may still decide that parental permission can/should be waived, knowing this is against federal law.

Birks et al. (2006) included signed letters by all consultants in participant packages to inform participants that they were aware of and supported the study, inviting participants to take part. Although no issues are mentioned in the study, it is important to ensure that participants do not feel coerced into being involved in the study and their decision to participate should be independent of their treatment. Including consultants may have forced participants into taking part due to possible fear of retaliation regarding their treatment. Adolescents' assent needs to be carefully considered as younger adolescents may feel pressured to enrol; however, the reasons are not clear. One reason was parents not giving them a voice regarding their participation (Grady et al., 2014). These adolescents require additional support and protection (Grady et al., 2014). For this reason, continuous consent and check-in with adolescents throughout the research process is necessary. Researchers should be careful to make sure adolescents understand the value of participation without feeling pressured to enrol (Grady et al., 2014).

Even though adolescents want a voice, parental involvement is significant in decisions such as their involvement in health research and clinical trials (Grady et al., 2014). Gatekeepers play an important role in identifying research participants. Coad and Coad (2008) had an adult gatekeeper who was a senior play therapist and not an active researcher in the project. The role of this gatekeeper was to protect participants and to gain consent without coercion. Research specific to adolescent health identified that adolescents trust their parents to support them when making decisions about enrolment in health research, and this does not vary by age or severity of illness (Grady et al., 2014). Parents, as usual gatekeepers, may also feel forced to be involved in research studies labelled as 'therapeutic' for fear of harming their child or adolescent by refusing participation (Alderson, 2007).

Another important aspect to consider is legal status. Adolescents (under the age of 18 in most countries) have a different legal status from adults; therefore, adults have a duty of protection towards them. This introduces a logistical concern, as parents or guardians must give their consent for adolescents to be included in a study (Schelbe et al., 2014). Adults can deny participation for children or coerce adolescents into participating (Schelbe et al., 2014). This usually occurs if families are concerned about their privacy and topics adolescents may disclose (Schelbe et al., 2014).

A study carried out in New Zealand (Martel et al., 2019) decided to include adolescents over the age of 16 only, as this allowed them to include participants without parental consent. Apart from being legally allowed to do this, the authors explained that adolescents often visit clinics without parental or guardian awareness and, therefore, this would have been a breach of confidentiality. Adolescents who were not able to provide consent due to cognitive difficulties were excluded from the study. There is, however, no explanation of how these cognitive difficulties were evaluated.

Protecting participant identity is one of the pillars of ethics in research. It has been argued that anonymity, however, is not foolproof, as data can be reidentified (Berman & Albright, 2017). Data can often be either useful or anonymous (Berman & Albright, 2017). It is important to ensure anonymity in all parts of the study. For example, Flicker and Guta (2008) said that it was important to remind adolescents not to write their name at the top of forms or questionnaires. Surveys may be printed as booklets to ensure answers can be covered answers. Adolescents should be given identical writing materials to avoid being identified; for example, same coloured pens. Additionally, they should be given access to a drop box where they can return the material without it being recognised as theirs (Flicker & Guta, 2008).

Researchers need to be clear and transparent about the limits of confidentiality from the start, regarding for example child protection issues. Researchers have an obligation to report any disclosures of abuse, neglect, self-harm or if the adolescent poses a danger to themselves or others (Schelbe et al., 2014). Adolescents should be aware in advance of the risks of taking part in research, for example potential child protection issues that may be disclosed by a research participant (Shortt & Ross, 2021). This information should be explicitly included in participant information sheets and consent forms.

3.3.1 *Situated Ethics Approach*

Situated ethics consists of a constant evaluation throughout the research process to adapt accordingly to the development of the project (Olesen, 2021). Whittington (2019) used situated ethics, where all participants were given the opportunity to consent or withdraw along the life course of the study. The research topic was sexual consent. It was considered that sexual consent had to be 'sought every time' and therefore the researcher decided to model this approach in the research. The researcher described that this approach was not always successful and would sometimes 'get in the way', but she persisted as it was useful in the research process and the research topic.

Adolescents should be made aware that they can revoke their participation at any time, without any consequences for them (Østergaard, 2021). Adolescents may also be willing to engage with the research to protect their benefit entitlements as well as to maintain support from agency workers; however, if this is their motivation, they may disengage from the research very early on (Campbell & Trotter, 2007). Adolescents, however, need to be provided with examples of how to refuse or withdraw their participation, for example periodic check-ins to consider if they are willing to continue the research (Schelbe et al., 2014). Adolescents may also refuse to answer a question and concrete examples of how to do this can be provided: 'just say next please' (Schelbe et al., 2014). Materials and activities should explicitly indicate what participants should do if they feel uncomfortable about any aspect of their involvement in the research (Al Hweidi et al., 2022) or during a specific activity. Overall, it should be clear that refusal to participate in a study does not jeopardise adolescents' access to services (Flicker & Guta, 2008).

3.4 Technology, Research and Ethics

The first ethical consideration about the use of technology in research is that the existent evidence is conflictive about whether technology is beneficial or harmful for adolescents and in what context. Technology is reshaping research methodologies (Gibbs et al., 2020). The development of new media has been so rapid that research is failing to keep up with the pace (Patton et al., 2016). There is therefore a continuous debate over the impact of digital media, whether it is beneficial or negatively impacting on adolescents' social, emotional and cognitive development (Patton et al., 2016).

One very strong example of how technology has reshaped research methods is the adaptation and transformation of traditional research methods. Netnography is the method of conducting ethnographic fieldwork in virtual environments. It is based primarily on the observation of textual discourse, instead of traditional ethnographic face-to-face interactions.

One of the identified advantages of technology in research is the capacity to bridge the geographic and social distances (Gibbs et al., 2020). Social networking and media enable access to information, communication and sharing information with peers, and they generate contents and draw in resources (Patton et al., 2016). Chen et al. (2010) described how technology was an essential tool to attract adolescents and engage them in their project. It is fundamental, however, that equipment is 'right' for the research design and functioning well. Participants in this study, for example, identified that the use of digital cameras – capturing images, recording interviews and using software to create their final report – was their favourite part of the study (Chen et al., 2010).

Digital content that is age appropriate and viewed with adult supervision can boost academic achievement, literacy and improve social connections (Maftei & Merlici, 2023). Improved social network activity may lead to enhanced self-esteem, improved friendship quality, sense of belonging and identity exploration (Maftei & Merlici, 2023). Video games can also improve attention, visual and representational processing, executive functioning and visual spatial working memory (Maftei & Merlici, 2023). Digital media, such as the use of biometric devices, can foster positive approaches to eating, exercise and sleep patterns (Children's Commissioner, 2017). Seland (2024) found that digital engagement can be a coping strategy for young people who experience problems. Children and adolescents perceive digital media as leisure and pleasure as well as a huge potential for learning (Children's Commissioner, 2017).

Stafford et al. (2003) identified the views of adolescents themselves on online research methods. According to their study, these methods can reach many adolescents who are familiar with online methods and enjoy them. In principle, they offer privacy, and adolescents liked not having to travel to avail themselves of the research; however, they do recognise that not every adolescent may have a computer or access to the internet at home. Adolescents themselves have awareness of ethical issues, for example privacy as well as differential accessibility.

Potential limitations of technology in research start with the fact that research is struggling to keep up with evolving technologies that are shaping children's lives, and researchers tend to rely on old methodologies to investigate these new developments (Mallan & Singh, 2010). There are great benefits from social digital connections, but this can increase vulnerabilities, including for example social contagion, violence, mental health, suicide and self-harm and being targeted by extremist groups (Patton et al., 2016). Technology may expose adolescents to potential risks online (Gibbs et al., 2020). There is a growing concern for online safety. Adolescents can experience cyberbullying, grooming, exposure to sexual content and social contagion including self-harm, mass shooting, radicalisation and eating disorders (Patton et al., 2016). Digital media can instead become a promoter of consumer cultures and affect adolescent lifestyle, health and well-being (Patton et al., 2016).

Problematic use of media and the internet has been defined in several ways; however, there is overall agreement that these types of behaviours can be detrimental to adolescent mental and physical health (Maftei & Merlici, 2023). Sleep disturbance and gaming addiction have been linked to new media (Patton et al., 2016). Age-inappropriate and violent content can severely impact development and behaviour (Maftei & Merlici, 2023). Additionally, the more time spent online means less time spent on activities such as exercise, healthy eating and sleeping, which are conducive to a healthy lifestyle (Children's Commissioner, 2017).

The other significant challenge is that the capacity to conduct research online has expanded more quickly than the ethical guidelines for digital research (Hodges et al., 2023) that should accompany them. Online research is perceived as lower risk than in-person research and this may lead the risk of disclosure online to be underestimated (Hodges et al., 2023). According to James et al. (2009), for every young person who is an example of good citizenship online, there are many more examples of intentional or naïve misuses – or ethically ambiguous misuses of digital media.

Ethics in technology is fundamental. James et al. (2009) have described how carefully managed and informed sharing can result in an inspiration, an empowerment and building supportive communities for adolescents. The opposite – careless oversharing – may lead to long-term negative effects on adolescents and the friends or people they write about online.

Adolescents who experience empowering social roles online can build a sense of responsibility towards others, their community and society in general (James et al., 2009). The ethical challenge, therefore, is to maximise the benefits of technology without exacerbating risk and exposing children and adolescents to harm (Children's Commissioner, 2017).

3.5 Defining and Evaluating Risk in Health Research

Identifying and evaluating risk is challenging in health research with children and adolescents (Alderson, 2007). There may be extra risks as children and adolescents may be damaged by short- or long-term interventions and may be liable to live with the side effects for many years. Risk can be quantifiable based on incidence; how many people out of 100 may experience a harmful side effect, for example (Alderson, 2007). The other aspect of risk is magnitude. This aspect is qualitative as it depends on a person's evaluation of whether it is severe or minimal, which is subjective (Alderson, 2007).

Risk is not only present because of treatment or intervention but is also potentially present in other stages of the research; for example, research reports may inadvertently lead to humiliation, embarrassment or stigmatise disadvantaged groups including children and adolescents with mental or behavioural issues. Flicker (2008) carried out research with HIV-positive adolescents and highlighted potential risks regarding disclosure and stigma. Their participation in research could jeopardise the respect of their peer group and put them at risk of being tokenised.

3.5.1 Researching 'Sensitive' Topics

Topics that are 'sensitive' require extra ethical thought. It is important to consider what the meaning of sensitivity is. Overall, researchers should ask themselves who is this topic sensitive for? Is it a sensitive topic due to cultural or contextual reasons and, therefore, may not be as sensitive in another context? It may also be sensitive only for a group due to generational differences, for example. Is it sensitive as it may cause embarrassment or sensitive due to potential emotional reactions? And lastly, even if it is socially sensitive, what are an adolescent's approach, views and opinions about this? Is it sensitive for them also and, if so, how? This will help the research team to consider how best to approach the topic to ensure that sensitivity does not lead to upset or any negative consequence for a research participant.

There are, however, topics that have been traditionally considered as 'sensitive' for research, for example sexuality and mental health. According to Petrie et al. (2006), topics such as sexual behaviour in young people is a very personal topic in nature and it is also an area where adults are prone to make judgements and would often seek to control. Due to the research topic, Petrie et al. (2006) sought parental consent for every young person under 16 years of age to take part in their interviews, even though the research was taking place within schools. The research topic might attract adult disapproval and media attention. The topic could also lead to disclosure of information that may require child protection intervention. For this reason, researchers were clear about the limits of confidentiality and had an 'opt in', 'opt out' approach where adolescent could engage on a voluntary basis.

Adolescents with mental health issues are described and perceived as a vulnerable population (Olesen, 2021). Research in this population requires extra precautions; however, they should be given the opportunity to make an informed choice regarding their involvement in the research (Olesen, 2021). Excluding these adolescents without giving them the opportunity would be paternalistic and unethical (Olesen, 2021).

Researchers need to have reasonable expectations of adolescents' capacity to participate according to their abilities. This means that not all adolescents may be engaged in the research to the same capacity or the same way (Olesen, 2021). Whittington (2019) argues that alongside safeguarding procedures, researchers should develop robust participation and engagement strategies that consider the competences of adolescents, their agency and right to participate, independent of the sensitivity of the topic.

3.5.2 Safety and Vulnerability

An essential part of ethics is safety and supporting adolescents continuously through the research process by ensuring they are going to be well and feel well through every stage of the research study. There are several examples of good practice from the literature. Beresford and Sloper (2003) prepared 'help packs' for adolescents. These packs had contact details of key voluntary organisations that could provide extra support for adolescents. Independent project advisors were available to support adolescents. These advisors were knowledgeable about the different illnesses and conditions that adolescent participants might have (Beresford & Sloper, 2003). They were available to provide information and advice by telephone. They were also introduced to adolescents on the first group meeting (Beresford & Sloper, 2003).

Sartain et al. (2000) established a support network to help researchers manage research-related stresses to provide appropriate responses for participants and their families. Possible scenarios were discussed with professionals in child protection on how to deal with disclosures of abuse or other situations where confidentiality had to be breached due to child protection issues.

Specific groups of adolescents may have unique needs and characteristics that may leave them in a place of vulnerability in society that permeates any participatory research exercise carried out with them. One of the issues is defining 'vulnerability'. Holmarsdottir (2024) provided a definition of vulnerability which entails a person's lack of ability to protect their own interests with a lack of capacity for decision-making as well as environmental factors that impede their access to rights, opportunities and power. Some of these adolescents also experience significantly unequal access to technology. Some of them experience the consequences of a digital gap which limits the opportunities and the capacity of adolescents to meaningfully engage in the digital world and access the benefits of technology. Digital inequalities include innate vulnerability but also situational vulnerabilities such as gender, sexuality, race, ethnicity, disability, health, education, rural residence and global geographies (Holmarsdottir, 2024). Closing the digital gap is imperative as this would stop social and economic inequalities from worsening. This means that significant efforts are needed to ensure children and young people have access to develop the skills they need to use digital technologies effectively and safely (Ayllón et al., 2024).

Adolescents with healthcare needs may have a disability that requires medical technology to survive (e.g. tube-feeding equipment) (Watson et al., 2006). Watson et al. (2006) described the way they obtained consent from this group of children, which included adolescents also (0–15 years). Ten participants were non-verbal and three had assisted communication. Researchers spoke to participants about who they were, where they came from and used pictures to explain the research questions (Watson et al., 2006). In some cases, researchers relied on parents and carers for interpretation. According to the researchers, despite relying on parents for interpretation they were confident that they gained 'unique insights' from their participants.

Digital research should avoid replicating marginalising social experiences that could intensify participants' vulnerability. Hodges et al. (2023) worked with Black immigrant and refugee participants and consider that it is important to consult experts in immigrant and refugee issues to avoid negligence when designing studies and in the overall research process. Immigrant adolescents are at a higher risk of participation tokenism, as they are less likely to participate in research, particularly controversial or sensitive topics (Vyas et al., 2022).

Consent with African Americans is not an individual decision but a collective one (Hodges et al., 2023). Regarding research online with this population, Hodges et al. (2023) suggest that researchers must ensure that the recruitment and consent procedures honour cultural decision-making processes. According to Hodges et al. (2023) an iterative consent is appropriate for Black immigrant and refugee families. Iterative consent entails researchers proactively engaging in ongoing conversations with participants about their continuous consent process throughout the research. This becomes particularly relevant in online research where participants may perceive they have fewer opportunities for voicing concerns or queries to researchers (Hodges et al., 2023).

Researchers need to build long-term relationships with Black immigrant and refugee families to ensure community buy-in (Hodges et al., 2023). Recruitment most often occurs in face-to-face community gatherings and places of worship where researchers can build relationships with leaders, community representatives and become partners in the communities. Due to this sense of community, an individual's negative experience in a study may dissuade others from participation by word of mouth or 'snowballing' effect (Hodges et al., 2023). Research teams should include or be led by Black researchers who are cultural insiders as this can provide a suitable pace and direction (Hodges et al., 2023). Additionally, researchers would benefit from training on social positionality and ongoing support regarding their ethnic-racial identity (Hodges et al., 2023).

Another population with specific needs and characteristics is LGBTQ+ adolescents. Gaining access to LGBTQ+ adolescents can be challenging (Schelbe et al., 2014), as some of them may not be 'out' to their family or community. Some may attend LGBTQ+ groups without the knowledge of their parents and guardians, therefore obtaining consent for their participation in research may not be possible. The standard of seeking parental consent could expose LGBTQ+ adolescents to greater harm (Whittington, 2019). Schelbe et al. (2014) described an example where a researcher advocated for a waiver of parental consent. These waivers can be warranted in cases where parental consent may result in harm for the child or adolescent, or parental consent infringes rights to privacy or leads to unjust exclusion. Following the waiver, Schelbe et al. (2014) used 'youth research advocates'. In this case, they were licensed social workers who had individual and collective meetings with the young people to ensure they understood the research, assess any emotional vulnerability and provide any other support needed.

Some adolescents may come from very specific social and cultural backgrounds. Martel et al. (2019) carried out a research study with Maori adolescents to evaluate a screening tool for early detection of mental health issues in New Zealand. This is an interesting example of research that is designed and carried out within a specific cultural group, respecting their culture and values, specifically, the design and ethical considerations that need to be considered to ensure the research is undertaken with rather than on people. Digital research methods, without careful consideration, could instead distance researchers from communities (Hodges et al., 2023).

This study was not designed as a Maori project; however, most participants were and therefore the researchers opted for a co-creation design where Maori culture, values and beliefs were validated, respected and protected. Non-Maori researchers worked in partnership with Maori, allowing them to understand context, specific requirements and challenges, working alongside each other in bicultural research (Martel et al., 2019). YouthCHAT is an electronic, multi-item screening tool developed in 2016 to assess mental health and risk behaviours in young people. Martel et al. (2019) translated YouthCHAT into the Maori language and tested it among Maori youth and clinicians. The study consisted of the design of YouthCHAT, which was informed by clinicians and adolescents and explores information on sexual health, youth stress, conduct disorder, eating issues, substance abuse, depression and anxiety (Martel et al., 2019). This electronic screening tool helped adolescents prioritise concerns and identify areas where they were ready to accept support. Adolescents completed YouthCHAT using a tablet.

3.6 Rewards and Incentives

Providing rewards or incentives for adolescent participation is conflictive. Children's and adolescents' level of vulnerability should be evaluated before making decisions about the use of rewards or incentives. Crane and Broome (2017) consider that young children may not have a full understanding of the value of money and it would be more suitable to give them incentives such as toys, books and movie tickets. Parents and adolescents may be consulted about suitable and age-appropriate incentives. Careful consideration should be given to children and adolescents who may be homeless or financially disadvantaged (Crane & Broome, 2017). Participants should never be exploited and should never be coerced into taking part in research (The British Psychological Society, 2021). Researchers may also want to discuss the most appropriate incentives or compensation with organisations involved in the study, depending on what was useful and significant for a research participant, as well as avoiding any harm (Schelbe et al., 2014).

Compensation for participants may go beyond money. It may include technical assistance and training (Israel et al., 2005). Different examples of rewards and incentives have been reported. For example, students received an incentive (e.g. a water bottle or a key chain) for completing the form whether they took part in the study or not (Ozer & Douglas, 2013). Adolescents received two movie tickets (Oridota et al., 2023). Participants were given gift cards after completing their interview (Østergaard, 2021). Participants received cash incentives for completing the survey and for recruiting new participants (Powers & Tiffany, 2006). Valdez et al. (2021) used 'student dollars' to recognise the participations of adolescents in the study. These dollars could be used to purchase snacks and school promotional items (e.g. t-shirts) from their school's student store.

Rewards may be given in more indirect ways as well in exchange for participation. For example, Harragan (2021) spent time running sessions in the youth club. All adolescents, even those that did not want to take part in the research, could benefit from these sessions. Flicker and Guta (2008) administered their research questionnaire with adolescents but provided them with an educational activity. Adolescents could write down questions and they were answered in the workshop by the adolescent advisory team, and an adult member of the research team was present as a support.

The timing of these incentives should also be considered. To avoid participants feeling coerced into participating, they were given a monetary incentive at the time of assent/consent (Schelbe et al., 2014). According to Lightfoot and Sloper (2002), payment for participation should be offered once adolescents have agreed to be involved in the research. Additionally, payment is needed when involvement is high and over a period. Treats, trips and meals make adolescents feel appreciated as much as cash.

Rewards can have a deep societal impact. Hampshire et al. (2012) described, for example, that a 16-year-old participant used the money obtained from his participation to buy textbooks for school. A 15-year-old used the money to buy fertiliser to contribute to the food production business of his household. Adolescents may experience significant benefits when taking part in the research. Adolescents can become paid researchers in the project (Powers & Tiffany, 2006). This role meant adolescents oversaw surveys, data collection, educational sessions, data analysis and co-authored a journal article (Powers & Tiffany, 2006).

Paying adolescents can also be perceived as exploitation. According to Campbell and Trotter (2007), involving adolescents as co-researchers, paying and training them, has questionable ethical implications as this may not have any use to them, to the extent of possibly exploiting them. Therefore, the benefits and risks should be carefully considered in every case, for a specific group of adolescents and their circumstances.

3.7 Relationships and Collaborations

Research with adolescents requires a systematic communication, collaboration and developing good relationships (Schelbe et al., 2014). Promoting a healthy, working social relationship with adolescents is crucial for success (Vyas et al., 2022); however, the timing and characteristics of these relationships must also be mediated by ethical principles and behaviours.

Different studies emphasise the need to approach and create a relationship with adolescents before starting the research study (Wrede-Jäntti et al., 2021). Whittington (2019) worked with adolescents before ethical approval was sought. The researcher consulted with adolescents over the age of 16 regarding the methodology as well as to determine what was realistic in a collaborative study. Adolescents were also involved in co-developing research methods. This engagement helped develop rapport and interest for the adolescents to participate in the project. It is important to consider the potential risk of approaching participants before seeking consent from them or their parents and carers. In some cases, for example for funders, this might also be considered unethical behaviour instead of good or recommended practice which may jeopardise success in obtaining funding. If, however, there has been an ongoing relationship with an organisation as a worker or facilitator then having pre-existing relationships is expected.

Collaborations are very important in order to access adolescents. These collaborations should be clear about the research objective, risks and benefits. Researchers need to invest time and energy with the gatekeepers before accessing research participants. These collaborative relationships are crucial if problems arise, as mutual decisions can be made based on mutual respect and understanding (Schelbe et al., 2014). Researchers need to identify key personnel who are enthusiastic about the project, have access to the adolescents and are willing to assist in pragmatic tasks (recruitment, obtaining consent, access to physical space) (Schelbe et al., 2014).

From an ethical perspective, organisations (schools, charities, agencies) are usually not compensated with money or any other tangible method, therefore it is crucial to identify how the study will benefit the organisation (Schelbe et al., 2014). Researchers have also worked in partnership with children's charities, for example Children in Scotland (Shortt & Ross, 2021). Researchers were given a contact number for Children in Scotland if they needed to discuss any issues (Shortt & Ross, 2021).

Overall, researchers need to recognise that they need organisations and should negotiate with them as to how the research can be carried out, respecting their culture and ethos as well as ethical practices. If these are compatible with the research then these collaborations will be very powerful and capable of supporting the study and the research team, which is fundamental to the research success and development.

3.8 Inclusion

Inclusion, in Chapter 2, focused on participation in the research process. In this chapter, it is focused on the implications for ethics.

Researchers should carefully ensure children and adolescents involved in research are fully informed about the project and what their participation entails. Having their name or signature on a piece of paper does not mean they have that understanding, but it could be a response to obeying to an adult figure or just assuming it is expected of them. This may translate into children and adolescents dropping out of the study or not participating meaningfully as they were not interested to begin with.

The emotional, cognitive and language ability of children and adolescents varies. Not all adolescents of a similar age function at the same level (Schelbe et al., 2014). Researchers must be ready to accommodate different levels of skills to meet the variety in developmental needs of adolescents (Powers & Tiffany, 2006; Schelbe et al., 2014).

Adolescents can have the capacity of deciding themselves to participate or not in health research; however, this involves an assessment of their cognitive development, psychosocial circumstances, emotional state, judgement and personal circumstances (Rogers et al., 1994).

Rogers et al. (1994) have provided guidelines for adolescent participation in health research; however, these principles are relevant to inform any study with adolescents:

1. Design research in which adolescent identity and data cannot be linked.

2. Ensure the privacy and confidentiality of participants in all stages of the research: a) selection, b) setting, c) question design, d) collecting and storing data.
3. Interact with community representatives.
4. Ensure that researchers have made reasonable effort to obtain parental/adult consent.
5. Unemancipated adolescents can take part in the study if they are already obtaining healthcare services and the research is carried out with these services.
6. Adolescents may only be allowed to consent independently if the study involves minimal risk.
7. Adolescents who will participate without parental consent should be evaluated by a trained professional to ensure they have the cognitive ability to comprehend the research and risks, judgement around their personal health and long-term benefits of participation or non-participation, as well as their sense of health responsibility and capacity to comply with research protocols.

3.9 Data Management Online

This section is not solely focused on adolescent research online, as these considerations should be taken for all research carried out online, but they are mostly applied to child and adolescent research. According to The British Psychological Society (2021), internet-mediated research can make it difficult to adhere to existing offline ethical principles. Online research also means participants may often be in many different countries and therefore situated and governed by different cultures and legal jurisdictions (The British Psychological Society, 2021). The British Psychological Society (2021) provided the following guidelines for online research:

1. Privacy and anonymity. The distinctions between public and private spaces may be unclear. Data that was anonymised could eventually become identifiable when data sets are linked or specific analyses or algorithms are applied to it. The fact that internet communication is often public, visible, traceable and permanent does not mean that it can be used for research purposes. The opinions of users on this matter vary and are unclear. Personal webpages may seem like public documents; however, the copyright remains the property of the web hosting company. Consent should still be sought. Consent online should be simple, as lengthy consent may be quickly skimmed

through or not read at all. The British Psychological Society (2021) also recommends that the General Data Protection Regulation (GDPR)/UK Data Protection Act (2018) information is included: 'I understand that information will be used only for the purposes previously outlined and my consent is conditional upon the university complying with its duties and obligation under the Data Protection Act 2018.' The names of forums or website where information was obtained should not be revealed if this compromises the safety and anonymity of participants. Pseudonyms used by participants online should be treated with the same respect as personal names would be treated. Data transcription services online, such as AI, may not be compliant with participant confidentiality policies and should therefore not be used (The British Psychological Society, 2021).

2. Data storage. Careful consideration should be given to where data is stored. Vulnerabilities can emerge when data is stored in third-party software which may become compromised. This may lead to a higher risk of linking data sets and releasing personal or sensitive identifiable information. Identifiable data collected automatically by software (e.g. location, IP address, email address) should only be used to check for multiple completions and should be deleted immediately.
   If researchers need to match existing data with participant responses over time, participants should provide a memorable code instead.
   If personal information is still needed, this information should at least be stored separately from participant responses. Unencrypted emails offer low security (The British Psychological Society, 2021).
3. Scientific integrity. Online research usually means the researcher has less control over the research procedures and environment, for example who has access to participate, the conditions in which participants are responding, participant feelings or reactions to the research process and variations generated by different hardware or software used by research participants. Another risk to research integrity is the use of AI or 'bots' to complete information; particularly if these are paid surveys, these may be false. The use of open-ended questions, captcha or skip logic can help identify false respondents.
4. Social responsibility. Researchers have the duty to act responsibly and, for example, to refrain from intruding in spaces considered private by users. Online research can also, unintentionally, lead to promote inequality by benefiting a privileged sector, which in this case has access to technology and services online. Researchers should make the fundamental decision of whether their research would be better

carried out offline to protect participants or reduce the negative impact on them. Researchers should also mind themselves and reduce risks for themselves and their integrity as people and as researchers. This means refraining from accessing websites designed around illegal services, goods or activities without being compliant with relevant legislation and authorities.

3.10 Big Data and Ethics

Big data is an umbrella term encompassing the vast amount of digital data continuously generated globally, at a high speed, frequency and variety of sources (Berman & Albright, 2017). Big data is a technological issue, but it is also the social and cultural dimensions related to its use, expectations of applicability, robustness and accuracy across several domains and disciplines (Berman & Albright, 2017). It is characterised by several features (Berman & Albright, 2017), being:

1. digitally generated
2. produced passively
3. collected automatically
4. trackable temporarily and geographically
5. constantly analysable.

This rapid development of data and technologies that facilitate collection and analysis means more data will be collected on young people over their lifetime than before. The issue is that the impact that big data will have on their futures is still unpredictable (Berman & Albright, 2017). Ozer and Piatt (2017) say that the possible implications, when disseminating results online, is that big data creates a permanent digital footprint, which remains over time. This must be understood by participants before they consent to posting any materials or images related to the research, but since the long-term impact of the digital print is still unknown, participants' decisions may not be fully informed.

Data collected from children and adolescents may be used and analysed by indeterminate algorithms to create digital identities of which individuals may be unaware of, and digital identities may be created and shared over social media and by digital service providers who may even profit from this (Berman & Albright, 2017). For this reason, online consent is fundamental. Berman and Albright (2017) highlighted that there are no clear guidelines on the nature of informed consent for websites, and the terms and conditions may be written in legalistic or technical language which makes understanding difficult. Adolescents and parents may be faced with a binary choice to accept these terms without understanding them or forsake the website completely.

The introduction of GDPR has contributed to safeguard children's and adolescents' information. The Right to Erasure is concerned with data being unlawfully processed due to lack of free and informed consent. Additionally, if data were disclosed to a third party, the individual affected must be informed and all links or records of personal data must be erased, unless it is impossible or requires a disproportionate effort to do so (Berman & Albright, 2017).

Empathy Card Game

This game was used by Geppert (2023) to introduce empathy in adolescent research.

Adolescents had a card on their foreheads. The group would treat the person according to the label they had on their forehead but could not see themselves.

This was a fun way to get adolescents thinking about how social systems include or exclude people.

Here is an example of an adolescent consent form used in an online study exploring the impact of maternal cancer on adolescents (Rodriguez, 2016):

Adolescent Adjustment to Maternal Cancer

Participant Consent Form

Purpose of the Study
You are invited to join a study which examines the psychological impact of adjusting to maternal cancer diagnosis. This is a difficult and distressing time for you but the information you provide will be used to enhance understanding of what you are going through and to establish if a web-based intervention is a good way to help adolescents facing this situation.

What will be involved if I agree to take part in this study?
If you agree to take part in this study, you will be involved in four different phases.

The researcher will have an online video chat (Skype) interview with you to understand your current situation further. This session is audiotaped. Participants will fill in a survey online which will help understand the psychological impact of maternal illness on adolescents. Adolescents will complete an eight-week intervention. Half will complete the intervention first and the other half will participate in the intervention later. The survey will be filled in again at the end of the intervention and at a six-month follow-up.

Can I withdraw from the study?
Even if you decide to take part in all phases of this study, you are free to withdraw at any stage without having to explain why and there will be no consequences for you or your family.

Confidentiality
All the information you provide will be anonymous. Your name or family name will not appear in any report resulting from this study. A research number will identify you in the databases. Findings will only be reported as group data. The researcher, however, <u>must</u> break confidentiality if:

1. Your physical and/or emotional well-being is at risk and another adult (parent, guardian) must be informed to guarantee your safety.
2. You are being harmed or at risk of being harmed by issues specified in the Child Protection Policy NUI Galway (2011) and *Children First: National Guidance for the Protection and Welfare of Children* (2017).

However, the researcher will always inform you first about this situation and the procedure that must be followed after the situation has been reported.

If you have any queries, please contact [add relevant research contact details here] ______________________________

Adolescent Adjustment to Maternal Cancer

Participant Consent Form

I confirm that I have read and understood the information sheet about the study which is examining the psychological impact of adjusting to maternal cancer diagnosis.	Place a circle round either Yes	 No
I am satisfied that I understand the information provided and have had enough time to consider the information.	Yes	No

I understand that my participation is voluntary and that I am free to withdraw at any time, without giving any reason and without my legal rights being affected.	Yes	No
I understand that any information I give to the researcher is anonymous and will be treated with confidence.	Yes	No
I understand that I can ask the researcher questions about the study at any time.	Yes	No
I confirm that I have competent reading writing and comprehension skills in the English language to be able to take part in this online study.	Yes	No
I confirm that I have access to the internet and parental/adult permission to use it for the purpose of this research project.	Yes	No

Name:________________
Signed:________________ Date:______

Please send back one signed copy of this Consent Form. The other copy is for you to keep.

CHAPTER 4

Mobile Apps and Video Games

Chapter Highlights
1. Mobile apps and video games design should take into serious consideration the needs, interests and recommendations of adolescents.
2. Mobile health (mHealth) has shown benefits in illness management and changing health-related behaviours.
3. Apps and video games should have a solid scientific and theoretical foundation. The impact of interventions should be properly evaluated.
4. Data management online and ethical guidelines should be put in place from the start to ensure the safety of participants and their data.

This chapter is focused on exploring the potential of mobile apps and video games to improve the mental and physical health of adolescents. These are methodologies that continue to evolve quickly, and the potential for researchers is very significant. As with any other methodology, there are benefits but also challenges. Important recommendations are provided on good practices and the perspectives of adolescents themselves on what they would like to have from a mobile app, or a video game targeted at them.

4.1 What Do Adolescents Want from Technology?

An important aspect of participatory health technology regarding adolescents is understanding their wishes and needs, to ensure that interventions and studies using technology are attractive to them and get their attention and engagement. Otherwise this could lead to a waste of valuable resources, time and adolescent expectations and motivations. Livingood et al. (2017) carried out a consultation with adolescents to design a digital intervention to reduce adolescent obesity. Some of the recommendations provided by adolescents themselves are described in Table 4.1. Some of

Table 4.1 *Adolescent recommendations for digital intervention design*

Messaging: messaging emerged as an important component for adolescents. This could be through mobile texts or free messaging apps. Future health interventions with adolescents should include this type of communication by sending text messages about health and project meeting reminders.
Mobile and computer apps: youth identified that mobile apps would be suitable for a digital health intervention as adolescents use them frequently.
Gaming: incentives such as group competition and socialisation are incentives that, according to adolescents, could enhance a digital health intervention.
Wearable technology: these items may be expensive for adolescents; however, they are willing to use them if provided. These would be particularly suitable to increase physical activity.
Shifting youth communication: social and mobile technology is rapidly changing; therefore, interventions must be adaptable to this swiftly changing pattern.

these methodologies are explored in the following chapters, as these have been identified by adolescents themselves as useful tools that they would be interested in.

Researchers and app developers should be aware of the preferences of their target audience to ensure that the app is accepted and used effectively. Best practices for adolescents have been identified by research.

4.1.1 *Activities*

Adolescent app users want activities that require active engagement and contribute to developing useful skills (Cheng et al., 2018). One challenge, however, is that adolescents engage more meaningfully with games or apps that are entertaining, yet they should also be educational (Patchen et al., 2020). Therefore, finding this middle ground successfully may be a fundamental component of app design.

4.1.2 *Customisation*

Service users want to be able to customise their own app experience by selecting their own display images or avatars (Cheng et al., 2018). Adolescents want to control the flow of information, for example by including collapsible text boxes, as well as having information presented in different formats like videos with subtitles and transcriptions (Cheng et al., 2018). Key information can be presented in different formats for participants to select the option that suits them best and to avoid unnecessary repetition.

4.1.3 Personalisation

Participants expect apps to be personalised. This means apps should save personal information and remember information the participants had entered about themselves before. This information should improve participant experience and overall well-being (Cheng et al., 2018). Participants want to be able to track their health and well-being using apps (Cheng et al., 2018). Participants were willing to complete a registration process that would enable the app to provide personal information; however, these questions should be few, short and not too detailed (Simons et al., 2018).

4.1.4 Ambassadors

Ambassadors can be useful to make games engaging and attractive for adolescents. Cheng et al. (2018) included a selection of players from the Australian Football League to promote the game to the football industry and the public.

4.1.5 Language

Language needs to be considered carefully and possibly piloted with the target population. Cheng et al. (2018) found formal tone was sometimes perceived as intimidating, but some participants took content less seriously if it was written in an informal tone. In the case of Patchen et al. (2020), language was crucial in the design of an app promoting healthy sexual relationships. According to the authors, topics like sex and sexual behaviours needed to be talked about directly, in a trauma-informed and non-judgemental manner, as well as in a familiar and realistic tone. In this type of app that included a sensitive topic, this aspect of language was extremely complex (Patchen et al., 2020). An advantage of apps, as well as increasing acceptability and use, would be to make the app available in several languages to make it usable for more target groups (Simons et al., 2018).

4.1.6 Comparison/Competition

Introducing comparison and/or competition abilities in the app may be inadequate depending on the issue that is being targeted. In the case of health and well-being apps, this may be particularly inappropriate as users may be in distress (Cheng et al., 2018) and the information they are sharing is generally sensitive and confidential. Adolescents wanted a reward system to encourage health behaviours. These could be rewarded with money, points or an improvement in their health and perceived attractiveness which could also improve their relationships with others. Unhealthy behaviours decreased the awards in these same meters. (This was all relevant for the study carried out by Patchen et al., 2020.)

4.1.7 External Information

Adolescents expressed a liking for pop quizzes, pop-ups and trivia, as well as links to reliable and useful external information (Patchen et al., 2020).

4.1.8 Ease and Comfort of Use

The app described in Simons et al. (2018) included wearing a fitness tracking device. Regarding this device, users liked that it was easy to wear, use and had a long battery life. The device could track activity automatically, even if participants did not carry their smartphone with them during the day or during working hours (Simons et al., 2018). This device should also be waterproof (Simons et al., 2018).

4.1.9 Cost and Accessibility

Cost for participants is an important issue to consider. Apps and devices should be affordable for the target population (Simons et al., 2018).

4.2 Considerations for App Usage in Adolescent Research

Apps are not a replacement for face-to-face interactions. Doctor–patient encounters are face to face and continue to be a critical element of health provision. Apps can, however, improve efficiency, aggregate data and support the development of evidence to inform healthcare interventions (Whitehouse et al., 2013).

Apps depend on design and stakeholder engagement. Therefore, they can only work if they have a good design that engages target stakeholders; otherwise they will miss their targets (Whitehouse et al., 2013). In healthcare there are a variety of stakeholders that interact with technology that have their own expectations, priorities and limitations; therefore, successful apps need to address the perspectives, needs and priorities of these groups (Whitehouse et al., 2013).

Transferring validated scales from paper versions to digital ones can be challenging. Questionnaires may have long or inappropriate wording which can be unsuitable for electronic interfaces. Graphics can reduce the literacy level required for a user and can improve accessibility to a more heterogenous and young population.

Age is an important ethical and legal consideration which may vary from one country to another. Apps and games should consider the developmental capacities and needs of the target population, beyond simply their age as a number. Davis et al. (2018), for example, set the lower age of their health app at 15, since this is the youngest age at which health apps can be accessed without parental consent. The use of apps and games is bound by the ethical and legislative context in which these are designed and the contexts in which they will be used.

4.3 eHealth

eHealth is the use of technology for health. Technologies such as smartphones, health, fitness apps and wearable devices can be very useful to assess and promote physical activity for all ages (Simons et al., 2018). These devices can measure physical activity and provide individualised content for the user (Simons et al., 2018). Waller et al. (2006) consider that eHealth enables communication between adolescents and health professionals through an interface which is less threatening and embarrassing and increases approachability and accessibility to health professionals. eHealth can also be significantly beneficial for services as it is a way to make them scalable to a minimum cost and more accessible for outpatients who may struggle to access regular care (Firth et al., 2016).

One of the challenges with eHealth is the lack of evaluation and use of this technology (Firth et al., 2016). The efficacy of smartphones is particularly underresearched (Firth et al., 2016). Additionally, eHealth trends worldwide are unequal. Higher-income countries have more eHealth activity than lower-income ones. Specifically, Europe has the highest activity and Africa the least (World Health Organization (WHO), 2011).

4.4 mHealth

mHealth applications consist of mobile phone apps. Mobile phones facilitate reaching people directly, wherever they are (Whittaker et al., 2012). Mobile phones are always carried by the user and they are almost always on, which means information and services can be delivered at set times (Whittaker et al., 2012). Mobile phones also have the capacity to monitor patients remotely, manage risk factors and increase treatment compliance (McCurdie et al., 2012). This increases the probability of detecting medical issues early and preventing non-essential hospitalisations, as well as enables patients to engage in self-managing their conditions (McCurdie et al., 2012). Information on user behaviour recorded on the app can be used to design tailored interventions (McCurdie et al., 2012).

mHealth apps have the potential for the prevention of and early intervention in mental disorders in adolescent and young adults (Bidargaddi et al., 2017). mHealth apps have been described as very suitable for required patient behavioural change for illnesses, such as the health effects of smoking (heart disease, bronchitis, lung cancer), diabetes and obesity (McCurdie et al., 2012). mHealth programmes can also reach those from different backgrounds, including underserved and disadvantaged populations (Whittaker et al., 2012).

Health apps have great potential, but this technology can have limitations because these apps are usually not always developed in conjunction with healthcare professionals or academics who can provide evidence-based theoretical content, such as behaviour change techniques (Bidargaddi et al., 2017; Simons et al., 2018). Some apps also do not include citations or privacy policies, making access more difficult for users to make an informed assessment about the app quality (Bidargaddi et al., 2017) or to have a guarantee that their data will be safely stored and they will be safe online.

Adolescents need the knowledge and skills to identify high-quality mobile apps that will help them change their health and lifestyles (Bidargaddi et al., 2017). Readily available apps may not achieve improvement in the well-being of non-clinical samples but can, at least, prevent a decline in their mood, energy, rest and sleep patterns (Bidargaddi et al., 2017). People use app store ratings as indicators of app quality; however, these are based on usability and aesthetics but not necessarily on their capacity to improve health outcomes (Bidargaddi et al., 2017).

Apps are suitable to support adolescents with chronic illnesses. Davis et al. (2018) have suggested that this population often has difficulties accessing timely and ongoing healthcare due to several issues such as lack of health literacy, cost and the transition between parental supervision and independent illness management. Apps provide an opportunity for adolescents to engage with health support outside the support of their families and healthcare services by providing self-management guidelines, the capacity to monitor health over time and reminders and feedback.

The development of mHealth depends on a strategic approach to its planning, development and evaluation (WHO, 2011). There is also a need for country-based eHealth strategies. These polices need to be supported by standards and partnerships to enable initiatives to develop and reach their full potential (WHO, 2011).

One of the other uses of mobile apps has been the creation of screening tools for adolescent health (Whitehouse et al., 2013). For example, the TickiT app was used by adolescents to input data prior to a visit to the clinician. The app generated a report that would alert clinicians (if needed). Mobile phones can also facilitate the use of text messages in research and in strategies to improve adolescent health. Text messages have been used to design support systems for adolescent patients. Waller et al. (2006) designed a text message system to support adolescents with diabetes. Using text messages is a good way to deliver behavioural interventions as text messages have been described as 'an integral part of teenage culture' (Waller et al., 2006, p. 305) and this can, therefore, facilitate adolescent engagement with the system. Text messages are also a method to provide support proactively by sending information to the user rather than waiting for it to be actively sought. It is also a relatively inexpensive method, according to the authors. It is important to also consider the cost of the phones, the accessibility of data and the guarantee of connectivity (internet, phone chips). One of the usual disadvantages of using technology in research is ensuring that adolescents have access to the hardware and software required to be actively involved. This can be costly for some adolescents.

Text messages, to be effective, should reflect core messages including relevant topics for the adolescent and their health condition, for example insulin injections, blood glucose testing, healthy eating, exercise, carbohydrate counting and pump therapy (Waller et al., 2006). Messages should also be appropriate for the adolescent's age, sex and disease management and treatment (Waller et al., 2006).

One of the significant concerns about mHealth and eHealth is data security. According to the WHO (2011), there are legitimate concerns regarding citizen information about programmes that use mobile health technologies. Data security involves how this information is kept, managed and potentially shared. Important decisions about data security and data management need to happen. Recommendations in Chapter 3 about managing digital data may be very useful to inform these decisions.

4.5 Participatory Research Methods

One of the biggest challenges with mHealth apps is the lack of a systematic methodology to design engaging and effective ones. There have been different methodologies used in the design of apps, such as co-creation, storyboards, pilot studies and participatory designs.

Co-creation has been used in the design of apps. It can improve patient and adult (e.g. healthcare providers) engagement, communication and experience (Whitehouse et al., 2013). Whitehouse et al. (2013) had co-creation sessions with adolescents. These sessions were documented, and participants could provide feedback in person or via email, before and after the sessions. Additionally, adolescents were involved in open-ended interviews about the development of the app.

Pilot studies and feasibility studies can be used to evaluate functional apps. This will contribute to understanding how the app is being used or any issues that happened during implementation. Storyboards, for example, were used to present the trajectory of patients' visits to evoke the variety of contexts in which the app could be used: before appointment, registration, waiting room, after the appointment and back home (Whitehouse et al., 2013).

Waller et al. (2006) used a participatory design to use a text message system to support adolescents. Participatory designs have the advantage of involving users at every level of the design process. Participatory design also involves cooperation with all relevant stakeholders. Waller et al. (2006) carried out their design process within a clinical setting; this facilitated the cooperation between designers and medical staff. Waller et al. (2006) used paper and computer-based prototypes to evaluate ideas. One of the limitations of this design is that adolescents were not included in the design process, and they were the end users. Like Waller et al. (2006), Davis et al. (2018) used a participatory design to develop a self-management app for asthma in adolescents. The methodology followed consisted of two iterative cycles of testing and feedback with involvement of adolescents at all stages of the process as well as input from clinicians to ensure accurate medical content (Davis et al., 2018). The active engagement of adolescents in the app design was critical to design an engaging app. The app uses language, features, colour schemes and even a name relevant to adolescents, their context and their cognitive and social development.

Goal setting was used by Davis et al. (2018) in conjunction with a participatory design; however, it is included as a separate method to highlight its significance. According to Davis et al. (2018), few apps have been built founded on evidence-based behavioural models or self-management tools. Including goal-setting facilities in apps correlated positively with improved self-management and clinical outcomes for adolescents (Davis et al., 2018).

Table 4.2 *User-centred design stages*

Concept generation	Identify end users. Determine the intended use and goal of the application by carrying out a needs analysis using different methods such as focus groups, ethnography and interviews. Identify the environment in which the app will be used. Find the social and organisational culture of the user, e.g. cultural bias.
Design and system development	Analyse user data transcripts. Themes identified are then used to inform design principles. Prototypes can be sketches and/or wireframes to inform the goal of the application. Designs are evaluated and refined by the feedback provided by users.
Evaluation	A user and a facilitator use the application. They think aloud and provide feedback on their experience using the app. This testing provides an objective evaluation of the design, once a functional prototype is available. The user is in a controlled environment experiencing different scenarios of typical app use, while thinking aloud. Observers take notes of the user's behaviours, comments and issues, which help identify functional and design flaws. Usability testing provides an objective evaluation of the design, once a functional prototype is available. Usability testing can also happen in the user's natural environment (home, work) by remote data collection, videos, etc. Users perform realistic tasks with working prototypes.

User-centred design (UCD) is an evidence-based approach based on the needs and understanding of the end users (McCurdie et al., 2012). The end user is taken into consideration at every stage of the design process. The design also consists of an iterative cycle of prototyping, user testing and improved ease of use. There are several stages in UCD (Table 4.2).

Participatory design methods can be costly in terms of time needed and resources required. The design process can be extensive, and some users can become tired in the process (Waller et al., 2006).

4.5.1 Theoretical Frameworks

Some apps have a clear theoretical underpinning which supports the design process. These pre-existing frameworks can inform design and development decisions. Other apps do not follow or do not report a specific theoretical framework; however, there is no evidence available to determine which of the two is better, more effective or more engaging. Overall, having an underlying theory is beneficial to the design and content of the app, as it can make the app evidence informed, which shows validity and effectiveness (Bidargaddi et al., 2017).

Some of the theories reported by the literature are behaviour change, ecological momentary assessment, social cognitive theory and problem-solving theory. Simons et al. (2018) included existing literature, a health behaviour change model and an exploratory qualitative study with their target population, who were young adults between 18 and 26 years of age. Bidargaddi et al. (2017) used evidence-based behaviour change techniques. Ecological momentary assessment can detect short-term changes in mood and sleep patterns on a day-to-day basis (Bidargaddi et al., 2017). Social cognitive theory (SCT) was also reported, which considers the multiple and reciprocal influences on health behaviours, individual experiences, beliefs and the contextual factors that impact on health (Patchen et al., 2020). Problem-solving theory was reported by Patchen et al. (2020). This theory consists of the process that a person experiences when they gain new information and identify the circumstances which affect or do not affect the conflict or difficulty they are experiencing. Self-determination theory underpinned the app in Simons et al. (2018). The theory is concerned with the content of goals and the way goals are communicated can explain differences in people's motivation and performance. The autonomy-supportive style includes motivation language (can, may, want) versus controlling language (should, have, to).

4.6 App Development

App development may have different methods and stages. According to Simons et al. (2018), app development requires a stepwise and iterative approach.

Selecting the correct operating system is crucial depending on the target population that the app is targeted at and the resources available to develop it. Android apps are compatible with Android operating systems, which also means they are compatible with smartphones' features and hardware (camera, GPS, accelerometer), and it guarantees a good user experience (Simons et al., 2018). The Android operating system has the highest penetration rate in the market of smartphones around the world (Simons et al., 2018). Developing an app for iPhone (IOS) can be more expensive and time-consuming (Simons et al., 2018).

There are several studies which have followed similar stages in their design, as described in the next few subsections.

4.6.1 Design

The target population was usually included in the design process. Different methods were used for this, for example design workshops (Cheng et al., 2018), advisory groups (Patchen et al., 2020) and focus groups (Simons et al., 2018).

4.6.2 Prototype

Designing apps and games involves the design of a prototype. Prototypes are tested to determine their usability. Different studies carry out this usability test using varying methods and strategies. Patchen et al. (2020) used focus groups to evaluate usability with adolescents. Other methods used are usability surveys (Patchen et al., 2020) and interviews (Simons et al., 2018). Interviews could have different styles; 'think aloud' interviews consist of giving participants the app and asking them to use it and say anything that came to their mind out loud. Other interviews were semi-structured. Acceptability and feasibility questionnaires were also used (Simons et al., 2018). According to Simons et al. (2018), conducting usability testing with five people can reveal 85 per cent of potential usability issues.

4.6.3 Usability Testing

Usability usually involves installing the app and targeting users trying the app for several weeks and identifying any problems with it. Researchers collect this information and pass it on to the developers to adapt and improve the app (Simons et al., 2018).

Simons et al. (2018) shared their interview schedule for usability testing (Table 4.3).

4.6.4 Programming

Games and apps are then programmed. This stage usually requires an interdisciplinary team, for example gaming experts, graphic designers, script writers and audio/visual specialists. Multidisciplinary teams, including health professionals, educators, game designers and psychologists, can inform intervention and design to ensure efficacy, safety and benefit for target users (Gkintoni et al., 2024). Patchen et al. (2020), for example, had a panel including experts in clinical service delivery of adolescent sexual health, developmental psychologists and mobile health development technologists. The panel oversaw informing content development, aligning the

Table 4.3 *Usability testing questions*

So far, what do you like or dislike about the app?
Are there certain parts of the app that you find confusing or that you do not understand?
What change(s) would you recommend to improve the app (design, colour, font, content, ease of use)?
Are there certain parts of the app that should stay the same?
What do you think of the use of the tracking device?
Are there any problems or difficulties while using the app or the tracking device?
What do you think of the daily and weekly goals?
What do you think of the tips you get?
What do you think of the facts you get?
Do you use the app regularly?
What makes you continue to use the app?
What would be the main reason for you to stop using the app?

project to existing research and identifying target behaviours. Simons et al. (2018) developed their app in cooperation with a commercial mobile app development company. The app content was also evaluated by public health researchers. Young adults (18–26) also contributed by evaluating the app's usefulness, applicability and comprehension of the content.

4.6.5 Evaluation

Games and apps are evaluated once again. This involves interacting with a more final version of the app/game. This new version is given to the participants already installed in a phone or tablet. Participants are asked to provide feedback on (Patchen et al., 2020): 1) instructions: clarity, language, length and comprehension and 2) content: artwork, design, games, dialogue and entertainment value. The feedback is recorded, and recommendations are carried out on how to improve the app/game. Google Analytics can be used to measure app usage statistics and identify participant usage patterns. It also has the advantage of being free (Simons et al., 2018).

***

Whittaker et al. (2012) designed a systematic methodology to develop and evaluate mHealth interventions: conceptualisation, formative research, presenting, pilot study and conducting a randomised controlled study.

Conceptualisation is the stage of the intervention mapping theoretical foundations and translating theory into materials that can be used for health promotion strategies and interventions. Practical techniques are turned into mobile-phone-friendly formats such as 160-character messages, 30-second videos, scheduled alerts and mobile websites. Formative research involves gathering information from the target population (focus groups, surveys, semi-structured interviews) to find out their patterns of mobile use and how this can be integrated to the health programme; for example, frequency of text messages and use of videos. Presenting consists of early intervention content and obtaining feedback from the target audience, such as on videos, style and content, credibility of the person in the videos, realism, positivity and clear messages. Pilot studies are used to obtain feedback from the target audience on the intervention as it would be delivered in its final form. The pilot study would also help understand processes like recruitment, registration, data collection and technical aspects of videos and messages. The last stage is the randomised controlled trial. These are used to provide rigorous evidence of the effectiveness of the interventions determined with objective health outcomes measures.

The methodology followed by Davis et al. (2018) to design apps is described in detail in Table 4.4, as this was part of a participatory design; therefore, these stages are relevant and suitable for this type of methodology.

Table 4.4 *App design stages*

Concept ideation and app design	Participants completed a questionnaire which included demographic information, medication, illness control, lifestyle, illness needs, concerns and goals. It also explored their goals, intended use, design and content preferences for the app. Participants also completed a paper workbook. Finally, participants suggested the creation of screen designs.
Drafting and developing the app	A creative specialist used the information gathered from adolescents to create wireframes – paper-based screen templates – which are visual representations of app navigation and core functionalities. Developers created 'personas' which are fictional user profiles. Possible scenarios and user flows are used to identify how users would interact with the app. This stage also involved the team developing evidence-based health information in a language and format suitable for adolescents. Different and improved versions were created until a high-fidelity version was created and tested by users.
Evaluation	Participants involved in the co-design process were asked to use the app in their personal phones and provide feedback. Participants provided vocalised feedback on their likes and dislikes, challenges, satisfaction with features and overall performance. Feedback sessions were also audio recorded and analysed to determine acceptability and more changes needed. Adolescents also provided a satisfaction score for the app (1 = least favourable, 6 = most favourable). Participants also helped to name the app to encourage acceptability.

Methodology: Mobile Diaries (Hagen et al., 2012)

Mobile diaries is a form of self-reporting using audio and visual technologies. Research participants document aspect of their lives with words and images, including daily experiences, attitudes, emotions, thoughts and aspirations.

Participants can be involved as contributors and interpreters in the research study, in real time and from different geographical locations.

Mobile and video diaries can be used to evaluate technology usage.

Considerations:

1. Privacy and data security are appropriate and guaranteed.
2. If participants capture images of others, permission and ethical approval guidelines need to be followed. (Please check Chapter 6 on Photovoice for concrete guidance on this topic.)
3. Sensitivity is needed regarding risk of filming. Researchers must know and follow policies around filming that some institutions may have.
4. Images may have different cultural meanings for different people.
5. Filming illegal activity can have implications.
6. Young people may require additional training on technology usage and/or ethical considerations.
7. Image-based methods can be very suitable for people with low levels of literacy.
8. This methodology relies on individual motivation; some will be more engaged than others.
9. Technology can break down.
10. The recommended sample size is 8–10 participants.

4.7 Video Games

Gamification is the 'use of game design elements in non-game contexts' (Cheng et al., 2018, p. 2). Gamification has been described as a 'promising strategy' to facilitate engagement in digital health interventions; however, an issue remains because the impact of electronic health interventions is poorly understood (Cheng et al., 2018; Gkintoni et al., 2024). Video games have the potential to improve health outcomes for a variety of socio-demographic groups, particularly in the areas of psychological therapy and physical therapy; however, further rigorous evidence, such are randomised controlled clinical trials are needed (Primack et al., 2012). According to Primack et al. (2012), video games can make potentially monotonous and repetitive tasks more compelling. Gamification can increase motivation and engagement in mental health interventions by including elements of gaming such as rewards, challenges and interactive components (Gkintoni et al., 2024).

Gamification also has risks such as overstimulation and addiction, reduction in intrinsic motivation and overreliance on external motivation (Gkintoni et al., 2024). Additionally, there are issues around privacy and data security due to the use of personal data and private information (Gkintoni et al., 2024).

4.7.1 Game Design

Essential elements of game design are space, goal, components, mechanisms and rules (Ugras et al., 2022). Game space is the world where the game inhabits. It includes the lighting, audiovisuals, colours, sounds, etc. The goal consists of something meaningful and attractive for players. They can achieve this goal when they obtain a high score in the game. All games need a story, particularly those that are based on strategy, adventure and role playing.

Ugras et al. (2022) described that industry and academia can benefit greatly from the involvement of children and adolescents in digital game design. Patchen et al. (2020) created a game specifically targeted at African-American adolescents (15–21 years) called Sexually Active Adolescent-Focused Education (SAAFE). The design of the game involved adolescents in discussions, co-design and cocreation. Ugras et al. (2022) proposed a participatory methodology to co-design digital games with children; however, this method can also be used with adolescents. Designing games with children and adolescents is a way to evoke their imagination during the design process (Ugras et al., 2022). Co-design also emphasises the empowerment of participants by actively involving them in the design process. The advantage of this technique is that it encourages children to be empowered, engaged, productive, creative and open to collaboration (Ugras et al., 2022). Additionally, the involvement of adults increases child–adult interaction. These adults should be flexible and willing to contribute and encourage children to do so too.

Ugras et al. (2022) described some of the strategies used to design games with children in co-design with adults. A brainstorming session is carried out with participants. The professional or researcher moderates the brainstorming session with participants while the designer creates sketches based on their answers. Implementation of participants' ideas should take place in a fun environment with access to materials and equipment. The ideal duration should not be too long it really depends on the age of participants. In the game narrative design stage participants provide ideas to create game ideas from scratch. The game narrative emerges from the game ideas created. These game narratives should include narratives in various genres.

Game design has challenges as well. User experience is significant in gaming. It is difficult for researchers to compete with large and fully funded corporations that can invest significant amounts of money on seamless, intuitive and engaging user experiences. This may result in unattractive interfaces for research purposes (Cheng et al., 2018). Timing can be an important issue as well. Research usually has a specific time frame which may be inappropriate. Cheng et al. (2018) found that the development and user testing needed to happen almost simultaneously. As a result, some of the needs and recommendations from participants might not be included in the final version.

Device compatibility is another important consideration about gamification. Device compatibility across smartphones, tablets and computers is crucial for accessibility, as well as reliable internet access (Gkintoni et al., 2024). Gkintoni et al. (2024) considered children and adolescents with different socio-economic backgrounds may have unequal access to digital devices, technology and internet access. Differences may also exist between digital literacy, which may impact children's and adolescents' ability to engage with digital health tools (Gkintoni et al., 2024). Literacy training is necessary for children and adolescents to use tools effectively (Gkintoni et al., 2024). Access can be facilitated by having inclusive designs. Gkintoni et al. (2024) suggest researchers and designers can establish alliances with community centres, NGOs or schools to provide access points. Overall, gamification must be designed and implemented taking into consideration age, inclusivity and ethical design (Gkintoni et al., 2024).

4.7.2 *Types of Games*

There are different types of games that have been used in health interventions with adolescents, namely active, applied, mobile and serious games. They differ in terms of design and purpose. There are conflicting reports in the research about their overall effectiveness and, in general, more evidence is needed.

Active video games integrate exercise and gaming in a digital interface to promote physical activity and reduce sedentary behaviour (Oliveira et al., 2019). Active video games have had a better than minimal intervention in improving health conditions, for example reducing BMI and body weight (Oliveira et al., 2019). The current evidence suggests that videos may not replace other healthy habits but may supplement them. Active video games can be used in conjunction with sports to improve adolescent health (Oliveira et al., 2019).

Applied games refers to the use of games and games for purposes other than entertainment, for example games for psychological therapy (Cheng et al., 2018). These applied games integrate 'effectiveness potential' where users can be motivated to explore interventions in more depth as a motivation besides self-improvement.

Serious games are a type of computer-delivered intervention which is educational and fun (DeSmet et al., 2014). Serious games have three important characteristics:

1. Immersion or transportation. The player is absorbed in the game without disbelief while creating personal experiences and developing affection for the characters.
2. Flow. A state of high concentration in which the player experiences a balance between the challenge and their skills.
3. Meets needs. The game provides mastery, autonomy, connectedness, arousal, fantasy or challenge.

Research found that serious games can increase the adoption of healthy lifestyles and can also improve antecedents that determine this adoption (DeSmet et al., 2014). DeSmet et al. (2014) emphasise that serious games can work in a variety of populations, particularly if the preferences of the target population are considered. Players of serious games are willing to spend more time learning by using games rather than learning with traditional methods. This fact can inform the design of future healthy lifestyle game-based interventions (DeSmet et al., 2014). Another important finding from DeSmet et al. (2014) is that it is insufficient to tailor games to behavioural changes only; effective games were also tailored to the specific socio-demographic characteristics of the target population (e.g. age, gender, body type). Previous game experience should also be taken into consideration. Games with high immersive features can overload the players and decrease their capacity to focus on the educational aspects of the game by focusing, instead, on mastering it (DeSmet et al., 2014). Fun and educational elements are critical in game effectiveness (DeSmet et al., 2014). DeSmet et al. (2014) found that play duration was not significantly related to game effectiveness.

Designing serious games for educational health interventions shares similar challenges to general game design. According to DeSmet et al. (2014), interventions should be explicit about the theories that underpin the change in specific outcomes.

Generating Research Questions (Chen et al., 2010)

1. Brainstorming activity: collage. Participants work in small groups to create a collage that represents the research topic.
2. Identify topics. Participants use the collage to identify important topics for them.
3. Turn topics into questions. Participants identify their most important topics and convert them to research questions.
4. Selection. Participants review and discuss the questions and together identify the top two to be included in the study.

CHAPTER 5

Sonification

Chapter Highlights

1. Sonification is a developing method, with great potential for data communication. However, it requires a level of skill and training which can be resource- and time-consuming.
2. Sonification is not intended to replace visual methods but is a way to complement data dissemination, particularly in already saturated visual environments or to target people with visual impairments.
3. Sonification can be used to disseminate primary as well as secondary data.
4. New applications of sonification, less reliant on technology, are also emerging and changing the field.

The increasing production and availability of data, the diversification of stakeholders as well as the need for data and information has transformed the ways in which data is analysed, visualised and used to build knowledge (Lenzi & Ciuccarelli, 2020). Due to the rapid growth in information in the world, ordering this information in a sensible way has become a priority (Alnihoud & Masi, 2010; Appiah & Martey, 2015). Sonification is an interesting alternative to visualisation as it can be used as part of public outreach/conveying data without breaching anonymity. Sonification can have practical benefits in situations where eyesight is already stimulated but information still needs to be communicated, such as in airplane cockpits. Sonification may also be a way to reach different groups with an interest or background in music by engaging them in the creation of music through research or to increase their interest in research findings through music. Overall, the chapter includes an example of the application of sonification in health research, but the method is lacking more application using a participatory approach nor has it been widely applied with adolescents. These challenges may be associated with the fact that sonification requires very specific skills in data programming and other sound-producing software, and it may be too costly and time-consuming to effectively teach these skills to a group of adolescents from scratch and then involve them in research. According to the United Nations (2023), there needs to be a consensus about sonification methods to develop specific and effective sonification training programmes. Currently there is a need for several experts in sound design and the field of study; the challenge is that these experts may come from a variety of fields which may have different goals and different norms for project design and evaluation (United Nations, 2023). This increases the cost and logistic complexity of sonification (United Nations, 2023). Despite the limitations of sonification, its benefits – such as enhancing scientific practice and enabling disability inclusion – provide the justification to develop the field further and achieve its maximum potential (United Nations, 2023).

5.1 Sonification

An auditory display can be defined as 'any display that uses sound to communicate information' (Walker & Nees, 2011, p. 9). Sonification is a subtype of auditory display. There is, however, no single definition for sonification. The United Nations (2023) defined sonification as 'the transformation of data into acoustic signals, namely a way to represent data values and relations as perceivable non-verbal sounds, with the aim to facilitate their communication and interpretation' (p. 14).

Sonification is the use of non-speech audio to convey information (Hermann et al., 2011; Hermann & Ritter, 1999; Supper, 2014). It is specifically the presentation of data using sound (Hermann, 2002), 'rendering sound in response to data and interactions' (Hermann et al., 2011, p. 1). It must be clarified that sonification is not intended to be a replacement for visualisation. Instead, it provides the possibility to integrate sound into multisensory experiences and data analysis (United Nations, 2023).

The theoretical underpinnings of research and design come from diverse fields including audiology, engineering, informatics, psychology, linguistics, mathematics and music (Walker & Nees, 2011). Sonification is interdisciplinary (Hermann, 2002; Hermann et al., 2011; United Nations, 2023). Sonification has been used in a variety of contexts and data sets including biology and genetic data (Supper, 2014).

Sonification can be used to make phenomena which are not accessible by direct sensory experience accessible to the senses (Barrett, 2016;

Table 5.1 *Sonification types*

Artistic sonification	These sonifications push the boundaries of music to creatively explore the data. Sonifications may engage the public with science and music, but these are primarily musical.
Outreach and education	Sonification can be an unusual tool to communicate science to engage non-expert audiences. These sonifications also inspire curiosity about STEM, to communicate a specific learning objective, or both.
Scientific research	These sonifications are used as analysis tools. The objective is to understand the underlying phenomenon of data analysis using sound.

Supper, 2014). Auditory displays are appropriate for data that contains complex patterns, time changes, warnings and calls for immediate action (Hermann et al., 2011). It can also be a tool to increase public understanding of scientific initiatives (Supper, 2014). According to Lenzi and Ciuccarelli (2020), sonification has become a communication practice to reach a wider public as it includes a range of languages and senses in order to understand complex data. Sonification can be used to engage non-expert audiences with data about issues that are socially relevant (Lenzi & Ciuccarelli, 2020). Auditory displays, such as sonification, can provide enhanced accessibility of information to visually impaired audiences (United Nations, 2023; Walker & Nees, 2011). Specifically applied to social issues, Lenzi and Ciuccarelli (2020) suggested that social issues are complex by nature and therefore alternative languages such as sonification can contribute to more effective, coherent and comprehensive communication.

The United Nations (2023) described three types of sonification: artistic, outreach and education, and scientific research (Table 5.1). Different research projects may fall into one or several of these categories (United Nations, 2023).

Väljamäe et al. (2013) provided definitions for sonification techniques, which may be very useful to understand how sonification can be used:

1. Audification. Data values are directly converted into a soundwave. This is the most simple and oldest approach to sonification.
2. Parameter mapping. Consists of mapping data to an intensity level of a sound.
3. Model-based sonification. Mathematical models generate sound according to the data input.
4. Generative music: Describes the systems that use musical rules and structures to create sound outputs.

Sonification has several advantages (United Nations, 2023):

1. Sound perception. The way humans perceive sound can have multiple benefits, for example the capacity to identify and prioritise sound in a noisy environment. Sound is multidimensional; therefore multiple data parameters can be combined in one sound: pitch, timbre, amplitude and duration. Sound is more appropriate than visuals for time-based information, patterns and changes. It also covers a wider frequency range. The ears can be actively operating in the background; therefore, people can listen to a sonification while engaging in other tasks.
2. Accessibility. Sonification is very suitable for people with visual impairments. This is not a homogenous group, and the needs of every individual must be considered as they will also interact differently with the sonification.
3. Engagement. Sonification can be a way to inspire curiosity and wonder.
4. Complex data analysis. Sonification enables the identification of patterns and signals in large and multidimensional data sets.

Sonification, as described, has many benefits; however, it is not without its challenges. Sonification is defined by its goals, methodology, design and evaluation (United Nations, 2023). Ultimately, sonification depends on the goals of the project, the intended users and the data source. This lack of standardisation is a core challenge of sonification (United Nations, 2023). Another challenge of sonification is its usability. It would be beneficial if sonification could be adjusted iteratively and quickly, so the best representation of the data can be identified (United Nations, 2023). The usefulness of sonification will be enhanced further as the ease of use also improves (United Nations, 2023). Sonification should also consider the needs of different users and evaluate the efficacy of sonification accordingly, taking into consideration aspects such as the cultural background, disability and their level of sonification training. Overall, sonification projects should be driven by rigorous evaluation to determine their efficacy. This requires time and resources. According to the United Nations (2023), the lack of scientific legitimacy of sonification may currently be a limitation to finding suitable funding for projects.

Sonification is an emerging and evolving discipline; therefore Supper (2014) described that there is a blurry line between sonification as a scientific tool and sonification as an artistic expression. It is often seen as an entertainment instead of a scientific tool to understand data (Neuhoff, 2019). People with no musical experience generally struggle to grasp the meaning of music

Table 5.2 *Stages of a sonification model*

Step	Definition
Set-up	Data is converted to the 'sounding instrument'; for example, selection of the data that will be converted into sound.
Dynamics	Dynamics consist of the production of pleasant sonifications. These dynamics are effective if they follow the rules of sound-generating systems. To comply with sonification dynamics, the choice of software specialised in music production will enable effective sonifications with pleasant aesthetics also. For example, Reaper is a widely used digital audio application; MIDI is a popular protocol for sound production. Another aspect of dynamics is the use of music theory, including existing chords, melodies, arpeggios, diatonic chords and beats. This supports the aesthetic aspects of the sonification to create meaning through a pleasant sound.
Excitation	Excitation consists of the expression of 'virtual' physics that produce external excitations. The excitation consists of the conversion of this message into sound by the synthesisers into the speakers.
Auditory observables	The final product and the message the sonification conveys to the listening audience.
Listener	The listener of this sonification project can have a passive or an active role. A passive listener will access the final product (sonification) but will not interact with any of the previous phases to produce it. The active listener will engage with the sonification and 'decode' the message it is conveying (or not if the message is ineffective or unclear).

terminology such as understanding 'up' and 'down' in term of pitch change. Therefore, variability in music cognition leads to variability in the comprehension of the majority of sonifications (Neuhoff, 2019).

For sonification to be effective, it is important to identify the appropriate sound type and sound character, considering the expectations of the user and context of use (Hermann et al., 2011) to ensure that the sonification message being transmitted will be effective. The capacities, limitations and experiences of listeners will impact their experience of auditory displays (Hermann et al., 2011). Hermann and Ritter (1999) define the stages of a sonification model in Table 5.2.

5.2 Participatory Sonification

Sonification had not been widely used from a participatory approach. E. Young (2021) created a participatory design method for qualitative data

Table 5.3 *Embosonic design*

Empower	Involve participants from the start of the project and include their knowledge, experience and inspiration in the implementation.
Make	Undertake activities and design goals to produce tangible artefacts.
Break taboos	Participants must be free to share experiences without feeling judged or offended.
Open discussion	Conversations and ideas should flow naturally and organically.
Safe space	The space should be private and suitable to share and make noise. Extraneous sound should be kept to the minimum.
Ownership	Participants should share their own experiences only and not attempt to translate the experience of other participants.
Neutrality	All sonifications are subjective, individual and unique.
Immerse	Complete deep listening exercises before the workshop to heighten understanding of the materials and enable participants to engage with the sound.
Connect	Be curious. Motivate participants to explore their experiences, deepen insights and strengthen their sonifications.

sonification called embosonic design. The method established that sharing deep stories through sound making facilitates the creation of narratives that go beyond the limits of language (Young, 2021). Although a participatory method, embosonic has not been used with adolescents. Young (2021) carried out a participatory workshop where women embodied their experience through this method. This workshop facilitated their self-reflection and the women acquired a deeper understanding of the issues they explored. Embosonic stands for the initials of the principles associated with this method. These are described in Table 5.3.

These embosonic workshops should be small, with three to five being the optimum number of participants (Young, 2021). Embosonic is unique as it is an instruments-based method and does not rely on technology or programming, which may mean it is more accessible. These workshops use Foley tools, which consist of a variety of sounding objects (Table 5.4).

Embosonic consists of three stages: ideation, meditation and translation (Young, 2021).

5.2.1 *Stage 1: Ideation*

This is the phase to gather information, to create a 'collection of feels'. This consists of the sensations, feelings, concepts and analogies that represent participants' subjective experiences of the subject. Topics and

Table 5.4 *Embosonic sound objects*

Solids	Liquids	Gases	Wood	Metal	Plastic
Sandpaper	Water	Air pumps	Solid	Solid	Solid
Steel/wool	Splash mats	Ballons	Hollow	Hollow	Hollow
Foil	Open vessels	Aerosols	Different surfaces	Serrated	Flexible
Cellophane	Closed vessels		Rollable	Mechanisms	Range of thickness
Paper			Range of weights	Range of weights	Spherical
Cardboard			Breakable	Spherical	Rollable
Fabrics				Rollable	
Small loose objects					

descriptions emerge naturally. Emerging concepts can emerge, and they are gathered in a flipchart. If categories emerge, concepts are classified into groupings.

5.2.2 *Stage 2: Mediation*

Participants immerse themselves in the medium. Participants will get to know their materials, sound sources and the impact of their spatial positioning on the sound. Participants spend 15 minutes listening to the sounds in their environment and determine their spatial positioning. Afterwards, the group can share their experiences.

5.2.3 *Stage 3: Translation*

The medium is used to formulate solutions, that is, start to translate the concepts into sounds. Participants are encouraged to enjoy themselves through the manipulation of the tools and explore their sound-generating talents. Work through the different 'feels' and enable participants to produce meaningful sketches.

***

Among the challenges of embosonic is the fact that sound design is highly subjective and, therefore, the sound content produced will vary between participants and designers, particularly in embosonic, as this is based on intuition and favourite design style (Young, 2021). Generally, translating concepts into sound will not 'come naturally' to participants and they will need encouragement and experimentation:

Is it heavy or light?
Is there a sensation of any movement?
Is there tension or friction?

5.3 Sonification and Health

Sonification has been used in health research with children and adolescents; however, the nature of these studies is not participatory in the sense that participants are subjects of research and are not actively involved in the design and decision-making process. Cibrian et al. (2020) carried out an interactive sonification for children with autism. Interactive sonification provided real-time auditory feedback which resulted in an increase in participants' awareness of their movements. Interactive sonification is the use of sound within a human–computer interface where the audio signal provides information about the analysed data. The study showed that children with autism are aware of the sonification of their movements and engage with the sonifications. Discrete sound structures are particularly suitable to engage participants in upper-limb movement and increase their ability to carry out movements correctly. A significant finding of the research is that the type of sound is a significant determinant of the therapeutic impact (Cibrian et al., 2020).

Walus et al. (2015) evaluated the use of sonification and music to support communication of alcohol health risk for young people. The experiment was unsuccessful as there were no statistically signficant changes identified between groups in their levels of health knowledge and risk perception. The authors suggested this was due to a lack of power from a small sample and not from the sonification method being ineffective. They suggest that using this method of communication is interesting for adolescents, as long as it does not overload their senses.

Pauletto and Walus (2018) created an immersive multimedia health communication intervention called Jane's story. It is a tool to stimulate discusson about chronic diseases and disorders in adolescents. The project was designed by an interdisciplinary team made up of health science researchers, sound and music theorists, practitioners and film makers. The aim of the project was to design an effective immersive, multimedia entertainment education intervention that combined video, voice, sound effects and sonification to communicate public health topics to adolescents, their parents and communities. The topic specifically chosen was the experiences of adolescents living with chronic illnesses. The script describes the stages that adolescents experience when they are diagnosed. It does not specifically identify with a disease, to remind the audience that it is still a fictional and general production.

Pauletto and Walus (2018) included a sonification of graphs showing the prevalence of chronic illnesses around the world. This display was perceived as unclear by the audience. In this case the visual display was more informative than the auditory one. The authors concluded that sound can be very effective engaging the audience at a personal and emotional level, much less to portray data.

The story was perceived as being generally effective; the choice of music and sound design strongly support the health message transmitted to the audience. A very important finding for the research is that sound might be very effective in communicating concrete and urgent health messages that need an urgent change, while visuals are better suited for portraying general health messages that require change over a long period of time. Pauletto and Walus (2018) therefore suggested that the two elements combined can produce a very effective outcome.

Østergaard (2021) defined music-talk as a narrative around a piece of music. The song is first listened to in an interview and then participants talk about its significance and meaning. Participants self-select the song and the music facilitates co-production of knowledge between participant and researcher. Music is usually experienced together with other things such as people, events, scenes, states of mind and life stages which contribute towards self-identity (Østergaard, 2021). When people listen to music in specific settings or in relation to specific life occurrences, when they listen to the music again, this becomes part of a strong memory interpreted from a point of view in the present (Østergaard, 2021). Researchers, therefore, are interested in understanding the stories music triggers in relation to self-perception and the meaning it has for the participant's life course. The focus of the research is not the music itself, but the 'talk' generated by the music (Østergaard, 2021).

Starting Questions for a Music-Talk Interview (Østergaard, 2021)

Why did you choose that piece of music?
What does the song mean to you?
What story do you want to tell with this piece of music?

5.4 Ethical Considerations

Sonification as a method or applied to research should take ethical principles into consideration as well. All the principles in Chapter 3 should be carefully considered but there are also specific ethics applied to sonification. Music, for example, can evoke strong emotions in participants; according to Østergaard (2021) this can lead to a therapeutic conversation that cannot be properly and ethically dealt with in the context of a research interview. Adolescents should be given contact information on counselling options, preferably free ones (Østergaard, 2021). I would add that, even if the researcher does not provide the therapy or support to the adolescents, they are responsible to ensure that the adolescent is engaged with and is getting the support they need.

Case Study: Sonification of a Longitudinal Mentoring Intervention with Adolescents

This project is an applied example of sonification to a database which consists of the findings of a randomised control trial with adolescents and their experience of being mentored.

The Irish youth organisation Foróige commissioned the Child and Family Research Centre, University of Galway, to carry out this evaluation in 2007. The evaluation consisted of a mixed methods longitudinal design carried out over two years. The quantitative data included in this sonification project consists of a randomised control trial to determine the impact of the Big Brothers Big Sisters (BBBS) youth mentoring programme on adolescents' development (Dolan et al., 2010).

The sample consisted of 164 young people between 10 and 14 years of age, newly referred to the programme in the West of Ireland. Young people were randomly allocated to the intervention (regular youth activities and BBBS) or the control group (regular youth activities). Young people in the control group could avail themselves of the BBBS service after the study was completed.

SELECTING THE DATA

In Western musical theory, there are seven 'natural' notes (A, B, C, D, E, F and G). It was decided to include only seven questionnaires/surveys in the analysis as each one could be represented by one of these notes in a sonification project design. This was the original idea; however, this original design evolved over time. The questionnaires that were removed were selected because they had the smallest number of items as these consisted only of a set of two or three questions. The excluded questions were school liking, alcohol and cannabis use. These were also non-validated questionnaires designed specifically for this study, therefore the validity of these measures may have been less than that of published questionnaires.

Questionnaire	**Statistic**	**Wave 1**	**Wave 2**	**Wave 3**	**Wave 4**
Hope	N	159	136	140	133
	Mean	7.5	7.65	7.46	8.04
	SD	2.76	2.88	6.71	2.74
Social acceptance	N	153	130	136	130
	Mean	17.68	18.55	18.80	19.25
	SD	3.80	3.43	3.66	3.39
Scholastic efficacy	N	149	127	134	130
	Mean	17.36	17.44	17.41	17.63
	SD	3.78	3.83	3.86	3.84
Plans for school and college completion	N	159	135	136	133
	Mean	9.1242	9.31	9.35	9.43
	SD	2.718	2.502	2.490	2.438
Misconduct	N	158	134	139	133
	Mean	8.39	8.46	8.53	8.36
	SD	2.80	2.68	3.05	3.33
Parental trust	N	155	135	140	131
	Mean	13.88	13.96	13.75	14.06
	SD	2.67	2.68	2.54	2.44
Perceived friend support	N	160	136	140	134
	Mean	10.62	10.79	10.70	10.85
	SD	1.655	1.498	1.521	1.474
Perceived parental support	N	160	133	140	131
	Mean	10.80	10.68	10.81	10.65
	SD	1.648	1.853	1.622	1.839
Perceived sibling support	N	153	127	136	125
	Mean	9.38	9.14	9.35	9.28
	SD	2.58	2.52	2.25	2.60
Perceived other adult support	N	161	132	138	131
	Mean	9.78	10.02	9.33	9.79
	SD	2.33	1.961	2.331	2.068
Total perceived social support	N	153	119	132	122
	Mean	40.52	40.29	40.14	40.48
	SD	5.909	5.831	5.338	5.889

PREPARING THE DATABASE

The BBBS young person questionnaire database was prepared to carry out the sonification project. Different changes and calculations had to be carried out for each of the versions and variations carried out on the data. The database was 'cleaned' to remove missing data and replace it by using expectation maximisation. Missing data is a common issue in questionnaire-based research (Laaksonen, 2018) and how researchers handle missing data can have significant implications for the validity of inferences made (Dong & Peng, 2013).

Due to participant attrition, the number of respondents from Time 1 to Time 4 was reduced. Young people who did not complete data collection at the four data collection times were eliminated. At Time 1 there were 164 responses and, after the data was cleaned, there were 126 young people included in the sonification project.

With the remaining respondents, the missing completely at random (MCAR) test (Little, 1988) was used to determine whether data was MCAR. This test was run using Statistical Package for the Social Sciences (SPSS) version 24 software. Significant results indicate that the data was not missing completely at random. The result of Little's MCAR test is Chi-Square = 1135.14, DF = 16455, Sig = 1.000. Little's MCAR test is not significant, therefore it can be concluded that data is missing at random. This means imputation techniques can be used to deal with missing data.

Those participants who completed data collection four times but were missing some data were dealt with, in this project, using expectation maximisation. This has been described as an excellent procedure for handling missing data when data is MCAR or when the level of missingness is minimal (Allison, 2001; Bennett, 2001).

SOFTWARE

To carry out this sonification project a set of software and technology was selected. Reaper was the music programme selected, which is a digital audio production application for computers. Musical Instrument Digital Interface (MIDI) is the protocol which enables recording, editing, processing, mixing and mastering sound. It enables the transmission of messages between devices, equipment and software. Its messages consist of numerical descriptions of an action (e.g. press keys) converted into sound which comes out of the synthesiser into the speakers (Centre for Electronic and Computer Music, 2021).

A MIDI message consists of four components which have specific ranges as follows:

Component	Range
Pitch (notes)	1–127
Velocity (volume)	0 (no sound) – 127 (loud)
Channel: independent path which carries the message to its destination. Each channel is independent.	16 channels

LoopBe1 is the virtual MIDI cable which connects the Python MIDI output to the Reaper MIDI input. The MIDI port created needs to be enabled. This is done by selecting Reaper Preferences MIDI and finding the MIDI port created. Double-clicking on it will enable it. Reaper also requires the insertion of an instrument. This is carried out by clicking on the Insert menu and enabling the Insert Virtual Instrument on new track option.

Python was selected as the programming console for this project. A Python MIDI library was created using a command line. Python was then used to programme all the different sonification trials.

Pandas is a software library specifically written for the Python programming language. It is specialised in data manipulation and analysis of data structures. Pandas was used to read the datafile more efficiently and create a four-dimensional array considering the young person, the period, the scales and the individual scores in the questionnaires.

Excel is another programme used to manipulate the data sets. The original data sets were stored as Excel files. These files were converted into CSV files that were read into Python. These Excel files facilitated the conversion of direct scales scores into MIDI notes (pitches). The complexity of these Excel sheets evolved over time until the latest version which included the manipulation of music channels (two instruments), velocity and duration. SPSS was used for data preparation mainly dealing with missing data in the original data set.

SONIFICATION TRIALS

Different sonification trials were carried out by modifying the code in Python to ensure the sonification project corresponded to a logical representation of the data findings as well as generating an aesthetically pleasant sound for the user. These trials were increasingly more complex over time, as the skills of the research team developed. For example, the sum of all the answers to the questionnaires were calculated per person, that is, for each column of the Excel sheet. The mean of all answers was also calculated in this way, per person. This generated a single column with one value per participant in the order that they appeared in the original data set. Each of these values was converted to a pitch (MIDI note). As a variation, breaks were added between the scores of each young person, per scale, by adding an extra note at volume 0; this enabled the identification of where a new participant began, and the database iterated through their scores. Here is an example of the code used in this phase:

```
hopetime1 = (24+int(statistics.mean(L[8:13])))
hopetime2 = (24+int(statistics.mean(L[63:68])))
hopetime3 = (24+int(statistics.mean(L[118:123])))
hopetime4 = (24+int(statistics.mean(L[173:178])))
```

An additional step was included in this phase which consisted of the use of NumPy to read the Excel file as lists and reduce the amount of manual coding needed to read the Excel file. Lists became NumPyf files. (This is a standard binary file format to produce a single arbitrary array on a disk. This array can be reconstructed correctly in other machines even if these have a different architecture.)

The final sonification includes the creation of groups of subjects and interpolation of scores. It also involves the manipulation of the channel, the pitch, the volume and the duration directly from the csv file. An example of the file is shown in the figure:

A	B	C	D	E	F	G	H
Channel	Chord	Volume	Duration	Channel	Chord	Volume	Duration
0	69, 72, 76	50	16	1	69	75	4
				1	72	75	4
				1	76	75	4
				1	88	75	4
0	67, 71, 74	50	16	1	67	75	4
				1	71	75	4
				1	74	75	4
				1	86	75	4

To keep two instruments only, all participants were split into two groups. Group 1 consists of participants from the minimum mean up to the median mean. Group 2 consists of those participants from above the median mean to the maximum mean.

The overall mean for each question per group is used to allocate the pitches using the ranges in the table. To represent these means, the notes selected were diatonic chords of the key C. Diatonic chords belong to the same chord family and therefore sound better together. The six notes selected were: C, Dm, Em, F, G and Am.

Group	Chord	Midi Note		Melody			Mean Ranges
1	C	60, 64, 67	60	64	67	79	1.1–1.5
2	Dm	62, 65, 69	62	65	69	81	1.6–2.1
3	Em	64, 67, 71	64	67	71	83	2.2–2.6
4	F	65, 69, 72	65	69	72	84	2.7–3
5	G	67, 71, 74	67	71	74	86	3.1–3.5
6	Am	69, 72, 76	69	72	76	88	3.6–4

Instrument 1 (piano) played the chords, Instrument 2 (strings) played the corresponding chord as a melody. An extra note (an octave higher) was added to the melody to make the song 4/4 beats, which is more widely used, also known as the 'common time'.

The example below is part of the code used in the main Python function in this phase. It shows specifically the for loop which iterates across the MIDI message (channel, velocity, duration and pitches).

```
if__name__ == '__main__':
  data = main()
 print(data)
 b = midiBuffer(device=3, verbose=True)
 tempo = 105
 dur = int(60.0 / tempo / 8 * 1000) #eight note duration in ms
 print(dur)
 t = b.getTime()

 # Nested for loop

 for row in data.itertuples():
 idx, chan,pitches,vel,sdur,chan2,pitches2, vel2, sdur2 = row
 print(chan, pitches, vel, sdur, chan2, pitches2, vel2, sdur2)
 if np.isfinite(chan):
  chan = int(chan)
  vel = int(vel)
  sdur = int(sdur)
  pitches = eval(pitches)
  if type(pitches) == type(0): pitches = [ pitches]
  print(type(pitches))
  b.playChord(pitches, sdur * dur, vel, chan=chan, onset=t)
 else: sdur = 1000
```

To make the change over time more evident, it was decided to include the intervention group only in the sonification as their mean scores over time would have increased more because of taking part in the intervention. To highlight the change over time for participants was to modify the database, turn the columns to rows and rows to columns, that is, to calculate the mean scores by individual and not by scale. Once again only individuals in the intervention group were included as it was known from the research findings that these would have larger changes in their mean scores over time because of taking part in the intervention. New mean ranges were calculated, and the midi chords allocated.

Midi Chord	Melody				Mean Ranges
60, 64, 67	60	64	67	79	1.0–1.3
62, 65, 69	62	65	69	81	1.4–1.7
64, 67, 71	64	67	71	83	1.8–2.1
65, 69, 72	65	69	72	84	2.2–2.5
67, 71, 74	67	71	74	86	2.6–2.9
69, 72, 76	69	72	76	88	3.0–3.3
59, 63, 66	59	63	66	78	3.4–4

RESULTS

The strength of this sonification is that it describes the change over time experienced by a young person throughout their involvement in the BBBS intervention. This corresponds to the overall aim of the BBBS study: to evaluate the impact of mentoring relationships on an individual and show the benefits they obtained because of being mentored. Therefore, this transposed database is in line with the initial objective of the research study, and this makes the message transmitted by the sonification more meaningful and clearer to understand. Changes over time in the scales can be effectively transmitted by sonification too; however, this was not the objective of the original study and the sonification only shows change over time in the scales, without specifying who experienced that change.

This sonification enabled the manipulation of more elements of a song including pitch, volume, duration and channel. This facilitated the creation of a more complex song that was more aesthetically pleasing than earlier versions. Duration and volume on this occasion served exclusively aesthetic purposes, whereas channel and pitches were determined by the data itself – mean scores of participants. It was in this phase that data and aesthetics were 'married' to generate a song that is pleasant and effectively transmits the research findings, capturing the changes over time per participant. This was also carried out in an automated manner which was a more effective way to manipulate data and generate the sonification project, faster and with a higher complexity element that was not possible in previous versions and research phases. This project also demonstrated the use of sonification as a tool for primary and secondary data dissemination. Even though it was not participatory in nature, this project could be replicated with adolescents themselves, creating sonifications for the research studies they are part of.

Additional Resources

The Sonification Archive is a collaboration between the Centre for Design at Northeastern University (United States) and the Critical Alarm Lab of TU Delft (Netherlands). This lab offers an archive of sonifications carried out by many different designers and researchers around the world. This can be found by accessing https://sonification.design/.

The Data Sonification Canvas is a useful tool to begin designing your sonification project. It includes four basic stages that all researchers should think about for their projects.

1. Use case. Define who your users are and what the goals and the context of your sonification are.
2. Mapping choices. Define how you map data parameters to sound parameters.
3. Sonification approach. Find out the position of your approach to the sonification.
4. Listening experience. Imagine how your users will listen to the sonification.

CHAPTER 6

Photovoice and Visual Methods

Chapter Highlights

1. Images can be suitable methods to elicit the thoughts, emotions and lives of adolescents.
2. Photovoice is an intrinsic participatory method that empowers participants and transmits these messages to the correct audiences that will enable the change they want and need.
3. Photovoice has been successfully used in health research to explore mental health issues, chronic illnesses and complex healthcare needs in adolescents.
4. The use of photographs and images requires specific ethical considerations about safety, identity protection and copyright.

This chapter is focused on the use of visual methods using photography and self-filming, including photovoice and other methods. These methods have been found to be powerful and empowering for populations that were seldom heard. These methods are a medium for participants to identify their voices, express their needs and identify the changes they want and needs for themselves and their communities. These methods include dissemination to key stakeholders and policy makers as part of their methodology; therefore, this is an essential part of the process and cannot be ignored.

Images provide insights into meanings created by adolescents (Hill, 2013). Visual data provides insights into adolescents' routines, material worlds, relationships and their sense of self (Holland et al., 2010). Photographs have been described as capable of providing rich and in-depth knowledge and which are 'unique footprints in time' (Coad, 2007, p. 489).

6.1 Photovoice

Photovoice is part of participatory action research as it provides a space for participants and communities to exercise their rights (Aboulkacem, 2023). Capous-Desyllas et al. (2019) defined photovoice as an arts-based research method within community-based participatory research, which uses photography to provide a voice to participants to share their experiences and expertise. These photos are then shared beyond research and academia to elicit social change. Photovoice is grounded in three theoretical frameworks: 1) participatory action research; 2) feminist theory; and 3) a community-based approach (Wang, 1999; Wang & Redwood-Jones, 2001). Photovoice is a method which combines documentary photography and empowerment education, providing participants with an opportunity to document and communicate important aspects of their lives (Foster-Fishman et al., 2005). It is important, however, to consider that no one method is suitable for every topic and/or every community. Photovoice should be designed to address the needs of a specific community and population to ensure they will benefit from participation in the project.

Photovoice consists of three stages (Stephens et al., 2023):

1. Participants are trained by researchers on how to use the cameras and the ethics involved before taking the photographs.
2. Participants talk about the photographs in a group discussion.
3. Participants analyse the data.

One aspect which authors generally agree on with photovoice is the capacity of reflection and discussion it elicits in participants regarding social justice, encouraging and targeting social and political change (Aboulkacem, 2023; Goodhart et al., 2006). 'Photovoice when coupled with strategic dissemination, can spark social change' (Aboulkacem, 2023, p. 195). Photovoice is an empowering method which can raise awareness about issues in communities and society (Aboulkacem, 2023). This is associated with one of the theoretical underpinnings of photovoice which is Paulo Freire's (1970) empowerment education and critical consciousness theory which encouraged dialogue and an a more egalitarian approach to meaning-making. Empowerment education theory considers people as experts in their own lives leading the change needed socially and politically (Aboulkacem, 2023). Photovoice enables this dialogue and 'coming together' of participants and encourages change in their communities and lives.

Photovoice engages and empowers people who have usually been marginalised, disregarded or undervalued (Fountain et al., 2021). This includes youth experiencing poverty, racism and different types of discrimination (Fountain et al., 2021). Photovoice can amplify the voices of research participants and foster change (Stephens et al., 2023). Photovoice can also generate metaphoric and emotional insights, which may not be accessible through other qualitative research methods (Stephens et al., 2023). According to Stephens et al. (2023), photovoice can generate complex, opposing and occasionally contradictory information as it can flexibly examine adolescents' experiences in a variety of settings and populations. Research participants can benefit from learning research skills, consciousness-raising, capacity-building, skills training, work experience, paid employment, leadership development, peer mentoring and self-advocacy (Capous-Desyllas et al., 2019). Stakeholders are invited to these forums or displays to give participants an audience with the power to effect policy and changes needed to address the issues they have identified as concerning for them (Fountain et al., 2021). According to Wang and Redwood-Jones (2001), photovoice does not attempt to shift the power from policy makers to participants, instead it enables people to reach policy makers and become advocates of their own lives and communities.

Photovoice has several advantages over other research methods, particularly with adolescents. Regarding participatory research, photovoice is highly dependent on visuals instead of literacy, which levels the power difference between adult researchers and adolescent participants (Wong et al., 2010). Photovoice enables participants to engage in all stages of it democratically, which means the research aligns with public needs (Stephens et al., 2023). Sommer et al. (2021) state that visual methodologies such as photovoice provide participants with an opportunity to bring their environments into the discussion space. Photovoice empowers adolescents by making them feel like researchers of their own lives and communities. It enables participants to focus on their own ideas, elicited by their own photos, reducing the influence from other participants and the research team, meaning that each participant can influence the research process strongly and independently (Cambaco et al., 2024).

Foster-Fishman et al. (2005) carried out photovoice with adolescents and identified that this method empowered adolescents as experts on their lives and communities as well as fostered deep reflection and provided a safe context where they could explore diverse perspectives. Participants described an increase in their self-competence, increased critical awareness and having additional resources for social and political action (Foster-Fishman et al., 2005). Photovoice has also been used with stigmatised, disregarded or undervalued populations with success (Cambaco et al.,

2024; Capous-Desyllas et al., 2019). Capous-Desyllas et al. (2019) used photovoice to represent the visual voices of LGBT former foster youth. According to the authors, this method encouraged self-representation in adolescents, and this raised community awareness, created knowledge as well as promoted action planning and advocacy in the community. Wilson et al. (2007) carried out photovoice in a school environment; therefore policy makers were school local leaders, including the school's principal and after-school programme coordinator. These discussions were based on school issues and not about policy per se, but it is an example of how photovoice can make a difference.

Photovoice is a flexible method; however, this has been interpreted as lacking standardisation. Stephens et al. (2023) argue there is a need to standardise conducting and reporting photovoice studies. Photovoice can be carried out with disposable or digital cameras; however, digital cameras are usually less expensive (Green & Kloos, 2009; Hill, 2013; Schjellerup, 2021). Disposable cameras have the advantage of reducing the likelihood of youth being robbed or harassed (Sommers et al., 2021). Participant safety is also an important aspect to consider. According to Schjellerup (2021), the quality of the photographs was not significant; however, with disposable cameras adolescents, cannot delete photos which they may regret having taken. Resources may be needed for purchasing disposable cameras and photo development; this extra cost should be considered in the research budget and a smaller sample size may be suitable (Sommers et al., 2021). Cameras can provide control to adolescents regarding the flash, colour, zoom, focus, size, quality, keeping or deleting images as well as deciding which images they will share or not (Hill, 2013). Photovoice usually consists of having participants take their own research-specific photographs; however, Coad (2007) described that there has been a tendency towards using photographs participants already had, such as photo albums.

The logistic side of photovoice (obtaining materials, distributing cameras, developing photographs) can add a layer of complexity to it, particularly in rural settings where the distance to access participants may be significantly far (Esau et al., 2016). The time given to adolescents to take photographs varies from two weeks (Hill, 2013) to five weeks (Foster-Fishman et al., 2005). Foster-Fishman et al. (2005), for example, provided a roll of film for participants every week and developed photographs were returned, with participants completing a reflection that was shared in a group. In the groups, three photos were selected by voting and these were discussed further in terms of the research topic, which was neighbourhood life and change. Researchers usually oversee printing the photographs;

therefore, they will have the opportunity to make an interview guide ahead of time. Some authors, however (Schjellerup, 2021), prefer young people to set the agenda themselves.

Photovoice can serve as an intervention but also as a qualitative data collection method (Fountain et al., 2021). Photovoice can also be used as a quantitative method. For example, themes and motives can be categorised and the number of references to these categories can be quantified in the data (Schjellerup, 2021). Wang (1999) suggests a sample of 7–10 is an ideal group size. However, studies may have to follow specific sampling criteria to maximise or minimise representativeness across specific characteristics such as age, gender, income, ethnicity and health status. Additionally, different studies have different criteria regarding the ideal number of photographs for a study (Cambaco et al., 2024; Green & Kloos, 2009). Cambaco et al. (2024) suggested that a clear limit should be established to simplify data management and analysis. This could reduce the time and cost of data collection and enable a more in-depth discussion with adolescents about their experiences.

Goodhart et al. (2006, p. 53) summarised the steps to conduct a photovoice project:

1. Conceptualise the problem.
2. Devise initial teams and taking pictures.
3. Define broader goals and objectives.
4. Conduct photovoice training.
5. Take pictures.
6. Facilitate group discussions.
7. Engage in critical reflection and dialogue.
8. Select photographs for discussion.
9. Context and storytelling.
10. Coding issues, themes and theories.
11. Recruit policy makers.
12. Prepare photos and captions for presentation at the reception.
13. Reach policy makers, donors, media, researchers and others who may create change.

Photovoice, in general, will generate qualitative data because of interviews and focus groups with adolescents. Not all studies report the specific methodology they followed to complete the analysis. This information is generally presented as themes but the underlying theory informing the analysis is not disclosed or specified (McMorrow & Smith, 2016; Yi-Frazier et al., 2015). This may cause issues around validation and replication of research findings. Some studies report strategies of validation for qualitative data analysis; for example Yi-Frazier et al. (2015) calculated interrater reliability. This is a measure of agreement between different people, data analysts in this case. Overall, data analysis should be underpinned by strong methodologies and theories, particularly if the findings will be used to elicit change from key stakeholders and policy makers.

Traditionally, photovoice has been carried out as a face-to-face methodology; however, due to the Covid pandemic and concerns about inclusion, different authors have transitioned towards carrying out photovoice online. Aboulkacem (2023) developed and evaluated a photovoice online framework targeted at the 'digital generation' in Algeria with six university students. Aboulkacem (2023) included a parallel process to photovoice of developing competencies in visual, media and privacy literacy in research participants. This methodology is known as Photovoice 2.0 and aims to conduct the entire research online using social media platforms (see Table 6.1). Participants in this study used their own mobile phone cameras to take the photographs (Aboulkacem, 2023).

Table 6.1 *Photovoice stages*

Phase 1: Initiation*	Step 1: Visual literacy and photo analysis	Participants met and engaged in visual analysis of photographs.
	Step 2: Ethics and digital privacy discussion	In-depth discussions of ethical considerations of photography and digital privacy were carried out.
Phase 2: Implementation	Step 3: Picture taking	Participants went into the field to take photographs and data to bring to the next meeting.
	Step 4: Sharing of pictures and discussion	Participants met to discuss themes associated with their photographs and selected the social media platform they would use to share them.
Phase 3: Publishing	Step 5: Techniques of social media discussion	Issues around how to gain visibility and media literacy topics were discussed.
	Step 6: Publishing and online exhibition	Participants then published their photographs on social media.
Phase 4: Engagement	Step 7: Seek engagement with policy makers/ authorities	Participants discussed the continuation of the project and were debriefed about the Photovoice 2.0 methodology.

* Before initiation, researchers should engage with participants to obtain their consent for participation and to ensure they are suitable for the study. Participants should also be provided with information about the study and the task at hand.

Table 6.2 *Online photovoice stages*

Basic training	Adolescents completed consent forms. Participants' previous Instagram experience was assessed. All participants were trained in Instagram; new users downloaded the application and created an account. Privacy settings were reviewed, and participants were given the choice of keeping their accounts public or private.
Create the photo feed	Participants posted photographs in their feed which 'represented anything about their diabetes'. Participants got $10 per week if they had posted three photos per week, for three consecutive weeks.
Hashtags	Hashtags can group messages within social media. Participants could use the hashtag '#diabetesteenproject'. This enabled a collection of public photos to be maintained over time. This also enabled searches and photos to be tracked.
Follow-up interviews and focus group	Participants were interviewed individually to assess themes and experiences. Photos were printed and discussed in a focus group also following the SHOWeD method (explained later in the chapter).

A significant part of photovoice online was social media. Participants selected the platform to create and post their online exhibition. They created a name for the exhibit and which captions to use for each photograph and the tags to attract visibility from stakeholders, policy makers and the public. Hashtags contribute by increasing content visibility, tracking content metrics and boosting audience engagement.

Another example of photovoice online was used by Yi-Frazier et al. (2015) who used Instagram as an application for adolescents with type 1 diabetes to share their experiences. The study was specifically examining the feasibility of combining photovoice with social media. Feasibility was evaluated with a record of rates of recruitment, retention and satisfaction. This study followed a four-step methodology (see Table 6.2).

Yi-Frazier et al. (2015) found that photovoice and social media was a promising method for adolescents experiencing chronic illnesses. The authors, however, considered the 'personal touch' critical to keep participants engaged and sharing photographs taken by themselves. In this study, the majority (67 per cent) of photographs were not taken by the adolescents themselves. This was probably not specified in the original instructions provided.

Besides using a photovoice method, other projects have incorporated different participatory components in their studies. Goodhart et al. (2006)

included a student photovoice coordinator who oversaw project logistics with student participants and staff. The student coordinator also selected the themes to address in the research study. Capous-Desyllas et al. (2019) had a community advisory board (CAB). The CAB consisted of six members, two of whom belonged to the target population, as well as practitioners with experience working with this population. The CAB was also multiracial, multilingual and all members had queer and/or trans identities, which was relevant for the research topic. This group met bimonthly for three hours and were given a small stipend as well as their expenses being covered. The CAB completed several tasks: create a name for the research study; revise recruitment materials and research instruments; review interview guide and photovoice prompts; and troubleshoot any ethical issues which might have emerged. The CAB had a crucial role in phrasing the questions in a way that would make participants feel less stigmatised about sensitive topics such as homelessness, self-harm and engagement in sex working.

Photovoice has many benefits, but the method and its application can be challenging. The skills and abilities of adolescents may vary. Engaging them successfully in a research project may require additional support and training. Wilson et al. (2007) discussed adolescents' cognitive abilities, particularly carrying out photovoice with 'underserved' early adolescents. Wilson et al. (2007) argued that adolescents must be supported in their engagement and programmes should accommodate potential lack of experience and skills such as critical thinking, resistance to writing and negative attitudes. Cambaco et al. (2024) identified that adolescents were unclear about the term 'health impact' which was the crucial topic of their study. It is therefore important to ensure adolescents are familiar with the research topics in order to facilitate their participation as meaningful.

McMorrow and Smith (2016) reported difficulties with participants taking photographs relevant to the research topic. The research team dealt with the issue by talking with participants and in response modified the question or mission adolescents had. Participants were given new cameras to take more photographs. This seemed to be a successful strategy; however, issues like this can significantly increase research costs, which not all studies may be able to cope with.

Photovoice, and particularly photovoice online, may not be a suitable method for all potential participants (Yi-Frazier et al., 2015). Some participants refused to take part in the study as they perceived themselves as private and therefore not wanting to share photographs on social media (Yi-Frazier et al., 2015).

6.2 Photo Elicitation

Photo elicitation is a research method, but it is usually paired with other visual methods such as self-filming and photovoice. Photo elicitation consists of inserting visual material into a research interview (Olesen, 2021). Visual material can include different types of media such as photographs, videos, drawings, maps or paintings (Olesen, 2021). These visual materials generate a dialogue between participants and researchers to help researchers understand the material from the perspective of the interview.

One of the qualities of this method is that it is 'auto-driven' as the photographs are taken by adolescents themselves in their everyday life contexts (Schjellerup, 2021). Hill (2013) highlights that listening to adolescents' interpretations is a way of shifting authority from researchers to participants. It enables an 'insider' approach defined as understanding life experiences from within to obtain insights that can only be obtained from participants themselves (Schjellerup, 2021). Researchers should not assume they are able to interpret photographs as participants desired or that the photographs 'speak for themselves' (Hill, 2013, p. 144). Photos can be read externally (what is seen in the photo) and internally (the message sent) (Epstein et al., 2006).

Schjellerup (2021) purposefully described photo elicitation as a 'talk' and not as an interview as adolescents would experience the process as a 'dialogue where the young person oversaw the rhythm . . . the agenda . . . [and] which photos to talk about and when' (Schjellerup, 2021, p. 98).

Foster-Fishman et al. (2005) used different questions to allow discussion. These can also be adapted to the objectives and needs of a particular research study.

1. I want to share this photo because. . .
2. What's the real story this photo tells. . .
3. How does this story relate to your life. . .

Once participants have selected their photographs, they will proceed to write captions for them following a method based on the original work by Shaffer (1983) called SHOWeD. This method has been readily used in other research studies (Flicker et al., 2008).

1. What do you **S**ee here?
2. What is really **H**appening here?
3. How does this relate to **O**ur lives?

4. **W**hy does this situation **E**xist?
5. What can we **D**o about it?

Aboulkacem (2023) elicited analysis and reflection with the following questions:

1. How does this picture make you feel?
2. What message is the photo trying to convey?
3. Could this photograph violate someone's privacy?

6.3 Photovoice in Health Research

Photovoice is a promising prevention approach, which provides adolescents an opportunity for participation, self-determination, new skills and their health as well as any safety concerns regarding their lives and communities (Wilson et al., 2007). Photovoice can be used in conjunction with health promotion to elicit dialogue to address health concerns of a given population (Esau et al., 2016). Photovoice can encourage participants to reflect on their health and act accordingly (Esau et al., 2016). According to Wang (1999), the visual image can provide a learning site that can impact people's health and well-being.

Self-filming has been used in a health context to understand communication between patients and healthcare professionals (Olesen, 2021). Patients used film to capture their experiences of living with a chronic illness. The method is based on the premise that patients are experts on their own circumstances; therefore, they can teach health providers, who are in turn the disease experts (Olesen, 2021). This 'insider' perspective is used to inform the design of interventions to fit individual needs. Olesen (2021) used consumer camcorders to document patients' daily lives, interview people relevant to their lives and they could also film themselves providing observations, views, opinions, or anything they wanted to express about their illness. The recordings, in this case, were then evaluated by researchers to identify the patient's medical, psychosocial and anthropological circumstances they are living in due to the illness (Olesen, 2021).

Photovoice has also been used with research in children and adolescents with complex healthcare needs (Watson et al., 2006). This method was suitable for participants with communication difficulties and cognitive impairments, and participants were given a disposable camera to take a photograph of important people in their lives. Overall, this method has been described as suitable for children and adolescents who are not literate or have language difficulties (Coad, 2007). The photographs enable researchers to understand adolescents' lives and issues that affect them (Watson et al., 2006). Watson et al. (2006) developed a topic guide for participants:

1. Things I like.
2. Things I do not like.
3. Who lives at home with me.
4. School.
5. Friends.
6. Adults who help me.
7. Short breaks.
8. Things that are difficult to do.
9. General happiness.
10. What they thought about visits with professionals.
11. What they thought about their designated worker (if they had one).

Photovoice was used by McMorrow and Smith (2016) as a method for needs assessment to inform obesity prevention programmes with African-American adolescent girls who disproportionately suffer from higher rates of overweight and obesity compared with their White peers. One characteristic of this study is that it included one of the longest training times. It consisted of six sessions where adolescents were provided with a variety of content and activities including:

1. Introduction to photovoice.
2. Introduction to research (question/purpose).
3. The ethics of photovoice.
4. A photographer, who taught participants how to use a camera.
5. A practice photo session.
6. A safety presentation by the school officer.

Participants were given a disposable camera with 27 photographs available to take.

Participant training takes different styles in different studies. In some cases, it was researchers themselves who trained participants (Olesen, 2019, 2021). Wang and Redwood-Jones (2001) included professional photographers as trainers. Photovoice facilitators were trained as well. Overall, the study identified that photovoice is a suitable methodology that can be implemented as a participatory, formative assessment tool to tailor prevention interventions and reduce health disparities (McMorrow & Smith, 2016).

Esau et al. (2016) used photovoice to understand current health priorities of youth in rural Uganda. Participants in this study were between 13 and 17 years of age. They were given disposable cameras and were asked to take photographs of 'situations that contributed or detracted from their health status' (Esau et al., 2016, p. 59). Participants were given a week to take photographs. They were given these guiding questions to support the exercise:

1. What makes you feel healthy?
2. What makes you feel unhealthy?
3. What do you see as the health goals of your community?

Cameras were returned to the investigators and individual semi-structured interviews were carried out with each participant. Photographs were analysed, coded and assigned into themes.

Importantly, in this study a decision was made that if participants did not explain why a photograph was taken, these photographs were eliminated to avoid research bias and assumptions (Esau et al., 2016). This study found evidence to support the theory that photovoice is an effective methodology to assess and express adolescents' health concerns (Esau et al., 2016).

Photovoice is also a suitable method to explore mental health among adolescents who may experience stigma and lack power (Stephens et al., 2023). Stephens et al. (2023) carried out a scoping review of photovoice within mental health research involving adolescents. This review concluded that photovoice is a compelling and promising method which can generate insights into the social determinants of adolescent mental health (Stephens et al., 2023).

Olesen (2019, 2021) explored the experiences of young adults with mental health problems in health and welfare services in Norway. Participants had been involved in these services since they were teenagers, as they had one or more psychiatry diagnoses. Participants were given a camcorder (a Canon Legria Mini X). They were given basic technological training. Participants filmed for a couple of weeks up to several months. The researcher edited the sequence and selected the parts that were going to be used in photo elicitation.

6.4 Self-Filming

Self-filming is another type of visual method. Self-filming is 'the act of switching on a camcorder and turning the lens to oneself' (Olesen, 2021, p. 74). This method is known by other terms such as video diaries. The method is suitable for adolescents as they are accustomed to video technology (Olesen, 2021). Self-filming has been identified as a suitable method to deal with vulnerable people (Olesen, 2021). The method is participatory as it gives the young person the control of producing data, allowing them to decide when and where they want to film as well as which footage they want to delete or keep from the researchers (Olesen, 2021).

Techniques for Adolescents to Be in Control of Time (Coad, 2007)

Card system:

Participants are given different colour cards which they can hold up if they wish to stop (e.g. red ones) or change subject.

Rotation:

Researchers can rotate different data collection methods and activities to ensure boredom is reduced.

6.5 Ethical Considerations

Chapter 3 in this book provided a general ethical approach to health research with adolescents; however, there are some specific ethical considerations that need to be made regarding video and photograph methods. When conducting research using photographs, it is fundamental to have and enforce ethical protocols that will protect participants, researchers and the overall integrity of the research process (Aboulkacem, 2023). Ethical considerations are crucial as, according to Aboulkacem (2023), they may hinder creativity. There should be a balance to protect the participants' wishes and creativity while guaranteeing the safety and ethical principles of those taking photographs and those included in them (Aboulkacem, 2023). Ethical considerations, however, may not fully protect subjects from poor judgement. Having ethical guidelines and considerations in place in the project will make these incidents less likely (Wang & Redwood-Jones, 2001).

6.5.1 Who Will See the Participant's Material?

In some cases, raw material may only be seen by participants and researchers. The findings are the only ones shared in public. In the study by Aboulkacem (2023), healthcare professionals were not shown the material although no specific reasons were provided by the authors. I suggest the reason was ethical to protect patient anonymity particularly from those that may not have a very positive opinion of the services provided or that may have other negative perceptions of specific individuals they encounter in the services.

6.5.2 *Including People in the Material*

Including photographs of children and young people without their permission and adult permission is problematic. According to Schjellerup (2021), the potential inclusion of children and young people can lead to primary caretakers and gatekeepers denying access. In the Rethink Ireland study of alternative education (Kovačič et al., 2021), which is the case study at the end of this chapter, adolescents were discouraged from including other people in their photographs, instead they could include objects, places or situations that represented this person.

6.5.3 *Disruptions*

One of the issues that can happen with visual methods is the 'misuse' of cameras. The adolescents may use the cameras for personal photographs and not as part of the study. It is important to ensure that adolescents understand that playing with the camera has a negative impact on the data and the study (Schjellerup, 2021). Overall, this topic needs to be addressed early on with adolescents to ensure this contributes towards making an informed decision about participation in the research and to fully understand what this entails.

6.5.4 *Public Use of Images*

Participant consent forms for visual methods should be explicit about how the images will be used beyond the research study (Schjellerup, 2021). For example, images will be released to the public or in publications. Adolescents should give written consent but also researchers should consult with them, once the photos are printed, which one they feel comfortable releasing and which one not. An issue that may emerge is if the participant wants to keep the work they produced. Coad (2007) explained that researchers could photograph the work to use it for analysis. It is important, however, to include clear guidelines about this to avoid disappointment in adolescents.

6.5.5 Law

Ethical considerations should adhere to local and global privacy laws. These laws relate to the intrusion into people's private space as well as community and group privacy. Law also exists around data sharing and data handling, data ownership and government surveillance. Photographs posted on social media become the property of the platform (Aboulkacem, 2023). Researchers and participants should be aware of the local and global laws that impact on photovoice, whether face to face or online.

Researchers working with visual methods should understand the local policies and legislations. In countries like the United States, there is a guarantee by constitution of freedom of expression for journalists, artists and scholars which allows them to collect, interpret and disseminate information and ideas. Wang and Redwood-Jones (2001) explained that something that is legally permissible may be morally questionable.

***

Ethics in photovoice is important as the camera provides 'power' to the photographer of creating meaning about the subjects in the photographs (Wang & Redwood-Jones, 2001). This means there is the possibility of intrusion of people's private space. If the interpretation of the events in the photo conflicts with the subject's thoughts or feelings, this might mean the subject's rights are compromised. For this reason, Wang and Redwood-Jones (2001) recommend having three separate consent forms:

1. Consent between project staff and participants. This consent outlines the participant's rights and responsibilities in the project.
2. Consent between participants and subjects. Participants obtain the signature from the subjects in the photograph to have their picture taken. Wang and Redwood-Jones (2001) created brochures to provide participants for their subjects. Participants were also given copies of the photographs to give to their subjects.
3. Publication consent. This consists of the permission given by the photographer to the researcher to publish the developed photographs. Participants can decide if all photographs or only some can be published. Depending on the type of camera, participants may have negatives. Wang and Redwood-Jones (2001) suggest that the negatives belong to participants and they may choose to lend or give the negatives to researchers. Additionally, Wang and Redwood-Jones

(2001) suggest participants should receive an honorarium if their pictures are published.

If the consent process involves a minor, a signature of a parent and/or legal guardian is required (Wang & Redwood-Jones, 2001). Consent is not required if the photograph includes a group photo where individual faces cannot be identified, photographs of objects or if it includes a person who just 'happens to walk by' (Wang & Redwood-Jones, 2001, p. 565). Wang and Redwood-Jones (2001) also refer to the 'art of patience' in photography where the researcher can wait for the subjects to 'forget' they are being photographed and behave as usual. Participants need to be fully aware that the subjects' safety is more important than the image itself. Participants should be cautious of the environment, potential dangers and obtaining their permission before taking the picture (Wang & Redwood-Jones, 2001).

Photovoice may elicit change; however, whether this change is sustainable over time is unclear and whether researchers have an ethical and professional duty of ensuring that change happens and is sustainable over time is also an ethical concern. There may be a lack of clarity of who is accountable for the change and ensuring it is positive and sustained over time. In the case of Goodhart et al. (2006), for example, policy makers expected participants to create guidelines and future solutions, whereas participants expected policy makers to be the ones to solve the problems they identified.

Fountain et al. (2021) described that the most significant outcome of photovoice projects was an increase in community awareness of the issues identified; however, it was not determined for how long this awareness remained or if it was sustained over time, long enough to maintain the momentum in the community to elicit change. Research is needed to study participant empowerment and long-term impact of participation in photovoice projects.

Case Study: Exploring the Experiences of Alternative Education with Photovoice (Kovačič et al., 2021)

Photovoice was used as the methodology for an in-depth exploration of adolescent experiences in alternative education in different projects and alternative schools in the Republic of Ireland. This case study belongs to a three-year research and evaluation study conducted on Rethink Ireland's Education Fund (2017–2020) by the UNESCO Child and Family Research Centre, University of Galway.

Photovoice methodology was used to explore participants' real-time lived experiences. The method was applied partly as a face-to-face methodology, but due to the first COVID-19 lockdown, it also became an online experience.

Information pack: The research team designed an information pack for participants explaining the photovoice method. This pack also contained the participant information sheet and consent form.

Preliminary workshop: Participants received information on the ethics of photovoice (not taking photographs of other people's faces), the use of disposable cameras in the study, as well as information about the research topic.

Collecting cameras: Adolescents returned their disposable cameras after a week. These were collected by a member of the research team. Participants were asked to provide between 10 and 27 photographs.

Online interviews: Participants carried out an online interview with the researcher to explain the meaning of their photographs and their lived experiences in alternative education. Due to the COVID-19 pandemic, this was a salient topic as well.

Data analysis: Thematic analysis was used to analyse the transcribed interviews.

Data verification: Participants were invited to an online focus group with the researcher to validate the findings obtained from the analysis.

FINDINGS

Photovoice identified four themes: 1) access to equal opportunities – students emphasised how alternative education provided them with access to study and financial support; 2) access to the study room was important to them, as this was a place where they found peace and spent a lot of time socialising or having refreshments; 3) study support was available as grinds (a form of private tuition), online study support and external supports were also funded to help students improve their grades and performance; and 4) mental health including physical and psychological well-being was significant for participants. They had access to classes and uniforms. Other groups of adolescents described their experience of education online as due to COVID-19 their exams were cancelled. Schoolwork and support were online. They missed face-to-face contact, their teachers and their friends.

DISSEMINATION

Due to COVID-19 restrictions, what was initially going to be an exhibition of adolescents' photographs became a website. This website can be accessed at https://rethinkphotovoice.wordpress.com/

CHAPTER 7

Videos and Animations

Chapter Highlights

1. Video is a suitable and cost-effective way of working with adolescents.
2. Video and animations have been used for health promotion and service delivery improvement.
3. Participatory videography can be empowering for participants and a way to amplify their voices so they are heard by the relevant stakeholders who will enable the change they want and need.
4. The use of videos has specific ethical considerations, for example, protecting identity of participants.

Digital media facilitates the use of online and social networks with adolescents as this is the way in which they are currently consuming information (Ito-Jaeger et al., 2022). Social media and digital films can be an effective and cost-efficient way to improve mental health literacy in adolescents (Ito-Jaeger et al., 2022). Video production for children and young people can be attractive and it is becoming even more accessible as technology advances. Mobile phones have enabled the use of video from case-specific and small-scale research to becoming an instrument of work to obtain larger data sets; however, usage and accessibility are still unequal around the world (Blazek, 2017). The first-person narrative is used extensively in documentaries and television as it facilitates identification and empathy and, therefore, engagement (Pauletto & Walus, 2018) from the audience. Video is an effective way to capture an audience.

Participatory methods are suitable for video and animations as it is suggested that media content should be a co-creation to maximise the impact on the target audience (Ito-Jaeger et al., 2022). These methods also contain an active voice that enables anonymity for subjects involved in the creation process (Ito-Jaeger et al., 2022). Additionally, unlike other research products, videos and documentaries can appeal to a variety of audiences as the use of academic language can be explained (Bautista et al., 2013). Video mixes visual and auditory stimuli and can incorporate a variety of stakeholder voices (Bautista et al., 2013), which makes it suitable for a variety of audiences.

Szabó and Laihonen (2024) argue that the inclusion of digital technology can be very useful to engage participants; however, this is not without its challenges particularly related to the technique involved and the technology required. It also requires a certain level of skills to produce a useful, impactful and suitable video to be accepted as a valid research output. It is also important to remember that participants are often constrained by the fact that they are within a framework that was defined previously by the researcher's topics and interest; therefore, they are not always themselves fully able to decide on the research topics or the limits of the study they are part of.

7.1 Participatory Videography

Participatory video (PV) is defined as the process of video-making conducted by the people or community, instead of it being produced about themselves (Blazek, 2017). Participants become 'directors of their own stories' and are therefore in control of the message they want to convey (Gregorious, 2017). Szabó and Laihonen (2024) describe PV as a participatory methodology that shifts the focus of the research onto the people. It is often regarded as empowering communities, mostly those that are trained and use the skills to document and create their own narratives with minimal interventions from outsiders (Evans, 2017), the researchers in this case. Evans (2017) highlighted the immediacy of short films to effectively convey participants' messages, enabling participant voices to be heard directly by relevant stakeholders. PV enables listening to children's and adolescents' voices more widely, without tampering with their contents and qualities (Blazek, 2017). Videos can also be more easily distributed and consumed than academic papers or reports; these can be an accessible advocacy tool to create awareness of specific groups, for example people with disabilities (Gregorious, 2017). Video has the potential to destabilise misconceptions about people with impairments and enable social changes (Gregorious, 2017).

PV can take several forms, such as short films and video diaries (Blazek, 2017). This method can be recorded by the participant or the researcher, which enables an understanding of the research topic but also framing, capturing, editing and the overall environment of research participants (Szabó & Laihonen, 2024). According to Blazek (2017), producing video in this collaborative way can be empowering, and possibly richer and more powerful than the messages presented in the video.

PV requires training participants in film-making and using cameras, enabling them to take ownership of the research and as a motivating factor (Blazek, 2017). Once the topic is defined (by the researcher, the participants or both), it is recommended to design a storyboard and a filming schedule (Blazek, 2017). PV takes time but it is an opportunity to understand what is important for participants. This shared creative process is the most valuable feature of this method (Blazek, 2017).

Szabó and Laihonen (2024) suggest participants should also be involved in analysing the research material generated. The ideal PV, according to Evans (2017), involves community members at all stages from the idea, filming, editing and dissemination; however, this may be time and cost demanding; therefore, it is realistic for researchers to include 'elements' of PV in their studies. Evans (2017), for example, emphasised participation in the dissemination of findings, and identification of key messages for policy and practice, filming and editing was not carried out by participants. This was still regarded as a valuable approach even if the technical skills and power remained with the team and not with the participants. More thought, therefore, should be given to how outputs are disseminated to ensure participants' concerns are voiced to those in power but also how to achieve radical change with PV (Evans, 2017). Appropriate dissemination is also an ethical responsibility (Evans, 2017).

One of the challenges of this method is the dissimilar prior experience of participants with technology (Szabó & Laihonen, 2024). As with any other method, particularly involving technology, adolescents' participation needs to be supported and enabled to be successful. Dunn and Mellor (2017) carried out workshops with adolescents. Duration and group size of the workshops should be considered carefully to maximise participation in a safe, creative and confidential environment where adolescents can have the time and space to think, explore, reflect and share their ideas.

Ito-Jaeger et al. (2022) carried out seven Youth Juries where adolescents' opinions were sought regarding the content and presentations of the video animations. Nine adolescents took part in workshops and identified five topics: perfectionism, independence, loneliness, isolation and competitiveness. An additional group of 40 young people confirmed the relevance of these topics. This group was involved in script and animatic production. A core group of five adolescents was then selected, based on their level of

Table 7.1 *Games and activities*

Games	Games contribute to team building, changing pace and mood, and facilitate problem-solving and fun. It is important for adults and participants to be involved together. Games can also help to introduce difficult and complex topics.
Characters	Characters help participants to explore and share experiences. Characters can be created with stories, puppets, drama, role play, images and body mapping. Materials such as sheets of paper, pens, pencils and sticky notes can be provided. Adolescents can identify topics and concerns, for example life events, family situations, mental health problems and friendships.
Scaffolded discussion	These are led by workshop facilitators to identify themes and draw meaning from the group sessions. Notes can be kept for future reference.

engagement. This core group was closely and frequently involved with the production team and provided feedback on the final film production. This core group also provided information on the public relation strategies and selected the influencer for the media campaign. Adolescents also provided the voices for the characters. Other methodological strategies to provide skills for participants were used by Dunn and Mellor (2017), including a film project summer school. This was a four-day period where adolescents built cohesive teams, explored topics of interest and generated audio and visual materials. Other activities suggested by Dunn and Mellor (2017) are: games, characters and scaffolded discussions. These are described in Table 7.1.

Creating quality videos may also require professional input. Dunn and Mellor (2017) had an animator and sound editor who carried out the image and audio selection as well as editing the material; however, they worked closely with adolescents to ensure their wishes were captured and respected. Adolescents were guided for filming behind the scenes and film-making techniques (Dunn & Mellor, 2017). Ito-Jaeger et al. (2022), for example, worked in partnership with the independent animation studio Aardman Animations.

Choosing the most suitable professional is important. Preferably, a professional must have experience working with adolescents in a participatory manner. This means that they need to understand the role of adolescents as central when using this method. Adolescents will have an active role in the video-making process, and the decision-making required or the creative process. Rodriguez et al. (2018) had a professional that, in essence, became part of the research team and facilitated workshops to seek the ideas of adolescents themselves regarding the storyline, the location and the production of the video. In this study, the adult professional even allowed one of the adolescents with a personal interest in and skills using video cameras to carry out some of the filming himself. This was a very powerful way of showing trust to the group of adolescents and was also a strong message to them that they were valued and included and it motivated their commitment and engagement with the project. For example, all adolescents except one continued to attend the sessions and were included throughout the video-making process.

7.2 Experience-Based Co-design

Experience-based co-design (EBCD) is a qualitative participatory action research method for service improvement and development which specifically places the voices of service users at the centre of the improvement in health services (Cooper et al., 2016; Larkin et al., 2015). This is crucial to the evaluation and development of healthcare services. It is important, however, to carefully plan the involvement of service users, so that it is genuinely meaningful and leads to change (Cooper et al., 2016). The method of EBCD enables staff and service users to co-design services in partnership (King's Fund, 2013). It has been described a suitable method to use in mental health settings as well as physical health settings (Cooper et al., 2016).

This approach was created for and within the National Health Service (NHS) in the United Kingdom, specifically for service improvement and development; this means the method 'puts service-user voices at the heart of improving health services' (Cooper et al., 2016, p. 36). The method involves using videos to support service development. It is qualitative in nature and uses data gathering techniques such as in-depth interviews, observations and group discussions to identify 'touch points'. Touch points consist of 'emotionally significant points' which are the most significant issues identified by research participants themselves at the end of their interviews (King's Fund, 2013). These are the key parts of the service users' stories (between 1 and 5 points) (Cooper et al., 2016). The EBCD method is focused on capturing experiences and emotions rather than attitudes and opinions (King's Fund, 2013).

The method also involves technology as the outcome is the creation of a short, edited film. This video is shown to staff and other key stakeholders to better understand patients' experience of the service. The video triggers a discussion between those key stakeholders on how to improve the service. This video should be about 30 minutes long. It includes all the key themes identified in the interviews.

The overall objective of EBCD is to improve services; therefore, this must be integrated in the methodology. For example, Cooper et al. (2016) collaboratively created SMART goals (specific, measurable, achievable, realistic, time-bound) to improve the services. Larkin et al. (2015) created a steering group in charge of monitoring and supporting the implementation of actions and agreements over the following year. Researchers also attended this steering group. It is important to consider that translating qualitative findings into tangible changes in complex services can and will be challenging (Larkin et al., 2015).

King's Fund (2013) has a comprehensive toolkit available online with the specific steps to carry out this methodology. This can be found at: www.pointofcarefoundation.org.uk/resource/experience-based-co-design-ebcd-toolkit/step-by-step-guide/4-getting-started-building-project-team/.

EBCD consists of six steps, as summarised by Larkin et al. (2015):

1. Collection of experiences from staff and service users through observation or interviews (recorded or not).
2. Identification of 'touch points'.
3. Feed back 'touch points' to participants.
4. Participants select the most important 'touch points'.
5. Co-design event where all stakeholders design improvements to the service according to priorities identified.
6. Celebration event to review achievements.

Regarding the use of technology, the guidelines provide some important recommendations (King's Fund, 2013):

1. Create a comfortable environment for research participants where they will feel safe sharing their stories and experiences. This includes details such as having comfortable seats, refreshments, tissues and ensuring privacy. Participants can also make suggestions of locations.
2. Research participants may bring a friend or family member to provide moral support. A plan should be put in place in case participants become distressed and need additional support, for example referrals or contact information to attend a debriefing session with a service colleague (deliberately informed of their role in the research study) or a patient support line. Larkin et al. (2015) had

a quiet room available where all participants could take a time break or seek support during interviews and events.

3. Send notes and interview schedules to participants to ensure they know what to expect. Interviews can take between one and two hours.
4. Consider using a tripod to record the interviews, as the presence of a cameraperson may inhibit research participants.
5. The person capturing the video should have basic recording skills (angle, framing, lighting) to make sure the video is of a good enough quality to be used in the final overall video. Also, avoid interruptions and external noises (phones, pets, children) to facilitate the editing process.
6. Anonymity with videos should be given careful consideration. In the case of mental health issues, for example (Larkin et al., 2015), anonymity may be crucial due to the associated stigma. Film also preserves participants' testimonies over time and, thus, researchers have the responsibility to ensure these videos are not used for other purposes. Those participants and practitioners that express negativity about the service need to be reassured that this does not put their treatment or jobs in jeopardy. All data protection procedures used with any other type of research material should be put in place with the videos (Larkin et al., 2015).
7. Check interview times and attendance the day before. Research participants may need to cancel at short notice due to illness.
8. All names or identifying information should be removed from videos.
9. Editing requires software. An external editing supplier can be used; however, videos can already be provided at 10 minutes per speaker to reduce the cost. Shortening videos can be time-consuming.
10. Include at least one video of each participant interviewed. Before releasing the final version of the video, ensure research participants have given their approval for their specific quotes and sections; do not include other participants. Ensure they are given time to provide feedback and make any changes before the public release.
11. Think carefully about the release of your video. (Dissemination is a crucial part of a research study and will enable you to generate the impact or change intended.) Make sure you book a suitable venue in advance; consider providing food and refreshments, accessibility, transport and provide clear signposting for people to find the venue. The shape within the venue will help encourage group interaction,

for example have tables for groups or chairs in a circle where participants can face and talk to each other. Consider running separate events for service users and staff depending on your research objectives but also, and probably most importantly, to tailor the findings in a way that they will be fully relevant and understood by your target audience.

12. The creator's credibility is important for adolescents. Participants in the study by Ito-Jaeger et al. (2022) recommended that the logos of universities and mental health organisations should be included in the outputs to increase credibility of the information and trust in the health sources. Future media should clearly present the involvement of established institutions in the outputs (Ito-Jaeger et al., 2022).
13. Films and animations should ensure inclusivity for people with special needs (the hard of hearing, non-native English speakers), but they have also proven to be beneficial for everyone as they improve understanding, attention and memory (Ito-Jaeger et al., 2022).

7.3 Videos and Health Research

Videos and animations have been created with adolescents which can be used to educate them and the general population on health-related topics. Dunn and Mellor (2017) carried out participatory projects with adolescents and the NHS and produced three films. One was targeted at adolescents experiencing depression, another was for children and adolescents attending or leaving NHS mental health services and one was for those leaving the services at 17 or 18 years of age.

Animations are useful to deliver mental health information for adolescents. Ito-Jaeger et al. (2022) designed short, animated films to promote health literacy. The What's Up with Everyone (WUWE) project was created to promote mental health literacy among adolescents (Ito-Jaeger et al., 2022). The videos are between 40 and 50 minutes long and focused on a variety of themes: loneliness, isolation, perfectionism, competitiveness, social media and independence. Dissemination of these videos was significant; the videos were shared on YouTube, Instagram, Twitter (at the time), Facebook and TikTok (Ito-Jaeger et al., 2022). Participants considered that watching the films improved mental health literacy and reduced stigma because they are relatable and reassuring to adolescents who have experienced similar challenges. Adolescents perceived that the animations included very little information about seeking help but may encourage them to look for support (Ito-Jaeger et al., 2022).

7.4 Ethics

Film-making has important ethical implications, as the camera would reveal the identity of adolescent participants (Dunn & Mellor, 2017). This becomes a more critical issue when participants are perceived as 'vulnerable'. In the case of Dunn and Mellor (2017), it was agreed that adolescents would not be identifiable; therefore names and faces did not appear on screen. Adolescents who had co-researching roles and were involved in data dissemination (conference poster, presentations) wanted to be personally identified, so their names were released. Participants should have the authority to decide on the dissemination process, including where and how are the videos shown and to whom they are shown (Gregorious, 2017).

Evans (2017) provided some strategies used in her study to ensure videos were complying with ethical considerations:

1. Encourage participants to talk about issues in a more general way, instead of their own personal circumstances.
2. Remove participant names from the video.
3. Participants could record their messages in audio recording instead of video camera.
4. Follow up with participants to determine if they are satisfied with the messages and editing.
5. Remove any unwanted personal information; participants have the right to veto the content. (This can be a limited role in editing.)
6. Select the target stakeholders to present the video; avoid public exposure (if not essential for the project), for example social media. This enables a more controlled dissemination, although it could also be a limitation to the potential of the video.

Another aspect related to ethics is the need to manage participant expectations. According to Evans (2017), active participation in dissemination may inevitably raise participants' expectations that the research will lead to direct, tangible benefits for them. Change requires effort, resources and time. Video production can be a lengthy process, and it may upset young participants if they do not see the outcomes of their contributions. Balzek (2017), therefore, suggests the need to share 'work in progress' outputs and to engage participants in editing and other phases of the video.

Evans (2017) considers that researchers should be aware of the limits of their role; they may not be able to provide ongoing support or training or to continue working with participants once the research has ended. Researchers may also lack the skills, language or experience to provide this support. Engaging strategic stakeholders – change enablers – may also be difficult (Evans, 2017); therefore, the messages may not reach them.

Case Study: Using Videos to Disseminate a Secondary Data Analysis with Adolescents

The video described in Rodriguez et al. (2018) originates from secondary data analysis that explored the impact of mentoring relationships on adolescent empathy. This research aimed to: 1) identify the role of mentoring relationships in adolescent perceived social support; 2) explore the role of empathy in the experiences of youth in mentoring relationships; and 3) disseminate the findings to inform policy through the creation of videos with young people currently involved in the Big Brothers Big Sisters (BBBS) programme.

Data for this secondary data analysis originated from the BBBS youth mentoring programme of Ireland, in an evaluation study undertaken by the UNESCO Child and Family Research Centre, University of Galway (Dolan et al., 2010). This was a mixed methods study consisting of a randomised control trial (RCT; n = 164) and nine longitudinal qualitative case studies of mentoring pairs, including the views of mentees, mentors, mothers and case workers. The original study did not include participatory methods, due to the nature of RCTs.

The findings of this secondary data analysis were:

1. Empathy and mentoring are crucially related. Empathy is the motivation for mentors to engage in the mentoring programme, but empathy continues to develop over time in the dyad. Adolescents 'mirror' their mentors.
2. Empathic behaviours have benefits for mentees, including interpersonal competence, less aggressiveness, less antisocial behaviour, improved friendships, increased prosocial behaviour and improved capacity to anticipate negative consequences of their behaviour.
3. Mentoring relationships can increase perceived social support in mentees.
4. Mentoring can engage vulnerable mentees in an activity that they enjoy while giving them important life skills, such as empathy, which can and will make a difference in their life in the short and long term.
5. Mentoring can improve mentees' understanding of others and facilitates engagement in their community, allowing them to become active and resilient citizens.

6. Empathy skills can be a protective factor for children and adolescents. This is relevant from a prevention and early intervention perspective, as it will avoid problems and difficulties for young people later in life.

The purpose of the video was the dissemination of the research findings, but, more importantly, the researchers wanted to verify the findings of this new study with adolescents themselves who were currently and actively taking part of the BBBS programme. The confirmation of these findings was important to be able to disseminate the evidence to inform and influence policy and practice.

PARTNERSHIPS

The research team and the UNESCO Child and Family Research Centre had a long-standing partnership with Foróige in Galway, where the BBBS programme was rolled out. The researcher had also been a volunteer Big Sister and, therefore, was known by the BBBS staff. This alliance facilitated the acceptance from BBBS staff, and they became gatekeepers.

RECRUITING ADOLESCENTS, AND CONSENT

A group of 15 adolescents were invited by BBBS staff to take part in the video. Parental consent forms and adolescents' assent forms and information sheets were provided. Parents and adolescents returned their signed forms to their BBBS case worker. Since this was a dissemination exercise that involved filming, BBBS staff selected adolescents with personalities compatible with this exercise and adolescents who were in stable dyad mentoring relationships. There was a mix by age and gender.

BRAINSTORMING MEETING

A brainstorming meeting was organised by the research team on a Saturday morning to avoid clashes with school and extracurricular activities. The professional film-maker was present and actively involved in the workshop to elicit the creativity and active participation of the adolescents. A workshop was carried out with adolescents to share the findings and verify them as relevant to their own experiences. Adolescents were asked to share memories or situations where they had experienced similar situations they could relate to. These examples, with permission from adolescents, were recorded and shared with the wider group.

There was a break in the workshop to have pizza and drinks and other goodies.

The second part of the workshop consisted of creating the storyline. From the stories identified previously, adolescents selected one and created a character and different situations that happened to that character. This demonstrated empathy and how the mentor of this character had acted with empathy and provided advice to the mentee.

The storyline consisted of an adolescent who was new in school and was bullied. This adolescent expressed what was happening to the mentor and he supported him on how to solve the situation assertively.

FILMING

Two weeks later, a second meeting was organised by the research team. This time, filming was going to take place.

The professional film-maker converted the adolescents' storyline into a script.

There were three scenes: at school, in the playground and in the football pitch.

The adolescents who wanted to do so were actors in the video. Other adolescents were interested in film and photography, and they carried out some of the filming themselves, under the guidance of the professional film-maker. Other adolescents contributed by bringing props and organising the scenes if they did not want to be on camera themselves. One of the strengths of the video was that adolescents could take an active part in it based on their own talents, interests, abilities and personalities.

Another strength of the video was that the research team was also actively involved in the process and acted in the video in different adult roles. A real mentor was also invited by the adolescents to play one of the adult roles in the film, and this person showed up and willingly took part in the film, guided by the adolescents' storyline, script and creative process.

EDITING

Editing and creating the final version of the video was carried out by the professional film-maker. The cost of the film and film-making had been budgeted for and already approved in the research proposal. The edits were approved by the research team together with the film-maker. It would have been best practice if adolescents had been included in this process as well, not necessarily in the technical part but certainly in the approval of the final version of the video.

COMPENSATION

Adolescents were provided with food and drink during the workshop and the filming. These expenses had been included in the research proposal. Additionally, adolescents were given Amazon vouchers worth 50 euros. They were given these gift cards as a thank you for their creativity and active engagement in the project. These vouchers had already been included in the research proposal.

DISSEMINATION

The final version of the video was presented at a conference held in the UNESCO Child and Family Research Centre. The video was also disseminated in the Foróige website where it was accessed by professionals, mentors, mentees and their families. One of the limitations of the study is that the impact of the video was not accounted for. Once the findings of the research were disseminated, there was no plan in place for continuation of the findings. The budget ended, the funding ended and therefore the project ended. It would have been best practice to be able to understand the impact, if any, of the research study and its findings over time.

CHAPTER 8

Visual Mapping

Chapter Highlights

1. Maps can be used to explore and understand the sense of place and space of adolescents.
2. Various technology and software is available to carry out mapping; however, some degree of training may be required to support participants in data registration.
3. Careful ethical consideration should be given as to how data is disseminated as maps can reveal identifiable locations of participants, which may even be a threat to their safety.
4. Maps can be used to promote civic engagement and changes required in the spaces and the landscapes of these communities.

Visual mapping is a creative, technology-based method which has not been widely used in participatory research; however, it has many advantages and possible uses for a variety of research questions for research with children and adolescents. Mapping has been more widely used within geography; however, the sense of belonging, place, space and having a better understanding of adolescents' lives and worlds can be relevant to many other social sciences and disciplines. Mapping method is also usually applied as part of a set of methods, for example in conjunction with interviews and photographs (Ponto, 2017), which shows its versatility as well.

Maps can capture geographical, emotional and abstract connections experienced by the mapmaker (Amsden & VanWynsberghe, 2005). Maps can, therefore, be tools for adolescents to share their stories about themselves and the places they live in. Maps created in a group setting reinforce a sense of collectiveness of the group and the collective map produced is a snapshot of how the community see themselves, their awareness of local problems and possible resources available to address them. Mapping therefore shares principles of participatory research by honouring community voices, identifying needs and strengths of the community and supporting community development (Amsden & VanWynsberghe, 2005).

Mapping has been used to investigate children's and adolescents' perspective of their social context and environment to determine the implications of these on their general well-being (Morrow, 2001) and health (Dennis et al., 2009). Maps help determine the extent that adolescents have a sense of belonging and feel safe in their neighbourhoods/communities. Maps can also be used to identify which parks, streets, buildings, etc. are available to be used by them, highlighting the relevance of these spaces for their social relationships (Morrow, 2001). Research suggests that the construction of subjective meanings of places is intertwined with daily mobility patterns (Ponto, 2017).

8.1 Participatory Mapping

Participatory mapping enables an understanding of space as participants' 'lived experience' from their own perspective and simultaneously challenging adult perspectives of the use of space and spaces adolescents have access to (Gregorious, 2017). Gordon et al. (2016) examined interactive mapping as a method to teach and practise critical spatial thinking.

Digital mapping pedagogy can provide students with an opportunity to develop awareness of what happens in the space but also how and what they can do to intervene to potentially modify their use and access to the space. This is also linked with civic engagement, which is part of the skill set that participation and technology can develop and promote in adolescents (James et al., 2009; Van Staa et al., 2009).

Civic engagement can be defined as an awareness of social issues, a recognition of adolescents themselves as citizens in these issues and the structures and forums that influence them, which are the foundations of democratic citizenship (Gordon et al., 2016). Critical spatial thinking is the link between participants' learning with geographic information technologies and their civic engagement, which can also be learnt through geospatial technologies (Gordon et al., 2016).

Mapping Youth Journeys (Gordon et al., 2016) is a participatory digital mapping curriculum developed as an after-school programme for adolescents. Mapping Youth Journeys consists of an interactive, open-source platform designed by the research team. This platform allows users to zoom in and out, place points on the map, mark lines and areas on it, make text annotations, take photos and make videos as well as comment on other participants' maps. When an object on the map is selected, the annotated content appears on the right of the map, in an adjacent window. Comments added by other users are streamed below the map and are visible when objects in the map are selected.

Participants engaged in an interactive and dialogic process to build their maps. These included digital and face-to-face conversations between the researchers and other participants. Participant baseline knowledge had to be evaluated before the actual data collection could begin. One of the challenges of mapping is that adolescents need to understand the importance of completing all the parts of the task. According to Wrede-Jäntti et al. (2021), some adolescents can be very successful at doing the markings but may forget to write comments about why they selected those spots on the map. One of the ways to mitigate the loss of information if this happens is to record adolescents' verbal accounts of why they selected specific spots (Wrede-Jäntti et al., 2021).

Gordon et al. (2016) asked participants to identify a place that was significant to the topic they were interested in and draw the place on a paper map and then map it using the digital platform. It was identified that participants had basic mapping and digital skills; however, they showed great variation in their spatial thinking abilities. For example, there was a confusion between a historic place and a historic event. Some had cartographic abilities developed in a way that they could identify localised places using cartographic symbols, whereas others just used large polygons to mark entire areas of the city (Gordon et al., 2016).

Wrede-Jäntti et al. (2021) carried out a pilot study with adolescents. They used paper maps of the town and asked students to mark with stickers the places they liked and disliked. This can be useful for adolescents to understand the concept of the method; however, as the authors suggest, paper maps can be inconvenient as they are very specific and cover a specific area only, they take up space and could get torn or the stickers can fall off (Wrede-Jäntti et al., 2021). Paper maps have also been used in other studies, for example Shortt and Ross (2021). Adolescents were asked to mark places that made them feel safe in green and unsafe in red, as well as places they wanted to visit with friends and families and places where they found litter (Shortt & Ross, 2021).

Mapping enables participants to understand space, and spatiality can be used to challenge social exclusions and marginalisations, for example mapping historical suffragette marches that took place in their cities (Gordon et al., 2016). Annotations and discussions enabled participants to understand how geographical restrictions produce inequalities in the everyday lives of specific groups. Mapping enabled participants to understand historically significant places as expressions of social processes and social inequalities, fostering critical spatial thinking and civic engagement. Social mapping can enable adolescents' understanding of space as fundamental in the negotiation of power in society (Gordon et al., 2016).

A subtype of participatory mapping is participatory photo mapping, which integrates a set of digital tools and participatory protocols that enable a community-based health partnership (Dennis et al., 2009). Dennis et al. (2009) used GPS systems to gather participant geographic information and link it to specific locations. This is an integration of experiential data with spatial data. Research participants can indicate where the experiences happened (maps), what the experience looked like (photos, drawings) and how these experiences unfolded (narratives) (Dennis et al., 2009).

Research participants used GPS units to track their neighbourhood walks. The researchers used software to place photographs along the routes and carried out focus groups with participants to explain the narrative behind the maps (Dennis et al., 2009). Relevant to this book, participatory mapping can help to identify social, economic and health trends (Dennis et al., 2009). Participatory photo mapping can lead the change in social and built environments to improve participant health outcomes (Dennis et al., 2009).

8.2 Story and Interactive Maps

Story maps identify multiple functional elements of participant environments, including sites that are part of everyday life, for example school, supermarket, park, and others (Reilly & Hughes, 2021). These maps include where participants like and dislike visiting and spending time in these places (Reilly & Hughes, 2021). Similarly, interactive maps draw on participants' local knowledge to create visual and non-visual data to explore social problems, issues and questions (Wrede-Jäntti et al., 2021). The use of technology for interactive maps is a suitable method for adolescents as the gadgets and apps are interesting for this age group (Wrede-Jäntti et al., 2021). Interactive maps can be defined as a participatory method because they enable a shift of the power balance between adolescents and researchers (Wrede-Jäntti et al., 2021).

Interactive maps can be used to capture important locations, institutions, social relations, everyday lives, education, working life and leisure (Wrede-Jäntti et al., 2021). They provide immediate visible information that is easier to compare than using paper maps (Wrede-Jäntti et al.,

2021). Interactive maps can be used in different ways, depending on availability of resources. Some researchers have used paper maps and others have used electronic ones (Wrede-Jäntti et al., 2021). Participants can draw their own maps, take photographs of places or use map applications for mobile phones, tablets, or computers (Wrede-Jäntti et al., 2021).

There are limited examples of application of interactive mapping to health research. Akom et al. (2016) used mapping to explore adolescent perceptions of food providers in East Oakland, California. Adolescents were given digital devices with mapping software, messaging and cameras. These devices were used to verify information about the location of retail outlets and grocery stores. Adolescents collected written and digital information, using photographs and audio notes to later verify and update the information via platforms such as Local Ground and Streetwyze community mapping. Streetwyze has a variety of ongoing projects which can be accessed at www.streetwyze.com/.

8.3 Technology and Software for Mapping

Global positioning systems (GPS) tracking is used to contextualise adolescents' daily environments (Ponto, 2017). This method helps to identify the different facets of children's and adolescents' places by obtaining insights of adolescents' lives and daily routines (Ponto, 2017).

GPS is easy to use, and it enables an effortless data collection process, as the device keeps a record of the routes travelled while the researcher can focus on something else (Ponto, 2017). However, GPS is limited by its poor capacity to identify and record meaning and feelings associated with a place or the people in it. Researchers must interact with participants to identify the meaning (Ponto, 2017).

There are technological challenges with GPS as well: the accuracy of location information can be compromised in highly built-up areas when signals weaken (Ponto, 2017). Ponto (2017) carried out manual adjustment to the routes when necessary. Software programmes, such as ArcScene 3D, can be used to build map illustrations of the routes. These can be created from a sloping or a bird's-eye view perspective, which creates a 3D effect of the buildings (Ponto, 2017).

My Maps is an application on Google which is free of charge. My Maps can be used with any portable device with access to the internet and it allows alternating localities (Wrede-Jäntti et al., 2021). My Maps can be used to produce individual maps but also enables groups to build maps, which may be very suitable for participatory group activities. The application allows users to personalise their maps with their own styles, icons and colours as well as add points or draw different shapes, which may be attractive and appealing for adolescents. One of the disadvantages of the method is that anonymity can be kept to a maximum by not using adolescents' personal accounts or names. The data, however, is still context-bound, increasing the risk of possible identification of participants (Wrede-Jäntti et al., 2021). Additionally, Google remains the app's owner and how it protects and uses data is still up to its own discretion (Wrede-Jäntti et al., 2021).

Wrede-Jäntti et al. (2021) provided adolescents with tablets which had My Maps installed and explained to them how the application worked. Adolescents were asked to mark places using colour codes:

Red: Places to avoid
Green: Places they like to spend time in
Blue: Neutral places

Symbols were used to identify adolescents according to gender and school type. This enabled researchers to determine patterns of movement based on these characteristics as well as quantify their favourite places (Wrede-Jäntti et al., 2021). Quantitative statistical analyses can be carried out to determine if these differences were statistically significant.

How to Identify the Research Topic Using a Participatory Approach (Ozer & Douglas, 2013)

1. Creation of an 'issue tree', based on experiences.
2. The branches are Post-it notes that represent a problem, organised as domains and 'root' causes.
3. Adolescents vote to identify the topic. Facilitators support the group to respect differing views and work together to reach consensus.

8.4 Ethical Considerations

Maps can be a threat to participant anonymity as their surroundings and everyday activities are usually the purpose of visual mapping research. To protect participant anonymity, Wrede-Jäntti et al. (2021) created accounts on My Maps from the researcher's Google account. I would suggest, however, that it would be better to create an account exclusively for the research, avoiding all personal accounts, which would protect both the adolescents and the researchers.

Colour codes on the map can prevent the inclusion of full names, addresses or personal information being marked on the maps (Wrede-Jäntti et al., 2021), contributing to anonymity. Adolescents used a pseudonym to add a short comment on the map as to the reasons why they chose those places on the map (Wrede-Jäntti et al., 2021). Ponto (2017), for example, removed participants' final destinations, such as home addresses, from the maps.

Adolescent trajectories and routines can be described but maps do not necessarily have to be shown to the public or printed in any dissemination documentation. Patterns and information can be analysed, without providing the images of the geographical locations in an identifiable way. There must be careful consideration given to the use of maps in research and protecting participant identity, as well as ensuring their safety in their neighbourhoods.

Case Study: Application of Community Mapping in Adolescent Health (Amsden & VanWynsberghe, 2005)

Community mapping is defined as groups meeting to draw, write or express some aspect of local knowledge and experience, which can also be a youth-friendly methodology (Amsden & VanWynsberghe, 2005). Community mapping can be used to document geographical information and other forms of abstract data (Amsden & VanWynsberghe, 2005).

The Youth Friendly Health Service project consisted of a participatory evaluation of health clinics by mapping an evaluation tool based on the maps (Amsden & VanWynsberghe, 2005). Research questions need to be broad for adolescents to create their own definitions and set their parameters for discussion, while at the same time meeting the overall research question.

The research objectives were agreed with adolescents:

1. Build capacity of youth participants.
2. Learn to conduct youth-friendly research.
3. Create recommendations for improving health services that could be implemented by local providers.

In community mapping, participants need to feel comfortable in order to share their experiences and perspectives. This included the trust between adolescents and the researcher. Amsden and VanWynsberghe (2005) argue that where there is no trust, adolescents will not even attend the mapping sessions. This process can be facilitated by researching groups of adolescents that are already established and are therefore used to working together and willing to do so. Validating the knowledge and experiences of adolescent participants is also fundamental. Adolescents should be validated as experts throughout the mapping sessions (Amsden & VanWynsberghe, 2005).

Map templates need to be designed to ensure that the research question is addressed by connecting it to the everyday experiences of youth (Amsden & VanWynsberghe, 2005).

Collaboration is also an important part of community mapping. Amsden and VanWynsberghe (2005) explained that they encouraged adolescents to talk and share with each other to facilitate and create a collaborative and open environment. This creates an enjoyable atmosphere, and this also benefits the data analysis.

Researchers, the advisory committee and youth worked together to code and summarise data. A subset of this group took part in the analysis of all the information created in the mapping sessions. Each adolescent was responsible for analysing the map their group created.

1. The graphics and text were transferred into sticky notes that could be manipulated and moved around into different categories.
2. Notes were grouped into categories that 'made sense' to the adolescent in charge of the map. This process was underpinned by grounded theory where categories emerge from the data and not from pre-existing theories or assumptions.
3. Once the categories were created, data was revisited within the categories to ensure the final set of themes accurately reflected the data set.

Including adolescents in data analysis can be complex and 'messy' (Amsden & VanWynsberghe, 2005). For example, discrepancies may happen between groups as to how to categorise data. Creating a space for participation meant researchers must accept and find the meaning in possible unexpected responses from adolescents (Amsden & VanWynsberghe, 2005).

Another challenge experienced by the researchers was adolescents' lack of familiarity with participatory research methods (Amsden & VanWynsberghe, 2005). By providing more opportunities to initiate and design their own projects, adolescents can dispel the myth of research as something boring carried out exclusively by adult experts.

As a result of the mapping exercise, adolescents created a health service evaluation survey. They also created a zine to document their stories. Zines are self-published small booklets that are used to express ideas and experiences focused on a specific topic (Amsden & VanWynsberghe, 2005).

The final stage of the study was dissemination. Adolescents were involved in presenting the results at research conferences.

Community mapping is an open, unrestricted space where adolescents can choose how to represent their voices, using the map to link the research topic and aims with their local and lived experiences. Mapmaking also enabled dialogue and collaboration among participants.

CHAPTER 9

Internet-Based Participatory Research

Participation: knowledge from people who 'know where the shoe pinches'.

V. Krane et al., 'Youth involvement in research: Participation, contribution and dynamic processes'

Chapter Highlights

1. Online methodologies are versatile, cost-effective, time-effective and accessible to a wide variety of audiences, making them very useful tools.
2. Researchers should be very aware of the ethical guidelines and legislation that applies online and offline as well as that specific to the platforms they are engaging adolescent participants with.
3. Data management and participant safety online should be a priority.
4. Adolescents have very clear ideas of what they want online. These wishes should be given due consideration to ensure online research will engage and interest them successfully.
5. Participatory research can be applied to online methods and health research online successfully.

The internet can be used for qualitative and quantitative research and analysis. As a tool, it is also low cost, high quality and is a means of fast data collection (Clifford, 2013). It is a versatile medium ideal for carrying out high-quality research. This chapter will focus on several internet-based research methodologies that have been applied to participatory, health and adolescents' research. Although research combining all these elements has been limited so far, potential for its use is granted. The methods' advantages and limitations are described. Evidence of good practice and recommendations from adolescents themselves are included.

Clifford (2013) identified some of the advantages as well as the disadvantages of using the internet as a methodological tool (Table 9.1).

Table 9.1 *Advantages and disadvantages of internet research*

Advantages	Disadvantages
Data can be collected from large samples, thus increased statistical power.	It can be time-consuming to set up at the start.
Data collection can happen 24/7.	Samples may be non-representative.
Samples can come from different geographical locations.	Some data may be meaningless.
Possible faster turnaround.	Potential lack of control over some variables.
Data can be automatically entered, facilitating coding and analysis.	Participants may take part more than once.
Diverse samples can be identified for cross-cultural studies.	Dropout rates can be unpredictable.
Experimenter demand and expectancy effects can be prevented.	Participants may complete the task to an undesirable standard (lack of care and attention).
Participants may feel more at ease with anonymity.	Frivolous questions can be frequent.
There are reduced research costs.	Internet-based is still less acceptable than other methods.
Studies yield similar results to those using traditional methods.	Disgruntled or angry responses may also occur.

9.1 Adolescents' Views and Wishes

Martin et al. (2023) carried out a study to identify adolescent ideas for a web-based intervention, in this case a sexual health promotion intervention. The principles and ideas used for this can be useful for other types of web-based interventions also.

1. Participatory and interactive. Adolescents wanted these dimensions included in the intervention, for example as fun activities, peer interaction, interaction with competent professionals that would validate the content and personalised features. Activities could include vote systems, quizzes and games.
2. Security and confidentiality. Adolescents expressed needing a moderate, secure, confidential space where they would feel confident to participate. Adolescents proposed the creation of a portal to ask questions anonymously and to address diverse topics without feeling embarrassed.
3. Engagement. Adolescents want regular publication of messages, reactivity and positive reactions to their messages.
4. Inclusivity. Inclusivity was important for adolescents regarding gender, sexual identity and adolescents with disabilities or illnesses.

Other studies have contributed to identify what adolescents want online websites and platforms targeted at them to do and look like. Adolescents want a website, particularly a home page, which is welcoming and makes them feel comfortable without compromising its authenticity and professionalism. They want a banner, testimonials, reliable resources, information on how to support other adolescents, a frequently asked question section and a brief explanation of how the website works (Ospina-Pinillos et al., 2018).

One feature that can be very useful and ethical at the same time was included by Ospina-Pinillos et al. (2018). This is known as the 'triage system' that ensures distressed adolescents could access immediate care by having a very accessible button, for example stating: 'need help now'. Adolescents experiencing distress or a crisis could easily access help this way.

Easy and free access is important for adolescents. Web-based interventions were generally free to access and this was a way to increase access to web-based preventive interventions (Leeman et al., 2016). THRIVE is a web-based alcohol intervention targeted at undergraduate students in Australia, New Zealand and the United States (Leeman et al., 2016). This web-based intervention is accessed via email.

Some interventions had more than one delivery option to facilitate access or as part of a pilot/trial. Standardised interventions were delivered in the same way to all participants (Leeman et al., 2016). Personalised versions included messages that were tailored and, therefore, more targeted, focused and brief (Leeman et al., 2016). Personalisation also included the capacity to choose their own text types and colours (Ospina-Pinillos et al., 2018).

Adolescents were happy to complete assessments online; however, they expected to obtain feedback or results (Ospina-Pinillos et al., 2018). Adolescents preferred short surveys but understood that these may not be comprehensive enough. They preferred Likert scales, close-ended questions and multiple-choice questions instead of open-ended questions (Ospina-Pinillos et al., 2018). Results from surveys and assessments should be presented in a visually attractive and comprehensive manner, for example simple bar graphs, traffic lights, etc. Adolescents wanted the option to save and print these results, to share them with a health professional in the future. Comprehensive assessments could be used to provide adolescents with detailed dashboards and subsequent well-being plans (Ospina-Pinillos et al., 2018). A crucial and ethical aspect of these assessment features is that these systems can help identify vulnerable adolescents who may need additional support or face-to-face interventions. Healthcare professionals should be able to identify these adolescents and make sure emergency interventions are put in place to support them.

Although it may not be relevant for all projects, adolescents want to be able to book appointments online. They also wanted an online 'waiting room' where they had a choice of activities to do while they waited for the healthcare professional. Some of their suggestions were watching relevant videos or breathing exercises (Ospina-Pinillos et al., 2018).

Adolescents wanted information that was reliable and, evidently, relevant to the topic of the website. They requested links to outside sources that were safe and reliable, for example links to App Store or Google Play where they could access the information accurately and safely (Ospina-Pinillos et al., 2018). Information on the website had to be clean and tidy. Adolescents prefer the use of icons instead of text and videos instead of lengthy instructions (Ospina-Pinillos et al., 2018). Short videos were also welcomed; however, these should not be in autoplay mode to avoid privacy issues in public spaces.

The duration of web-based interventions was varied. Duration is a decision that needs to be carefully considered and it should be evaluated prior to delivery. Leeman et al. (2016), for example, found that interventions with a higher number of components were counterproductive. In the case of their intervention, which was intended to reduce drinking, it had the opposite effect. For example, THRIVE (Leeman et al., 2016) has a duration of nine minutes.

Adolescents were willing to share personal information if there was a guarantee that it was private and confidential and got them the help they needed (Ospina-Pinillos et al., 2018). Some adolescents, however, suggested that websites should be public, part of social networks, as this would enable them to share the website with their friends or communicate with them through private messages (Ospina-Pinillos et al., 2018). These decisions around public and private sharing of information need to be carefully evaluated considering ethical considerations and legislation in the specific contexts, both online and face to face.

9.2 Health Research Online

The internet is a major provider of health information; evidence suggests that it can be useful for mental health promotion, screening, prevention, early intervention, referrals and even platforms to deliver real-time care services, low-intensity treatments and the identification of the needs of patients as their illness progresses or intensifies (Ospina-Pinillos et al., 2018).

Internet-based methods are less established than face-to-face methods and there are concerns about the representativeness of online samples (O'Reilly & Parker, 2014); for example, access may be restricted in some areas of the world or even to a sector of society who can afford the hardware and the connectivity required. One disadvantage of online research may be validity. According to O'Reilly and Parker (2014), users oscillate between the 'world of social media' and the 'real world', meaning research participants may act differently when using social media than they do in their regular lives. It may also be confusing for researchers to decide whether to ask for consent to use data on blogs, chat rooms and social media (O'Reilly & Parker, 2014) which can be perceived as public and usable automatically.

O'Reilly and Parker (2014) identified the benefits of recruiting participants online. This is a useful strategy to recruit participants for health research as there is a significant increase in the use of the internet by the public to find out about health conditions, therefore it is possible to find research advertisements this way and potential participants willing to take part in research (O'Reilly & Parker, 2014). The internet has become a significant tool for adolescents as they are increasingly using it to find answers for their health-related queries (Ospina-Pinillos et al., 2018).

Email may be used for recruiting participants; however, ethical approval should be granted before and it probably also requires gatekeepers, such as parents, to allow access. Emails to gatekeepers (e.g. parents) should include a hyperlink to the project website. Emails should be personalised instead of group messages. Online discussion boards can be useful to post the link to the research project. It is best to request permission from board administrators to ensure the posts are not removed or treated as spam (O'Reilly & Parker, 2014).

The internet can enable several health-related activities online, which can be also used in online research. Online screening has been shown to be reliable and effective, and it also has the advantage of avoiding face-to-face interviews regarding sensitive subjects (Ospina-Pinillos et al., 2018). Online screening can also have disadvantages as symptom-based assessments may recommend unnecessary professional care, putting more pressure on services when alternative options, such as self-management, may be more appropriate (Ospina-Pinillos et al., 2018). Videoconferencing has been used for several years as it has an advantage over telephone interventions, enabling professionals to have information based on visual cues that inform patient assessment, for example their appearance, physical expressions, motor activity, movements and mannerisms (Ospina-Pinillos et al., 2018). Videoconferencing has been found to be as reliable as face-to-face assessments and even capable of negating risky behaviours such as suicide and violence. At the same time, it is highly cost-effective (Ospina-Pinillos et al., 2018).

Remote psychotherapy can have several benefits such as improving access to patient care, increasing service efficiency, saving time and money, and achieving more effective outcomes in some circumstances. This type of psychotherapy also has disadvantages such as technological glitches, operational hassles and the lack of a personalised connection due to online platforms that limit non-verbal communication (Biancalani et al., 2024). Biancalani et al. (2024) evaluated the impact of a psychological intervention called psychodrama that was carried out online, instead of face to face as it usually was, due to COVID-19 but also as a possibility of providing psychological psychotherapies online in the future. Psychodrama consists of a guided role play for participants to gain insight into interpersonal problems and possible solutions. Participants can role play current or past episodes of their lives, giving life to characters and symbolic stories. Each session of psychodrama consists of three phases: warm-up, action and sharing (Biancalani et al., 2024). The methodology online was as follows:

1. Google Slides was used to create a virtual theatre, representing a real one in the background. The computer screen of one member of the team was shared to show the virtual theatre. A photograph of each participant was included to represent the movement that would take place in a face-to-face session. Faces could be visible on screen, faces could be moved around the virtual theatre to portray a scene, and participants could also communicate using a microphone. In other cases, protagonists had their camera on while others did not.
2. Each participant had a session where they became the protagonist and enacted their own experience in the virtual theatre. Other participants could act as an 'auxiliary self', playing roles of other significant characters in the protagonist's life.
3. The double technique was used when another member expressed the inner voice of the protagonist.
4. A guided imagination activity was used to help participants identify and express their emotions. These experiences were then drawn out on paper and could be acted out by a protagonist or a double.

5. Contact was simulated with the use of props. For example, a pillow was hugged to imagine participants were hugging a person.
6. Zoom breakout rooms were used to divide participants into small groups to facilitate sharing and collaboration.

This online psychotherapeutic intervention improved participants' well-being, self-awareness, self-confidence, relationships and future perspectives. One of the limitations identified by the online methodology was the lack of physical contact, which was defined as unhelpful by participants, yet not affecting the quality of the treatment. There was also a lack of the socialisation activities that are usually associated with this technique when it is delivered in person and there was also a limited use of non-verbal expressions (Biancalani et al., 2024). The authors consider that the art of the success of the intervention was creating a non-judgemental atmosphere that made participants feel comfortable, reduced their anxiety and stimulated their spontaneity and creativity (Biancalani et al., 2024).

Digital health technologies consist of an array of technologies that promote or manage adolescents' health and physical fitness (Lupton, 2021). Digital platforms consist, according to Malloy et al. (2023), of any technology which can be defined as eHealth or mobile health (mHealth), including web, social networks, blogs, wearable devices, social media, SMS (short message service) or general health information technology. Within these digital platforms are digital health tools which aim to improve chronic disease states, mental health, dietary habits, physical habits and risky behaviours (e.g. binge drinking or smoking).

eHealth interventions can potentially promote empowerment, improve relationships between users and service providers, and improve information exchange (Coyne et al., 2016). eHealth intervention design that lacks service user input will be inappropriate or fail, therefore a participatory approach to the design can be crucial (Coyne et al., 2016). Researchers should be supported by stakeholders and software experts when developing digital health tools to ensure quality, feasibility and optimal use (Malloy et al., 2023).

Several digital health interventions have been developed for adolescents, including social networks, apps, websites, animated films and video games. They can be useful tools to disseminate health advice and clinical support for this age group (Malloy et al., 2023). Digital technologies can also be challenging as some adolescents who have used self-tracking apps and wearable devices do not continue with them over time. The designs are usually not specifically developed for adolescents and, therefore, may not suit their needs. These technologies may also limit adolescents' privacy, agency and autonomy. They may also become overly obsessed with their body shape and size or compare themselves with influencers on social media (Lupton, 2021). Coyne et al. (2016) designed a website to support the transition of adolescents with long-term illnesses to adult healthcare services. Adolescents expressed a need for trustworthy and empowering information written in non-patronising language. Information about how to become independent, managing their illness, information about medication and tips about how to transition were also considered useful. The website should be colourful and provide downloadable information online. Video testimonials of adolescents who had successfully completed the transition were considered helpful (Coyne et al., 2016).

Effective platforms should be targeted to the population of interest as well as provide accessibility and adaptability. Malloy et al. (2023) recommend pilot testing to determine the feasibility of platforms. It has been found that there is often a contradiction between what participants say they want and the features they finally use when the platforms are launched and accessed. Malloy et al. (2023) identified some of the characteristics that digital health platforms should have to effectively target adolescents (Table 9.2).

There are examples in the literature of research studies which created their own 'built for purpose' websites for their research purposes. The experiences and successes of these studies are varied and there are several factors which can explain these differences and contribute to increase the success of these types of methodologies in the future. Online resources can support adolescents when traditional sources of information are unavailable or perceived as less helpful (Coyne et al., 2016). This can be particularly useful for adolescents with chronic conditions who may experience infection risk around peers, as this would increase access to relevant testimonials that will contribute to improve their experience.

Mallan and Singh (2010) designed a website with an online forum to enable adolescents to evaluate the question 'what does it mean to be a young person in a world characterised by rapid social, economic and cultural change?'. Research participants were provided with the opportunity to generate their own anonymous usernames and given a password to access the website. The website had a public area promoting the study, sharing research findings and biographies and contact details of the research team. In the secured area adolescents could ask questions and respond on the discussion forums with their peers and the research team (Mallan & Singh, 2010). Researchers explained that having membership

Table 9.2 *Digital health for adolescents*

Social connectivity and networking	Platforms should enable direct connectivity between others who share similar experiences. Connectivity should also be provided with community support services.
Privacy and anonymity	Adolescents are concerned about privacy, and this stops them from disclosing personal health information on platforms. Platforms should therefore allow anonymity or separate user profiles, for example when using social media such as Facebook. Links should not exist with other social media accounts and chat history should be cleared following online sessions.
Trained moderation	Adolescents appreciate the inclusion of moderators (trained facilitators, clinicians) to enable safe health communication. Adolescents are more prone to speak, and speak honestly, in the presence of a moderator who provides additional support. Moderators can also increase trust, credibility and safety. Efforts should be made to introduce unknown moderators for participants to get to know them and build rapport.
Goal setting and progress tracking	Adolescents wanted to set goals and use trackers (preferably automatic) to evaluate progress over time.
High-quality interfaces	Interfaces (such as games) should be of a high quality and be realistic.
Personalisation and tailoring	Platforms should meet the needs of different cultural needs. Messages should be tailored and appropriate for participants.
Accessibility and inclusivity	Platforms should be designed and adapted to meet the needs of participants with disabilities or vulnerabilities. For example, including subtitles in videos and making resources multilingual.

cards was successful, as it showed an eagerness for participation; however, the actual level of discussion in the forums was minimal (Mallan & Singh, 2010).

Curtis et al. (2004) developed a website for data collection and provided feedback to participants. The website continued to be used after the study, to facilitate dialogue between services providers and adolescent users. Participants used the website to vote on their priorities for changes identified in the study (Curtis et al., 2004). Therefore, websites can be useful during the study but also contribute to sustainability over time.

Social media is now a significant part of adolescents' lives, having a significant impact on other aspects of their lives. Social media is one of the forms of communication most widely used by adolescents to share information, experiences and moments they consider as important in their lives (Ortiz-Pena et al., 2019). A significant part of adolescent social support is now virtual (Ortiz-Pena et al., 2019). Social media platforms represent important and emerging settings for participatory design research (Hagen et al., 2012). The flexibility of social media means design and research can be moved to where communities and adolescents are (Hagen et al., 2012). It also facilitates a more informal, ad hoc and relevant research (Hagen et al., 2012).

Social media has several advantages over face-to-face interactions, with the anonymity allowing individuals to experience low social risk and more privacy, as well as facilitating self-presentation and disclosure (Zhang, 2023). Perceived social support obtained through social media has been linked with alcohol consumption in adolescents (Ortiz-Pena et al., 2019). Adolescents with more virtual social support tend to have a higher alcohol consumption (Ortiz-Pena et al., 2019). Research has identified that social media has a significant role in forming a collective identity particularly among marginalised groups (Zhang, 2023). Zhang (2023) found that social media can provide a supplement for offline social interaction for adolescents who were affected by HIV/AIDS. Social media provided a sense of belonging and 'us' which contributes to maintaining social ties. The internet, for adolescents, can be a significant source of social support, including information, friendship, a sense of belonging, emotional support and facilitating a sense of collective identity.

Daniels and Willard (2023) investigated social media interaction in adolescents and young adults diagnosed with cancer. Their research is important in terms of the needs of this specific group regarding social support and social media online, but the study also identified how social media platforms themselves promote and facilitate very different types of interactions. This is an important finding for researchers wishing to carry out online research using social media platforms. Specifically, Snapchat was described as the platform that allowed adolescents to interact with friends online in a similar way to an offline space. TikTok was used to access entertainment and pass the time. Instagram enabled active social interaction with friends and content to be observed passively (Daniels & Willard, 2023).

Research participants described their typical social media habits changes because of treatment, specifically that the treatment changed the frequency and the type of engagement. Differences were identified between participants; for some, however, it remained as an important tool for connecting with friends, but for others, it was a source of entertainment and not a tool for social connections. Some adolescents felt self-conscious, and this prevented them from posting online and others even experienced critical remarks. Some participants received social support through likes and comments, but for some, this was also temporarily uplifting (Daniels & Willard, 2023). This study found that there is no 'one-size-fits-all' for navigating the social interaction on social media during cancer treatment. Again, this is an important finding for researchers wishing to carry out research with social media and adolescents experiencing cancer.

Using social media can have several challenges (Fisher & Jensen, 2013). Managing communication online can be challenging as people are usually distributed across different geographical locations. This can be particularly difficult if there are also cross-cultural differences that would require culturally specific communication cues as it is harder to establish common ground across the group. To ensure communication is suitable, the right technology needs to be used to ensure effective communication. Leadership is essential when participants are dispersed, as is usually the case with online research (Fisher & Jensen, 2013). Leadership is needed for effective communication, negotiation and collaboration. The input of all parties needs to be taken seriously. Communication and decision-making processes should be put in place early on. For example, this could include keeping minutes at meetings or having guidelines and protocols in place. The skills, knowledge and background of all team members are important for the success of a team. Understanding the purpose and importance of the research study is crucial for success and it is fundamental to encourage and support the adolescents involved (Fisher & Jensen, 2013). Everyone involved in a creation process, for example a research study, is also a participant and a change agent. Having different roles can benefit the research in ways that may not have been foreseen at the beginning.

Researchers need to be respectful when entering social media spaces, particularly without invitation (Hagen et al., 2012). Researchers have a duty to add value and clarity as to why they are there. Researchers also need to develop very clear guidelines or procedures about how to handle negative online or inadequate responses (Hagen et al., 2012). These guidelines should be publicly available for participants to be aware of and access. They should specify issues around disclosure, boundaries and confidentiality (Hagen et al., 2012). Information should also be available if participants become distressed; referral arrangements with partner organisations should also be clear and accessible for participants (Hagen et al., 2012).

Social media can also have other uses, for example chatbot. This is a computer programme or software used to mimic or stimulate human conversation with human users, usually online and through text or voice exchanges. Greer et al. (2019) created Vivibot, a chatbot that delivered positive psychology skills to adolescents and young adults treated for cancer. This was a four-week intervention which included daily emotional ratings and video material recorded by cancer survivors. The feasibility study evaluated participants at baseline, week 2, 4 and 8. The intervention was delivered through Facebook Messenger; however, due to issues with privacy policies, the authors recommend using other platforms such as WhatsApp or mobile apps.

Participants liked chatbot as it was 'non-judgemental'. The authors emphasised that participants were explicitly told and reminded that they were chatting with an automated system, not a 'real' person (Greer et al., 2019). In terms of benefits, it was identified that participants in the intervention group experienced a reduction in their anxiety, particularly those who engaged more with the sessions. Participants in the control group were given access to the intervention after four weeks. The control group provided reports of daily emotions, the same as with the intervention group. Greer et al. (2019) found Vivibot was like other digital health tools in terms of reducing anxiety symptoms in participants. The interface was also cheaper than a human-delivered intervention.

Online researchers need to be aware of the potential risk of technology and online environments. Caplan (2003) found that the preference for online social interaction over face-to-face interaction can have a role in developing negative consequences that can be associated with problematic use of the internet. Individuals with a predisposition to excessive and compulsive computer-mediated social interactions may find the internet can worsen their issues (Caplan, 2003).

It is important to understand that technology and internet use per se does not lead to social issues, compulsive use or psychological issues. Using the internet for mood-altering purposes can have a positive impact; for example playing games can bring joy and excitement, reading can be relaxing and fun, and viewing art online can be soothing and stimulating (Caplan, 2003).

9.3 Participation in Online Methods

Internet-based methods have been used to enhance adolescent social justice, which is an important goal of participatory methods (Rodriguez

& Brown, 2009). Kornbluh et al. (2016) created an online-based social network using a private Facebook group. Adolescent participants shared posts, updates and research activities and posted on social media the changes they were achieving in participatory projects they were involved in within their schools. Adolescents were given time in class to visit the group, twice a month. Participants were also allowed to engage in the group outside of class if they wished to. Social network analysis was used to determine how the social network influenced, or not, adolescents' use and adoption of participatory practices. For example, 'tagging' someone was a way to alert an individual towards an action, and these relationships were evaluated. This type of study provides insights as to how social networks contribute towards engaging adolescents in social change efforts. Kornbluh et al. (2016) found that adolescents with limited civic engagement may take longer to engage in social justice activities and may require additional structural support to do so. Social networks, however, may enhance the speed at which innovative approaches are diffused and utilised to address potential disparities in civic engagement. Connecting groups with similarities may also enhance diffusion processes (Kornbluh et al., 2016). This study, overall, shows that online social networks have the potential to promote and enable social justice in adolescents.

Coyne et al. (2016) used a participatory iterative process to design a website for adolescents transitioning to adult health services. This participatory method enabled the design of a website tailored to the specific needs of the target group. Coyne's study followed different stages to achieve this participatory design (Table 9.3).

Theoretical foundation was very important in the content and design of some programmes and interventions online. For example, cognitive and behavioural intervention was used by Greer et al. (2019) when delivering a pre-existing programme developed by Moskowitz et al. (2017) which had already been evaluated in a randomised control trial and therefore had credibility and certainty that it worked before running the feasibility study. Researchers use different strategies to find out the perspectives of their end users. For example, Greer et al. (2019) carried out interviews and focus groups with adolescents in their target group to refine content.

Participatory web-based interventions are usually designed with an iterative process consisting of several steps (Ospina-Pinillos et al., 2018) (Table 9.4).

Wikis and blogs are another modality of online media that can be used in participatory research. Fenge et al. (2011) used blogs and Twitter scripts

Table 9.3 *Participatory website design*

1. Consultation and cooperation with relevant stakeholders	A survey was used to identify adolescents' needs. Information and communication needs were identified. A co-design group was created with adolescents with chronic conditions. The group played a key role in reviewing the website materials, layout and content. An advisory group was created with stakeholders from illness and voluntary organisations.
2. Experimentation	Participatory workshops were carried out with adolescents to develop information materials and co-design the website. This included advice, key steps and questions. The group included adolescents who had completed the transition and some who had not. Finally, the website was populated with the information relevant to the user group.
3. Contextualisation and iterative development	Demo designs were tested as well as alternative designs that were modified based on the feedback received. Participants were included in a survey to name the website.
4. Consultation and cooperation with relevant stakeholders	The website was launched and the information disseminated with participants, voluntary organisations and mass media. The intervention was subject to evaluation. The number of visitors were tracked with Google Analytics.

Table 9.4 *Stages of participatory web-based interventions*

1. Participatory design	Studies that had a participatory design usually included workshops or consultations with the target audience. The knowledge obtained from service users is then used to produce mock-up versions of the websites and interventions.
2. Prototyping	Early designs, drawn or wireframes, are produced based on participant input.
3. Usability testing	Target users are asked to provide individual feedback, to assess the usability of the intervention.
4. Real-world testing	The website is then tested with the general target population and the public.

in participatory research with marginalised young people. Blogs can be used as a form of virtual diaries (Fenge et al., 2011). They can be kept private, and this will give adolescents the confidence to post (Fenge et al., 2011). Fenge et al. (2011) had separate group discussion forums for public group conversations. Some areas were password protected to encourage and protect individual reflection. One of the advantages of using multimedia in research studies is that it can 'ask' the audience, and collect and value their input, which is fundamental in participatory research approaches (Fenge et al., 2011).

Wikis are websites created collaboratively. They are a web-based open editing tool where different contributors can select, evaluate, revise, edit and publish information (Lamb & Johnson, 2007). One the advantages of wikis is that they do not require special software and these environments can include text, graphics, audio, video and animation (Lamb & Johnson, 2007). Wikis have been used for sharing ideas, collaborative problem-solving, generating lists, debating, making suggestions, voting, collaborative writing, brainstorming and organising information, portals, study guides and virtual conferences (Lamb & Johnson, 2007). Wikis, particularly those that are targeted at adolescents, should be well maintained and supervised to avoid offensive or damaging content. Disclaimers can be used to inform users about the type of content that is allowed or prohibited. Further procedures may also be followed such as removing content and blocking users and IP addresses.

Wikispaces: a wiki hosting service which hosts educational wikis for free. A fee can be paid to host business and non-profit organisations, for example.

phpWiki: a web-based wiki software application; https://sourceforge.net/projects/phpwiki/.

pmWiki: a wiki-based content management system for the creation and maintenance of website; www.pmwiki.org/.

Example of an Adolescent-Focused Wiki

Teen poetry wiki: www.ipl.org/div/teenpoet/

Example of a Design Software: Balsamiq (Balsamiq Solutions, LLC, Sacramento, California, USA)

Balsamiq is a tool for wireframing which is like using the whiteboard for designing on any computer.

There is a 30-day free trial that may be useful to make sure the software is suitable to the needs of the project before making any commitment.

The software can be found at https://balsamiq.com/.

9.4 Safety and Ethics

Ethics is a fundamental consideration for any research study using online technologies. Researchers should be familiar with local and international policies they must comply with. For example, in the UK there is the 'Age appropriate design: a code of practice for online services'. The code recognises that children are 'datafied' and this means companies and organisations are recording thousands of data points about children and young people as they are growing up (Information Commissioner's Office, 2022). The code requires services to put the best interests of the child first when designing apps, games, toys and websites that are going to be accessed by children online. The code is an application of the General Data Protection Regulation in the context of children and adolescents using digital services. There is a recognition that children warrant special protection in terms of how their personal data is used, while enabling opportunities for them to explore and develop online (Information Commissioner's Office, 2022). 'This code seeks to protect children within the digital world, not protect them from it' (Information Commissioner's Office, 2022, p. 5).

In terms of content validation and protection, you can nominate authorised users to add or delete pages and content. A moderator may also approve changes before they are released on the web publicly (Lamb & Johnson, 2007). Regarding age limits, some projects that have participants under 12 years of age require registration or guest access (Lamb & Johnson, 2007). This can be useful with research projects, to ensure only participants have access to the wiki and age limits can be determined by the research and its characteristics. Pseudonyms are a way to protect adolescents' identity online (Lamb & Johnson, 2007). In terms of preventing data loss, researchers should keep a record of participants' usernames and passwords in case these are misplaced or forgotten. Research participants should be encouraged to produce their own material. To avoid plagiarism and other issues for the research, content should be checked to ensure the appropriate permissions are in place. Proper referencing skills may also be needed.

Methodology: Crowdsourcing (Hagen et al., 2012)

This methodology can work online and offline. A person or an organisation taps into a network of people (a crowd) to solve an issue or develop an idea or solution. It can be introduced at any point in the research study.

Considerations:

1. Transparency and clarity are needed around intellectual property, ownership, copyright and ongoing communication with participants.
2. Crowdsourcing must be achievable and compelling, preferably through existing communities.
3. Incentives may be needed to promote interest from the crowd.
4. Mitigation plans should be put in place to manage inappropriate or non-constructive contributions.
5. This method can enable large-scale participation from diverse adolescents.
6. Crowdsourcing can build interest and build community momentum as well as ongoing relationships.
7. The method relies on voluntary participation and, therefore, there is no guarantee.

Case Study: Understanding Adolescent Adjustment to Maternal Cancer: A Study of Personal Experiences and Psychosocial Factors That Promote Adjustment (Rodriguez, 2016)

This study was carried out online. Adolescents completed scales at baseline and after they had completed an intervention online. Adolescents were part of an eight-week online intervention (adolescent adjustment to maternal cancer (AMC) intervention). Each weekly session had a specific theme: cancer, social support, self-perception, staying calm, assertiveness, emotions, communication and asking for help. All sessions provided information on these topics and included activities based on them.

A built-for-purpose website was developed using Wordpress, with the support of an IT specialist. The researcher mostly built the website herself, reducing the research costs. The website, however, was very text heavy. It was not interactive and adolescents could not have a personalised experience. Generally, activities had to be carried out offline and then adolescents provided written feedback. Due to ethical concerns, it was decided not to include a forum or any space where adolescents could interact with each other. Overall, there was big room for improvement; there should have been more resources and a more in-depth understanding of the guidance and considerations around technology and adolescent online activity. It would have been ideal to have had a larger research team to be able to monitor activity online and enable more interaction among participants, as one of the findings of the overall study was that the adolescents wanted peer support as the shared experience would have been of benefit to them. In hindsight, this was a lost opportunity that more modern online technology could have facilitated. This study was carried out over 10 years ago. The researcher's knowledge and skills have evolved since.

Examples of the session are included in Figure 9.1.

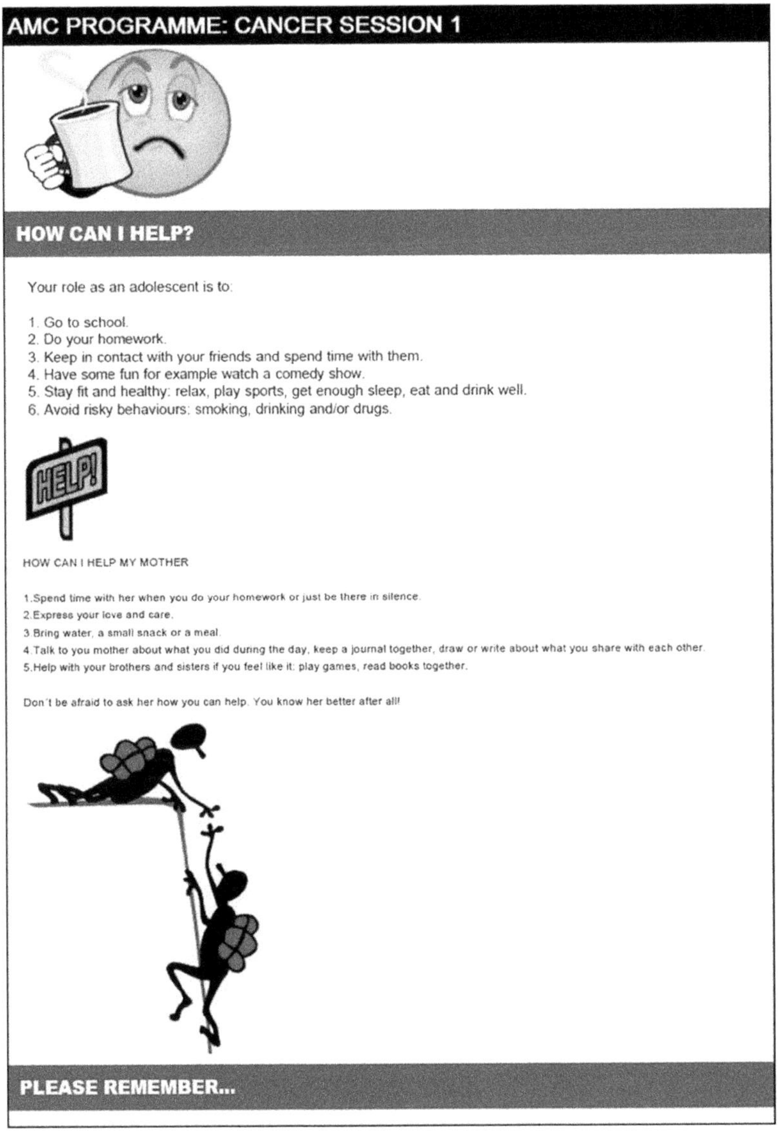

Figure 9.1 Online intervention examples

AMC SESSION 7

YOU CAN PROVIDE HELP WHEN:

1.Recognize the other person needs helps.
2.Listen carefully to what is being said.
3.Make sure you understand the petition.
4.Think if you are the right person to provide help.
5.If the petition is not direct but if it is clear that the person needs help, approach the person and ask them.
6.Help the person in a way they feel comfortable and you as well.

YOU CAN'T PROVIDE HELP WHEN:

1.Petitions are not reasonable or they are excessive.
2.You don't know or can't do what they asked for.

Specify your reasons to say no.
Apologize to the person asking for help.
Suggest who else may be willing to help.

EXERCISE: MY HELP JOURNAL

Keep a record of how many times you asked for help during the day and how many people asked you for help.

***6. Who did you ask for help?**

***7. How did you do it?**

***8. How did it make you feel?**

***9. How many people asked you to help them?**

Figure 9.1 (*cont.*)

CHAPTER 10

'Meaningful' Participation

> Adolescents . . . are central actors around their health and well-being. Their meaningful participation and engagement is essential for effective action aiming to enhance their health and well-being.
>
> G. Patton et al., 'Our future: A Lancet commission on adolescent health and wellbeing'

Chapter Highlights

1. Meaningful participation entails several different factors such as individual, social and cultural, which may facilitate participation or hinder it.
2. Adolescents' voices are more widely heard but require a more significant impact on policy, practice and service delivery.
3. Participation is a continuum; adolescents may have different levels of participation and engagement in a study.
4. Participation should not be a replication of the exclusion and marginalisation of specific groups of adolescents in society.
5. Participation may not be sustainable if the correct organisational structures are not in place to support it.

Meaningful participation depends on a complex combination of factors: the context, personal characteristics, the motivation and perception of parents, family members and other relevant adults (education, welfare, justice systems) and organisational, local and national regulatory structures (Gal, 2017). Research has found, for example, that older adolescents and girls tend to participate more. Ethnicity, affluency and deprivation create uneven levels of participation for adolescents, in general (Kirby & Bryson, 2002).

Participation of children and adolescents in private and public matters is partial and their voices are still having little impact on public decision-making (Kirby & Bryson, 2002). A minority of children and adolescents are involved in public decision-making; these groups are also not necessarily representative of all children and adolescents in the target populations (Kirby & Bryson, 2002). This is due to several issues including professionals' reluctance, child and adolescent contingency beliefs, and institutional barriers (Gal, 2017). Policy makers may perceive that they lack the skills, or actually do lack the skills, to speak with children and adolescents directly (Gal, 2017); however, there is also a dearth of research on how adults (e.g. facilitators and decision makers) benefit from taking part in participatory projects (Kirby & Bryson, 2002).

According to Kirby and Bryson (2002), researchers have more knowledge about how to support adolescents to express their views, but not so much about how to turn those identified issues into practice in a way that will affect change. Token participation is more damaging than non-participation, as involving children and adolescents creates expectations that will remain unfulfilled, leading to frustration and anger (Gal, 2017). Participation can instead produce feelings of being important and influential (Gal, 2017).

Meaningful participation requires effort. Hagen et al. (2012) described the conditions that must be in place to facilitate and ensure meaningful involvement for adolescents:

1. Adolescents need to be fully informed about the topic and project.
2. Adolescents need to be given non-tokenistic opportunities to participate.
3. Adolescents need to be listened to and their feedback used to inform the project.
4. Adolescents need to be aware of what is expected of them from the start.
5. Researchers/staff need to be available to answer questions or assist if problems happen.
6. Adolescents need to have the skills, knowledge and support to participate meaningfully. The conditions for these may require time and resources to be created.
7. Organisations must have a culture of participation to support meaningful participation.
8. There is no right way. There might be a need for experimentation to find the best way. Researchers should be flexible and prepare to adapt.
9. Adolescent participation should be given value and the benefits of their participation should be clear. This may take the form of

incentives or opportunities for engagement that are fun and rewarding for them.

10. Adolescent expectations should be properly managed. They need to be aware of what is going to happen, what is being asked from them, who is involved, the impact of their involvement and the steps involved to reach the results.
11. Adolescents must provide their input and advice; it is recommended to test and pilot methods.
12. Researchers need to promote inclusiveness through a diversity of methods. This enables participation from a variety of adolescents with different learning and communication styles. Methods should not unintentionally exclude certain groups. In the case of web technologies, these may not be accessible to adolescents with impaired vision, disability or special needs. There should not be differences of sex or cultural background in participants' ability to take part in the research.

10.1 Models of Participation

Several models of child and adolescent participation can be identified in the literature. Some of these models define participation slightly differently and enable it to different degrees.

The ecological model of child and youth participation (Gal, 2017) is based on Bronfenbrenner's (1986) model (Table 10.1). This model is composed of several layers with the person at the centre and subsequent circles surrounding and including them.

Hart's ladder (Hart, 1992) is a model of participation based on the premise that children and adolescents have the confidence and competence to engage in the highest levels of participation in the ladder but they may be offered to engage in the lower levels (Gal, 2017). This model consists of eight levels, from lowest to highest participation.

1. Manipulation is the lowest level of participation based on adults' unawareness of children's and adolescents' abilities (Hart, 1992). Manipulation can also happen when children are consulted but not given any feedback, therefore they do not know how their ideas were used.
2. Decoration. Children and adolescents have little idea of what their involvement is about and are not involved in the organisation. Children and adolescents participate for what they get (e.g.

Table 10.1 *The ecological model and the ecological model of participation*

Ecological model (Bronfenbrenner, 1986)	Ecological model of participation (Gal, 2017)
Person: resources and force.	Individual characteristics: age, gender, appearance and ethnic background.
Microsystem: parents and families.	Families, teachers, social workers and other adults affect children's and adolescents' expectations of their capacity to participate. Within families, children can develop and practise participation skills.
Mesosystem: professional practices.	Personal skills of professionals involved in decision-making; their moral standing regarding participation affects their level and effectiveness of children's participation.
Macrosystem: regulatory regime.	Society reinforces explicit and implicit messages for children and adolescents that their views matter in some areas but are not relevant in others. Participation is more effective if relationships are based on trust, respect and encouragement. Laws, regulations and guidelines provided by states. States provide the budget for participation.
Meso-exo-macrosystem: sociopolitical landscape.	
Paradigm system: universal human rights.	

refreshments) but not for the 'cause'. Children's and adolescents' role is to bolster the adults' cause in an indirect manner (Hart, 1992).

3. Tokenism. Tokenism happens when children are 'apparently' given a voice, but they have little or no choice about the topic, their style of communication and an opportunity to have their own opinions (Hart, 1992).
4. Assigned but informed. At this stage, the children understand the intentions of the project, they are aware of the decisions concerning their involvement and why the decisions are made. Children also have a meaningful role, and they participate voluntarily in the project after it was clearly explained to them (Hart, 1992).
5. Consulted and informed. Children and adolescents work as consultants for the adults with integrity, meaning the project is designed by adults but children understand the process and their opinions are seriously taken into consideration (Hart, 1992).

6. Adult initiated, shared decisions with children. Projects at level 6 are started by adults; however, the decision-making is shared with children and adolescents (Hart, 1992).
7. Child initiated and directed. Children and adolescents conceive and carry out their own projects, even complex ones (Hart, 1992). With the correct support, even younger children can cooperate in large groups (Hart, 1992).
8. Child initiated, shared decisions with adults. Children and adolescents design and manage their own projects and incorporate adults (Hart, 1992). Projects at this stage are rare; however, according to Hart (1992), this is not due to lack of interest from children and adolescents but because of the absence of caring adults tuned into their interests (Hart, 1992).

Hart's model includes a level where children make decisions independently from adults, which other models do not have. According to Shier (2001), this is because children make decisions separately from adults all the time when they play.

Shier (2001) created a model consisting of 15 questions that are used to plan for participation. This model uses the terminology 'children's participation' without specifying an age range. The model is based on Article 12 of the United Nations Convention on the Rights of the Child; therefore the term child, according to the UN, refers to anyone under 18 years of age. The model is based on five levels of participation as described in Table 10.2.

Each of these levels have different stages of empowerment (Shier, 2001):

1. Opening. This consists of a personal commitment or statement of intent to work from this perspective; however, the opportunity to make it happen may not be available.
2. Opportunity. The needs (resources, time, skills, knowledge) are met and the individual or the organisation can operate at this level of practice.
3. Obligation. The agreed policy reinforces an organisation and its staff to operate from this perspective of children's participation.

Wong et al. (2010) created a typology of youth participation based on empowerment called the youth participation and empowerment pyramid (TYPE). Empowerment in this framework consists of a democracy, and participatory co-learning is the emphasis (Wong et al., 2010). Wong et al. (2010) described that participation approaches are a combination of types. These approaches can also evolve over time into a different type. TYPE

Table 10.2 *The Shier model of participation*

Children are listened to.	When a child expresses a view, this is listened to with care and attention by the adult responsible. At this stage, the worker/team is only expected to be ready to listen.
Children are supported in expressing their views.	This stage involves a commitment to elicit children's views and to support them in expressing their views.
Children's views are taken into account.	The organisation has included children's participation in their policy and, therefore, children are enabled and supported in expressing their views. Children's views are one of the factors that will be considered in policies and decision-making; however, they don't have to be implemented. Children are informed of the decision made and the reasons for this.
Children are involved in decision-making processes.	This stage involves a transition from consultation with children to their active participation in decision-making.
Children share power and responsibility for decision-making.	At this stage, adults make an explicit commitment to share their power and to give some of it away to the children. Children should not be forced to take responsibility and there should be careful consideration given to the areas where it is safe and beneficial for children to be involved.

should not be seen as a rigid framework, but it is intended as a tool to challenge researchers, practitioners and youth themselves (Wong et al., 2010). The types of models are vessel, symbolic, pluralistic, independent and autonomous.

Vessel is described as a traditional adolescent–adult relationship which is adult-driven with very little or no input from the adolescents. This has very low empowerment potential, meaning that adolescents may acquire skills and knowledge but do not contribute their own ideas (Wong et al., 2010).

Symbolic participation consists of giving adolescents the opportunity to express their opinions and perspectives; however, they do not have power in decision-making (Wong et al., 2010).

Pluralistic is the process of adults and adolescents working together and sharing control (Wong et al., 2010). Shared control does not mean equal youth and adult participation; instead, it means joint decision-making and deciding who has the best skills or strengths for a specific decision (Wong et al., 2010).

Independent consists of an approach where adults give up their power and give it to adolescents. This, however, may mean adolescents miss out on the skills and experiences of adults (Wong et al., 2010). Independence can develop skills in adolescents including organising, controlling, planning, decision-making, competence, critical awareness and self-efficacy.

In the *autonomous* participation, adolescents have created their own spaces to express their voice, participation and expression of power without adult involvement (Wong et al., 2010). These models enable empowering; however, the lack of adult guidance in these spaces may be detrimental for adolescents' healthy development (Wong et al., 2010).

Another well-known model of participation is the Lundy model of participation. This is based on Article 12 of the United Nations Convention on the Rights of the Child, which gives children the right to have their views given due weight in matters that affect them (Lundy, 2007). Children's possibility of benefitting from Article 12 depends on adults who may not comply with it for different reasons, including (Lundy, 2007):

1. Scepticism about children's capacity to have a meaningful input into decision-making.
2. Worry that giving children more control will undermine authority.
3. Compliance requiring too much effort which would be better spent on other alternatives.

The Lundy model consists of four components, which are interrelated (Lundy, 2007) and described in Table 10.3.

Hart (1992) emphasised that the Convention of the Rights of the Child is focused on protecting children and less emphasis is placed on the responsibilities that rights bring. Children need to learn these responsibilities, and this can be achieved by engaging them in collaborative work with others, including those who may be older and more experienced (Hart, 1992). Participation enables children and adolescents to have a voice, but it is also a possibility for children to discover the rights of others to have their own voices heard as well (Hart, 1992).

There have been criticisms of participation models, as these have underlying assumptions. Ladder models, for example, assume participation is linear, whereby participation is preferred over non-participation (Wong et al., 2010). However, participation may be more complex than a linear process, in the sense that many factors may facilitate or impede it.

Table 10.3 *The Lundy model of participation*

Space	Children must be given the opportunity to express a view. Children must also be consulted in which matters they consider impact on them and whether they want to be involved in influencing the outcome of the decision or not, as they have a right to refuse to get involved. The space should be safe for children to express their views without fear of rebuke or reprisal.
Voice	Children must be facilitated to express their views. Children need time to understand the issues, access to child-friendly information and documentation. There should also be capacity-building for children and training for adults to overcome any limitations to children's participation.
Audience	Children's views mut be listened to and given 'due weight'. Children have the right to have their views listened to by those involved in charge of decision-making.
Influence	Children's views must be acted upon, as appropriate. State parties are required to ensure children's views are given 'due weight' in accordance with their age and capacity, which also requires real change.

10.2 The Limits of Participation

Participatory approaches may be successful but lack sustainability if no genuine structures are put in place. Youth engagement health projects usually lack sustainability, as they are adult-driven approaches (Patton et al., 2016) and may not have the organisational structure in place to support participation and to sustain it. Implementing participation has its challenges as this requires a modification of dominant principles and processes through which decisions are traditionally made (Zeldin et al., 2008). It is challenging to integrate innovation into already established systems and it requires extra effort from staff to act as advocates of adolescent participation, adding to their workload (Zeldin et al., 2008).

One of the major challenges of children and adolescent participation is not engaging them but translating their participation into practice that is meaningful to them and brings change that can become embedded in the ethos of an organisation (Kirby et al., 2003). Undertaking meaningful and sustainable participation is only possible if organisations develop the infrastructure and organisational capacity to enable that change (Kirby et al., 2003). It also requires commitment: staff support and an organisational learning approach (Kirby et al., 2003).

There is little research on how to create a culture of participation within an organisation or community (Kirby & Bryson, 2002). Chen et al. (2010)

carried out an organisational participatory evaluation with adolescent services users. Organisations need to ensure that they commit to take the findings seriously and there are several steps they should take to be accountable:

1. Self-assessment. The organisation should conduct an objective self-assessment of its capacity to engage in a youth-led evaluation before getting involved. Evaluation needs to be supported by top management to ensure staff time, resources, leadership and support are in place (Chen et al., 2010).
2. Follow-up. Research projects should include a follow-up phase where researchers will engage with different stakeholders in the organisation (staff, service users, parents) to collectively identify strategies to implement the evaluation findings and recommendations. This will enable shared accountability by facilitating stakeholder thinking and brainstorming solutions (Chen et al., 2010). Follow-up meetings should be scheduled with different stakeholders over time (Chen et al., 2010).

Participation cannot be effective without providing adolescents choice on the level of participation they can and wish to have (Gibbs et al., 2020). Some adolescents may genuinely not have the time to be highly involved (Gibbs et al., 2020). Therefore, enabling them to engage and disengage from the research as they will is a form of agency and assertion of their rights (Gibbs et al., 2020). Flicker et al. (2008) suggested adolescents should reflect on their participation. This included regular check-ins and impact evaluations. This enabled adolescents to determine the impact of their involvement and achievements and to celebrate success (Flicker et al., 2008).

Adolescents bring their own political, personal and relational agendas or they may identify and develop them by engaging in research. Therefore, this means adolescents may make requests and suggestions to researchers, which may not always be included in the research (Wulf-Andersen et al., 2021b). Participation may have to be negotiated.

Participation may exclude a sector of adolescents. According to Patton et al. (2016), adolescents who engage are usually already confident, articulate and 'natural' leaders. This means certain groups of adolescents – usually those who belong to ethnic groups, HIV positive ones, married adolescents, adolescents with disabilities, LGBTQ+ adolescents, those living in poverty with low level of education and very young adolescents – may be marginalised from participation (Patton et al., 2016). Research studies, programmes, work with children and young people, according to

Hart (1992), should be designed to maximise an opportunity for a child or adolescent to be able to participate at the highest level of their ability. Research should include alternative techniques to enable different children's voices to be heard (Hart, 1992). According to Purdy and Spears (2020), diversity is a collective strength, as there is not a single voice but many.

All programmes, however, cannot target all possible age groups and different kinds of personalities or issues; according to Hart (1992), the key is diversity. Diversity should enable different degrees of involvement for different people at different stages of the research process. Projects that are accessible and comprehensible at all stages can involve children, adolescents and adults with different developmental capacities and interests at various phases of the study (Hart, 1992).

Krane et al. (2021) described some of the possible types of participation of children and adolescents in research:

1. Objects and passive participants. Data collection methods are described as passive, for example completing surveys. Studies are usually led by adults. Participants only have some influence on the co-construction of knowledge.
2. Youth as partners. Adolescents are more involved in the research process. Participants are described as co-researchers.
3. Collaborative. This is the co-creation of knowledge through dialogue, interplay and collaboration between participants and researchers.

This categorisation has been criticised as it is static (Krane et al., 2021). It is an interplay of knowledge co-creation between researchers, adolescents and contextual factors (Krane et al., 2021). The model can be useful to understand that participation should be perceived as a continuum, where adolescents may have different roles and degrees of involvement. Scaffolding participation is a term coined by Gibbs et al. (2020) to refer to a smaller group of adolescents engaged in high-level and meaningful participation as research 'co-collaborators'.

10.3 What Is Needed for Meaningful Participation?

For successful engagement, the capacity of adolescents and adults to work in partnership should be highlighted. Adults must reject the belief that '*adults know best*' (Patton et al., 2016, p. 2461). Egalitarian relationships are crucial for meaningful engagement (Patton et al., 2016). Youth–adult partnerships, for example, are described as a method of practice grounded in the principle of engaging youth in the design and deliberation of policies and decisions that affect them (Zeldin et al., 2008). The method brings together diverse adults and youth to make decisions together through democratic and consensual processes (Zeldin et al., 2008). It has been suggested that this method can strengthen the culture, structure and programming of youth organisations and schools where it has been applied (Zeldin et al., 2008).

Researchers should also recognise multiple ways of knowing (Aldana & Richards-Schuster, 2021). This, in practice, means trying new research methods and approaches suggested by adolescents. This supports diverse young people to develop their ideas and strengthen their voices and enables their full participation in research (Aldana & Richards-Schuster, 2021). Researchers should ensure adolescents can access resources, training, mentorship and sensitisation to political and management processes, platforms and mechanisms for engagement (Patton et al., 2016).

Participation can be further supported with engagement from different government and non-government sectors: international agencies, global funders, civil society organisations, youth organisations, professionals working with youth, academia and private industry (Patton et al., 2016). This will help identify and engage a wider variety of adolescents.

Research has identified some of the reasons why participation may be challenged. Some of these reasons are contextual or a lack of resources, lack of availability or volunteer bias:

1. Lack of funding for participatory action research (PAR) (Shamrova & Cummings, 2017).
2. PAR is time-consuming (Shamrova & Cummings, 2017).
3. The political climate may prevent the dissemination of PAR results (Shamrova & Cummings, 2017).
4. Conflicting school schedules and adolescent commitment with other extracurricular activities (Tsang et al., 2020).
5. Adolescent participants may be subject to volunteer bias, including an interest in the research topic or an altruistic approach due to their past experiences (Tsang et al., 2020).

Research has identified that not all adolescents may be suitable to meaningfully engage with certain levels of participation. Tsang et al. (2020), for example, provide recommendations of the characteristics needed to recruit co-researchers. They should have:

1. Interpersonal skills in one-to-one and group settings.
2. Leadership characteristics in and out of school.

3. Communication skills in person and online.
4. Creativity and ability to share new ideas.
5. Proficiency in English (or in the language in which the research is being carried out).
6. Past or current personal experience in the research topic.

Adolescents may lack skills, expertise and connections to the social capital needed to conduct research appropriately, which may lead to frustration or unintended disempowering outcomes (Wong et al., 2010). Kirby and Bryson (2002) suggest that children and adolescents do not have to be involved in every stage of a research or evaluation process. It may be appropriate to involve them in one or two stages only, for example (Kirby & Bryson, 2002).

Another way to facilitate adolescent participation is for researchers to make sure there are benefits for adolescents when taking part in the research, and that they are aware of how the research will benefit them. These benefits should be realistic and honest.

Research studies in the past have described some of the benefits that research studies may have for adolescents. Some of these may be applicable to your study as well. These are personal growth, leadership and improvement in understanding of the research process (Tsang et al., 2020). Adolescents may also benefit from learning about several research skills: develop survey questions, understanding consent and assent, literature review, create and evaluate research presentation materials (Tsang et al., 2020). Other skills may include public speaking, improvement in cooperative learning, and teamwork and advocacy (Tsang et al., 2020). Adolescents may understand the importance of their role in the larger scope, for example in academia and research (Tsang et al., 2020).

10.4 Defining Problems in Collaboration with Adolescents

Developing a problem is a fundamental part of meaningful participatory research; however, there is little research about the process of how adolescents develop and define a problem that is feasible, significant and relevant for the research and adolescents' lives (Kohfeldt & Langhout, 2012). Identifying a research problem is, therefore, a fundamental step. Kohfeldt and Langhout (2012) applied the five whys method (Ohno, 1978/1987) as a tool to develop problem definitions in collaboration with children. This method is a reflective process where participants reflect on their lived experiences and develop a problem underpinned by second-order change.

Second-order change is an important concept as it entails change in the relationship among the system's parts, therefore is a change targeted at the origin of the issues themselves. Basic system structures must be modified to ensure change is sustained; it is not the result of changing a component within the system while leaving the system intact (Kohfeldt & Langhout, 2012). Problems, therefore, should be designed with second order in mind; otherwise they may not produce shifts in power and role relationships (Kohfeldt & Langhout, 2012).

The five whys method (Ohno, 1978/1987) consists of turning the problem into a question 'why'. It directly challenges the definition of problems as unidirectional, instead defining them as multidimensional (Kohfeldt & Langhout, 2012). The cycle repeats for five times (or less), or as many times as needed for the issue in question. The most plausible answer is turned into another 'why' in an iterative process.

I show a worked example by Kohfeldt and Langhout (2012) who worked with adolescents to explore why they did not have the opportunity to participate in budget decisions and resource allocation in their school. Applying the steps of the method, student problems were turned into a 'why', offering five possible answers to the question (Table 10.4). These iterations were stopped when participants felt they had reached the root cause of the initial problem. These can be carried out in small groups if there are several problem areas to address.

According to the five whys method and PAR, there is no one single truth but many (Kohfeldt & Langhout, 2012), as can be seen in Table 10.4. The original issue became an issue of the school's unaccountability towards students. Once the problem is defined, actions can be proposed. These actions are targeted at modifying institutional structures, not the students themselves, although these actions come from their own experiences (Kohfeldt & Langhout, 2012).

Students should (Kohfeldt & Langhout, 2012, p. 324):

1. Be able to sign out to use the toilet (one at a time).
2. Be able to borrow things they need (books, computers).
3. Be able to use the computers in the library during recess if they want.
4. Have their family members more involved in school.
5. Have a homework packet due on Friday rather than individual homework every night.

Table 10.4 *The 'five whys' method in practice*

Why are the toilets unflushed?	**Why are students lazy?**	**Why don't students care about school property?**	**Why don't students feel like school property is theirs?**	**Why don't students feel in control of school property?**
Students are scared of the noise.	They do not get enough sleep.	Students do not like mean people at their school.	Because they are not here all the time.	Students must ask before they can use school property.
Toilet handles are dirty, so students do not want to touch them.	They are physically tired from recess.	Students do not care about things in general.	Insults from other students do not make kids feel comfortable at home.	**Students do not have a lot of freedom at school.**
Laziness of students.	They are lazy from sickness.	Students like to play pranks.	Students do not feel like they or their parents pay for school property.	Students do not have any say in fixing or improving their school.
Students forget to flush.	They are born lazy.	**Students do not feel like school property is theirs.**	**Students do not feel in control of school property.**	Nothing from the school belongs to the students.
Students do not have time to flush.	**They do not care about school property.**	Some students do not like their schools.	N/A	Students cannot use school property in different ways. Students sometimes get in trouble for using school property.

Note: Entries in bold represent the final response chosen by consensus.

10.5 Policy

The relationship between research and policy is not often immediate or direct (Prout, 2002). There is also a lack of evidence regarding to what extent child and youth participation leads to policy changes that have an impact on their health (Yamaguchi et al., 2023). Yamaguchi et al. (2023) identified that adolescents are usually involved in situational analysis and policy design but not in policy implementation and evaluation. Overall, there is a lack of representation of adolescents from diverse backgrounds in mental health policy making; this is important as different characteristics such as gender, ethnicity, socio-economic status and educational attainment impact mental health (Yamaguchi et al., 2023).

In terms of child and adolescent policy, Banati and Lansford (2018) described that children under 10 years of age are usually covered by national child policies, whereas those over 16 are usually covered by policies that seek to empower them to enter the workforce and make an economic contribution. This means that those between 10 and 16 years 'slip through the cracks' (Banati & Lansford, 2018).

Children and adolescents are usually treated as 'objects' of local welfare policies, which means policies about provisions and facilities for children and adolescents are designed without including them or consulting them and their involvement is limited (Cavet & Sloper, 2004; de Winter et al., 1999). The message children and young people are given is that they are not social subjects whose opinions and involvement are important (de Winter et al., 1999).

Children and adolescent voices should have a greater role in developing policy and practice; this means a less 'top-down' view of policy making is required and achieved by having children as actors of a network of relationships (Prout, 2002). Some actors in this network will have more power; however, all the connections in this network are essential, including children and adolescents (Prout, 2002).

'Youth voice' is a widely used term; however, it does not distinguish between opportunities to express views versus enabling adolescents to hold power over decisions, policies and practices (Ozer et al., 2018). Voice is a physical attribute; however, it is socially constructed, depending on the degree of primacy given to different voices according to social hierarchies and power dynamics (Moran et al., 2021). 'Giving voice', however, may, to some extent, suggest that children are 'voiceless' without adult interventions (Moran et al., 2021). Centring the voice of adolescents does not mean always doing what they wish while diminishing the contributions of adults, it means prioritising adolescent perspectives and listening to their suggestions as an essential component of the research process (Aldana & Richards-Schuster, 2021). Listening to children can also be controversial because adults may intrude or distress children and adolescents by entering their spaces and lives (Moran et al., 2021). Therefore, listening should also be consented by adolescents.

Some of the barriers of including participant voices in policy include the complexity of bureaucratic organisations, internal politics, projects with an adult focus, short-term funding and perspectives against the effectiveness of adolescent participation (Cavet & Sloper, 2004). Often, children and adolescents are expected to fit into adult ways of participation, therefore institutional and organisational change is needed to facilitate and ensure children and adolescent participation (Prout, 2002).

Cavet and Sloper (2004) identified some aspects that can contribute to best practice in involving adolescents in service development. These are:

1. A listening culture among staff is needed so that children and adolescents can express their opinions and know these will be heard and acted upon.
2. Clarity is needed about the purpose, objectives and decision-making regarding adult involvement.
3. Flexibility is needed to include a variety of approaches and age-friendly methods and environments.
4. Resources are needed, for example about staff training and long-term funding.
5. Skills development and training for staff is needed to enhance confidence and competence.
6. Inclusion of marginalised groups requires attention to accessibility to ensure adolescents can participate in public decision-making.
7. Feedback should be provided about the results of the consultation and the changes which have happened, and those that have not.
8. Evaluation of participation is needed as well as improvement of relevant policies and standards.

10.6 Feedback and Dissemination

Enabling the voices of children and adolescents to prioritise research findings and engage in policy dialogue is crucial (Evans, 2017). Providing feedback for adolescent participants is also crucial, as it enables them to know the views of each other but also to understand why some of their ideas will not be turned into action and some will (Lightfoot & Sloper, 2002). Feedback can be provided verbally but also through noticeboards or newsletters. This feedback can also be ongoing – adolescents should receive feedback about the progress of changes or delays (Lightfoot & Sloper, 2002). Feedback is fundamental in shaping adolescents' attitudes towards participation (Lightfoot & Sloper, 2002). Overall, this enables participants to see how their contribution to the research can inform policy, practice and future research (Evans, 2017).

Successful dissemination requires time and effort from researchers to identify the correct audience and get them to dissemination events where adolescents will have an opportunity to share their projects and ideas. Percy-Smith (2007) organised a large event where 62 adolescents (13–21 years) were invited from different contexts as well as 36 professionals, including practitioners and directors of services; elected members from different sectors including education, health, youth services, voluntary sector and community organisations were also invited. Evidently, gathering this amount of people is crucial but entails time, resources and effort.

The second aspect of meaningful dissemination is going beyond adolescents expressing their concerns but engaging in a purposeful process of social learning. Percy-Smith (2007) facilitated a space where adolescents and professionals could engage in a dialogue to respond to identified issues. The methodology used by the author was a 'Knowledge Café'. Groups of participants – adolescents and adults – move around the space to deepen and share their understanding of different topics such as 'what a healthy life means to young people'. After the discussions, adolescents and adults used visual media to envision how to create a healthier future for adolescents, responding to the issues identified earlier. The final stage consisted of a plenary discussion where adolescents and adults discussed the learning and actions from the event. The findings from the event were analysed by adolescents themselves. An overall posterior analysis was carried out by the researchers using a grounded theory approach to write the research report (Percy-Smith, 2007). It is more likely that if professionals are present 'first hand' their participation will be followed by action, as reported research, unless it has been commissioned, may go unnoticed (Percy-Smith, 2007).

10.7 Involving Adolescents in Health Services and Health Policy Development

Adolescent engagement can lead to improving health policies and services and, therefore, an increase in improvements of their own health and societal outcomes (Patton et al., 2016). According to Patton et al. (2016), the definition of responsive and youth-friendly healthcare is similar in all countries of the world, independent of their level of income. Adolescents want patient-centred care including respect, coordination of care, provision of information, good communication, involvement in decision-making about care and being listened to by healthcare providers.

Participation also requires developing child/adolescent and adult relationships based on trust, respect and dialogue (Kirby et al., 2003). Involving adolescents in health service research requires developing a 'listening culture' (Lightfoot & Sloper, 2002). This means adolescents can raise issues at the right time for them and not just when staff request that information from them. A 'listening culture' also means staff listen to adolescents' views and act seriously on these issues. A listening culture will enable adolescents to express themselves to the staff they feel more comfortable with, rather than having to go to a solely designated person (Lightfoot & Sloper, 2002).

Percy-Smith (2007) carried out a consultation with adolescents to understand their health needs to improve local health provision. This study enabled adolescent participation by training adolescents in research methods and different interpretations of health. Adolescents were involved and supported in analysing and disseminating research findings. Therefore, involving adolescents means they need to be trained and supported.

Lightfoot and Sloper (2002) identified that involving adolescents in service development had benefits for staff. According to the authors, working with adolescents can have a profound effect on personal and professional development for healthcare staff. Involving adolescents enables healthcare staff to have a certainty of what is important for young patients (Lightfoot & Sloper, 2002). Informing professionals about adolescents' health needs is not only about increasing their awareness but ensuring they understand how health issues are experienced by adolescents and better informs health policy responses (Percy-Smith, 2007). Bringing adolescents and professionals together was an opportunity for professionals to learn from adolescents more effectively than only reading a report (Percy-Smith, 2007). More efforts at an organisational level are required to incorporate the voices of adolescents in service delivery, improvement and policy, to ensure their wishes and needs inform health systems.

CHAPTER 11

Conclusions

This book is the first to provide a critical and evidence-informed resource where the available information on participatory health research with adolescents has been explored. The book was written to become a useful tool for all who work in the field of participatory methods and adolescents, specifically exploring their health experiences and needs.

Participatory health research using technology with adolescents, as has been described in the book, is limited. There are some examples, but not many that have combined all these methods. Therefore, there is a vast field still to be explored and developed. The available evidence shows how these methods have been successfully combined and, if anything, provide the methodological and ethical considerations that researchers should follow in the future to ensure their experiences are successful for them and the adolescents involved.

In some of the chapters, the evidence is less. For example, not all chapters include a working example or a case study of how the method has been applied regarding adolescents or health research. Although this can be a limitation, it also shows a gap in research and practice waiting to be filled and explored. There is scope to make a significant contribution to this field.

As a result of writing this book, the 'Manifesto of Technological Innovations and Participatory Health Research with Adolescents' has been produced and described in detail, as follows:

1. There is no 'one-size-fits-all'.

Adolescents and researchers are not a homogeneous group; the umbrella of participatory methods can provide a variety of potential alternatives to meet the needs and characteristics of individuals. Research, therefore, should not privilege the views and perspectives of specific groups of children and adolescents over others. Researchers need to get to know the group they are working with, their needs and their specific cultural and social circumstances. They should learn the possible ways the group may benefit from the research and the best ways to keep them safe within that context. Participatory research offers many different approaches and methods to meet the needs of the research and those of adolescent participants.

2. Adolescents have unequal access to technology and unequal interest in engaging with it.

Adolescents' interest in and abilities related to technology should not be generalised. Not all adolescents have access to technology; although they should be given the opportunity to use it and benefit from it, they may not have the resources to access it, creating unequal opportunities for being heard and understood. Research should not replicate these differences; it should instead contribute towards lessening the gap. Resources are obviously needed. Even though adolescents are somehow perceived as tech-savvy and interested in technology, this may not be the case. Some technology-based methodologies described in the book require some level of expertise, for example sonification and mapping. Adolescents therefore may need training and support to be able to make a meaningful contribution in a true participatory context.

3. Adolescents have something to say, in the correct environment where they feel somebody seriously wants to listen.

The book has identified useful examples of best practice in adolescent participatory research applied to health and other contexts. The reality is that researchers need to consider many elements when engaging adolescents and their wishes and needs. Adolescents will not engage or continue in the research if they are not interested. Creating a safe environment, whether physical or online, will determine whether adolescents feel comfortable to speak and participate or not. Adolescents need the tools to participate successfully; they may need to be provided with a basic understanding of the research topic. Adolescents care about their safety and need to see evidence that thought and care has been invested into keeping them and their information safe, particularly in online platforms. Materials and language should be age appropriate. Some adolescents may also have other types of needs, for example language barriers or disability. Resources may be an issue; adolescents may be interested in a technological gadget but do not have the capacity to buy it.

4. Do not make promises you cannot keep, or that you are not willing to keep (yet!).

Researchers and adolescents should agree early on on what the research can offer them in the short term and long term and have a clear and honest understanding that change at a social, cultural and policy level may take time. Research may not impact adolescents' lives directly, but they may obtain some benefit when services improve, when organisations become pro participation and when major policy changes happen because of research findings. On occasion, adolescents may receive training and these skills can be transferable to future jobs and careers. Another important component is making decisions about adolescents receiving a reward, such as an economic one, for their participation. If these rewards are offered, they must be provided. Additionally, adolescents should know if the technological gadget used (e.g. cameras, iPads, etc.) are their own to keep or if they must be returned. Copyright is an important issue to consider when working in co-creation with adolescents. It should be clear if they are going to be owners of the final product and if their names are included in any research outputs.

5. If you make mistakes, be honest about it. We all make mistakes – children, adolescents and adults.

Relationships between participants and researchers should be open and honest. 'Real world' research, that is, research carried out in real-life contexts, may require adaptations and changes to fit the reality. For example, one of the studies included in the research began as a face-to-face project but became online research due to COVID-19. Circumstances may not change as extremely as that; however, adolescents may be disappointed if the researchers, for example, tried to invite specific stakeholders or policy makers, politicians, local celebrities, etc. but they declined to take part. Researchers should be always honest, showing adolescents that they can also be honest themselves. Adolescents can also provide possible solutions to issues or problems that emerge.

6. Participatory research takes time and effort; this is an investment.

Participatory research requires investment of time and resources. Adolescents may need to be trained and taught specific skills before the research study can even start. They may need to learn specific skills (e.g. programming, learning how to use a camera). Adolescents may also need to learn about ethics regarding research participants. They must understand that they should not develop personal relationships with participants, and they cannot include their face in photographs without their consent, among other considerations. Some research topics may theoretically be unknown for adolescents, for example research paradigms and methods. Research proposals need to consider this extra preparation time needed before starting actual data collection. Certain technology is expensive, for example iPads, biomarkers, mobile phones, etc. Researchers would have to include the costs of the technology required in research applications.

7. Change takes time and effort, but it is worth doing.

Research participants may not see immediate change happening, while other adolescents may see the impact of changes driven by research studies they had been involved in reaching future generations. Participatory research can generate different levels of change. For example, participatory research in schools may manage to make changes quickly within the school, while generating change within government institutions may take longer. Some organisations may demonstrate interest in child and adolescent participation but may not have the mechanisms to make this participation sustainable. Some people, even within the same organisation, may support participation, whereas others do not. There can be significant resistance to change at a personal and an organisational level; change make take even longer in these circumstances. The book has examples of adolescents achieving significant changes in their lives because of their involvement in the research.

8. Start small, persevere.

Starting small refers not only to the scale of the study but also the researcher's ability to carry out participatory research with adolescents. Researchers may need to improve their skills in the technology they want to use while also learning the skills to meaningfully engage and retain adolescents in research. The book proposes participation as a continuum, with different degrees of participation as suitable and valid. Participatory studies may include different levels of participation from peripheral to major involvement where adolescents will be involved in all parts of a study. Adolescents may inform parts of the study but not necessarily be involved in data analysis or data dissemination. That is all valid also. Some research topics, such as sensitive ones, may have clear ethical and safety reasons why adolescents should not be fully involved in data collection, for example. It may not be safe for adolescents to carry technological gadgets in the communities they live in, for example. All these elements should be considered when deciding the adolescent level of involvement.

9. Training is required and is available; you can also read, practise and learn from experience yourself.

Formal training for researchers should provide them with more skills in participatory research. I was not formally trained in participatory research methods. I have learnt through reading and engaging in independent studying myself. Participatory methods should be formally taught at university, like any other research method. There are courses readily available now, online and face to face; however, these can be expensive. Another way to learn is by engaging in participatory studies that other more experienced colleagues are carrying out.

10. Let adolescents be your teachers too.

Adolescents bring their own talents and abilities to the research. Some may already have knowledge of film-making, photography or programming. Some may have already been involved in game and app designing or may have even designed their own. Some adolescents may be more tech-savvy than a social scientist like me. Participation starts with the assumption that adolescents are experts in their own lives, and this is probably true. Researchers may have a lot of knowledge about a topic theoretically but lack the lived experience that adolescents can bring. They may know a community better than the researcher does; for example, they can identify important spaces and places that only a local would know. This can be crucial for the research to be carried out successfully and provide scientifically sound and impactful findings.

11. Ethics are not negotiable but mandatory.

The issue of power sharing has been thoroughly discussed; however, the basic ethical principle is that the researcher is still responsible for the safety and well-being of their participants (and their data), irrespective of their age. That is just a given fact. Depending on the definition used in a study, adolescents may be under the legal adult age in a specific context. In this case, researchers will be even more responsible for their safety. It has been comprehensively discussed that there are international ethical principles but also local ones or even specific organisational ones. Researchers must comply with all of them and have an obligation to research and become familiar with these guidelines before approaching participants. Ethical guidelines must be in place in every research study involving people, particularly with children and adolescents. How these principles are reinforced and applied in the study may be negotiated with adolescents and presented in age-appropriate and more creative ways. The book has included evidence that adolescents are interested in these topics, particularly when it comes to their identity and the protection of their data online. Adolescents are also interested in ethics, and they can contribute towards making decisions about ethics.

12. Technology changes very quickly; make sure you change with it.

One of the challenges of research with technology is how fast it can change. Research often takes a long time from start to dissemination. Ethics takes time, as does talking with gatekeepers, getting access to the target population, and identifying suitable dates and times for data collection – overall, research takes time. Software and products yielded from research should be able to update themselves or at least need to be easily modified or improved, otherwise a very significant investment of time and money can become obsolete very quickly. As explained in the book, having a multidisciplinary research team is crucial to support the design but also ensure the sustainability of products that result from the study. This applies as well to ethical guidelines and data management. Technology often advances faster than guidelines are produced and put into practice.

13. Surround yourself with like-minded people. Don't be afraid to disagree.

Not all adults find it easy or even logical to surrender some of their adult power to share it with adolescents. In general, children and adolescents have less power in society than adults. They require care to be safe and well. Some people advocate for the voices of adolescents to be captured, to give due weight to these voices; however other people may not. Beyond providing a discussion of who is right and who is wrong, it is important to carry out participatory research with people that support it. Researchers can benefit from identifying gatekeepers who will enable and facilitate access as they understand and see the value of participatory research. This will enable the research to be carried out as intended and with fewer limitations and hurdles to overcome.

14. Don't forget you were an adolescent yourself once; how would you have liked that to be?

As stated in the introduction chapter, I was once an adolescent, as were we all. It was not a period of my life that I can say I enjoyed fully. There were challenges and difficult moments. There were things I needed but did not know how to express assertively so I kept them inside until these became damaging. I am sure I am not the only one who has experienced this. This is why I want to make a difference, to provide adolescents with opportunities in which they can safely express themselves and maybe make their worlds a little (or a lot!) better in the process.

15. Never give up! For you and for them.

This is self-explanatory!

Manifesto

1. There is no 'one-size-fits-all'.
2. Adolescents have unequal access to technology and unequal interest in engaging with it.
3. Adolescents have something to say, in the correct environment where they feel somebody seriously wants to listen.
4. Do not make promises you cannot keep, or you are not willing to keep (yet!).
5. If you make mistakes, be honest about it. We all make mistakes – children, adolescents and adults.
6. Participatory research takes times and effort; this is an investment.
7. Change takes time and effort, but it is worth doing.
8. Start small, persevere.
9. Training is required and is available; you can also read, practise and learn from experience yourself.
10. Let adolescents be your teachers too.
11. Ethics are not negotiable but mandatory.
12. Technology changes very quickly; make sure you change with it.
13. Surround yourself with like-minded people. Don't be afraid to disagree.
14. Don't forget you were an adolescent yourself once; how would you have liked that to be?
15. Never give up! For you and for them.

Table 11.1 offers some resources and toolkits for further reference.

Table 11.1 *Resources and toolkits*

Resource	Description	URL
YPAR Hub	YPAR Hub was established in 2015 by UC-Berkeley as an online tool to support YPAR activities. The page includes guidelines as downloadable lesson plans including a variety of topics: observations, interviews, existing data, identifying community assets and strengths, surveys, photovoice, focus groups and developing research questions.	http://yparhub.berkeley.edu/

Table 11.1 (*cont.*)

Resource	Description	URL
EBCD: Experience-based co-design toolkit	This tool includes videos from staff and patients who were involved in experience-based co-design projects.	www.pointofcarefoundation.org.uk/resource/experience-based-co-design-ebcd-toolkit/
Consultation Toolkit	A practical guide about how to consult with children and young people on policy-related issues.	www.savethechildren.org.uk/content/dam/global/reports/advocacy/consultation-toolkit.pdf
Participatory evaluation with young people	A workbook with practical tools and learning activities to use in your community.	www.whatkidscando.org/archives/featurestories/2006pdfs/youthbook.pdf
Building a culture of participation	A workbook to involve children and young people in policy, service planning, delivery and evaluation.	https://resourcecentre.savethechildren.net/document/handbook-building-culture-participation-involving-children-and-young-people-policy-service/
Meet Them Where They Are	A handbook of PAR with adolescent girls.	www.icrw.org/wp-content/uploads/2016/10/Meet-Them-Where-They-Are-Participatory-Action-Research-Adolescent-Girls.pdf
Participatory research with adolescents and youth in the Middle East	A toolkit to explore how social, economic, environmental and political crises shape young people's well-being.	www.gage.odi.org/publication/participatory-research-with-adolescents-and-youth-in-the-middle-east-a-toolkit-to-explore-how-social-economic-environmental-and-political-crises-shape-young-peoples-well-being/
The Evaluator's Cookbook	Participatory evaluation exercises. A resource for work with children and young people.	https://eypagnet.eu/wp-content/uploads/2020/11/the_evaluators_cookbook_participatory_evaluation_exercises_for_young_people.pdf

References

Aboulkacem, A. (2023). *Photovoice 2.0: A research framework for the digital generation* [Doctoral dissertation]. Sam Houston State University.

Akom, A., Shah, A., Nakai, A., & Cruz, T. (2016). Youth participatory action research (YPAR) 2.0: How technological innovation and digital organizing sparked a food revolution in East Oakland. *International Journal of Qualitative Studies in Education, 29*(10). https://doi.org/10.1080/09518398.2016.1201609

Aldana, A., & Richards-Schuster, K. (2021). Youth-led antiracism research: Making a case for participatory methods and creative strategies in developmental science. *Journal of Adolescent Research, 36*(6), 654–685. https://doi.org/10.1177/07435584211043289

Alderson, P. (2007). Competent children? Minors' consent to health care treatment and research. *Social Science & Medicine, 65*(11), 2272–2283. https://doi.org/10.1016/j.socscimed.2007.08.005

Alderson, P., Sutcliffe, K., & Curtis, K. (2006). Children as partners with adults in their medical care. *Archives of Disease in Childhood, 94*(1), 300–303. https://doi.org.10.1136/adc.2005.079442

Al Hweidi, S., Jones, N., Małachowska, A., Pincock, K., Presler-Marshall, E., & Youssef, S. (2022). *Participatory research with adolescents and youth in the Middle East: A toolkit to explore how social, economic, environmental, and political crises shape young people's well-being.* Gender and Adolescence: Global Evidence.

Allison, P. (2001). *Missing data.* SAGE.

Alnihoud, J., & Mansi, R. (2010). An enhancement of major sorting algorithms. *The International Arab Journal of Information Technology, 7*(1), 55–62.

Amsden, J., & VanWynsberghe, R. (2005). Community mapping as a research tool with youth. *Action Research, 3*(4), 357–381. https://doi.org.10.1177/1476750305058487

Anselma, M., Chinapaw, M., & Altenburg, T. (2020). "Not only adults can make good decisions, we as children can do that as well": Evaluating the process of the youth-led participatory action research 'Kids in Action'. *International Journal of Environmental Research and Public Health, 17*(2), 625. https://doi.org.10.3390/ijerph17020625

Appiah, O., & Martey, E. (2015). Magnetic bubble sort algorithm. *International Journal of Computer Applications*, *122*(21), 24–28. https://doi.org.10.5120/21850-5168

Ayllón, S., Lado, S., & Symeonaki, M. (2024). Digitally disengaged and digitally unconfident children in Europe. In H. Holmarsdottir, I. Seland, C. Hyggen, & M. Roth (Eds.), *Understanding the everyday digital lives of children and young people* (pp. 27–55). Palgrave Macmillan. https://doi.org/10.1007/978-3-031-46929-9

Ballonoff, A., Soleimanpour, S., & London, J. (2006). *Youth action for health through youth-led research*. The Haworth Press, Inc. https://doi.org.10.1300/J125v14n01_08

Banati, P., & Lansford, J. (2018). Introduction: Adolescence in a global context. In J. Lansford & P. Banati (Eds.), *Handbook of adolescent development research and its impact on global policy* (pp. 1–24). Oxford. https://doi.org/10.1093/oso/9780190847128.003.0001

Barrett, N. (2016). Interactive spatial sonification of multidimensional data for composition auditory display. *Computer Music Journal*, *40*(2), 47–69. https://www.jstor.org/stable/43829321

Bautista, M., Bertrand, M., Morrel, E., Scorza, A., & Matthews, C. (2013). Participatory action research and city youth: Methodological insights from the council of youth research. *Teachers College Record*, *115*(10), Article 100303.

Bennett, D. (2001). How can I deal with missing data in my study? *Australian and New Zealand Journal of Public Health*, *25*(5), 464–469. https://doi.org.10.1111/j.1467-842X.2001.tb00294.x

Beresford, B., & Sloper, P. (2003). Chronically ill adolescents' experiences of communicating with doctors: A qualitative study. *Journal of Adolescent Health*, *33*(3), 172–179. https://doi.org/10.1016/S1054-139X(03)00047-8

Berman, G., & Albright, K. (2017). *Children and the data cycle: Rights and ethics in a big data world* (no. 2017-05). UNICEF Office of Research – Innocenti, Florence. https://www.unicef-irc.org/publications/907/

Biancalani, G., Orkibi, H., Keisari, S., Guglielmin, M., Bertagna, G., Meola, P., Viezzoli, D., Finco, N., & Testoni, I. (2024). Italian adolescents' perception of tele-psychodrama treatment during the COVID-19 pandemic. *Arts & Health*, *16*(1), 1–14. https://doi.org/10.1080/17533015.2022.2154942

Bidargaddi, N., Musiat, P., Winsall, M., Vogl, G., Blake, V., Quinn, S., Orlowski, S., Antezana, G., & Schrader, G. (2017). Efficacy of a web based guided recommendation service for a curated list of readily available mental health and well-being mobile apps for young people: Randomized controlled trial. *Journal of Medical Internet Research*, *19*(5), Article e141. https://doi.org/10.2196/jmir.6775

Birks, Y., Sloper, P., Lewin, R., & Parsons, J. (2007). Exploring health-related experiences of children and young people with congenital heart disease. *Health Expectations*, *10*(1), 16–29. https://doi.org/101111/1369-7625.2006.00412.x

Blazek, M. (2017). Participatory video with children and young people. In R. Evans, L. Holt, & T. Skelton (Eds.), *Geographies of children and young people: Vol. 2. Methodological approaches* (pp. 243–260). Springer. https://doi.org/10.1007/978-981-287-020-9_20

Bowler, L., Wang, K., Lopatovska, I., & Rosin, M. (2021). The meaning of "participation" in co-design with children and youth: Relationships, roles, and interactions. *Proceedings of the Association for Information Science and Technology, 58*(1), 13–24. https://doi.org/10.1002/pra2.432

Bronfenbrenner, U. (1986). Ecology of the family as a context for human development: Research perspectives. *Developmental Psychology, 22*(6), 723–742. https://doi.org/10.1037/0012-1649.22.6.723

Burstein, K., Bryan, T., & Chao, P. (2005). Promoting self-determination skills among youth with special health needs using participatory action research. *Journal of Developmental and Physical Disabilities, 17*(2), 105–201. https://doi.org/10.1007/s10882-005-3688-1

Cambaco, O., Cossa, H., Farnham, A., Macete, E., Winkler, M., Gross, K., & Munguambe, K. (2024). Applying the photovoice method with adolescents in mining areas in rural Mozambique: Critical reflection and lessons learned. *Global Health Action, 17*(1). https://doi.org/10.1080/16549716.2024.2305506

Campbell, C., & Trotter, J. (2007). 'Invisible young people': The paradox of participation in research. *Vulnerable Children and Youth Studies, 2*(1), 32–39. https://doi.org/10.1080/17450120701214053

Caplan, S. (2003). Preference for online social interaction: A theory of problematic internet use and psychosocial well-being. *Communications Research, 30* (6), 625–648. https://doi.org/10.1177/0093650203257842

Capous-Desyllas, M., Mountz, S., & Pestine-Stevens, A. (2019). Unpacking the layers of community engagement, participation, and knowledge co-creation when representing the visual voices of LGBTQ former foster youth. *Engaged Scholarship and Arts, 5*(2), Article 161. https://doi.org/10.15402/esj.v5i2.68342

Cavet, J., & Sloper, P. (2004). The participation of children and young people in decisions about UK service development. *Child: Care, Health & Development, 30*(6), 613–621. https://doi.org/10.1111/j.1365-2214.2004.00470.x

Centre for Electronic and Computer Music. (2021, July 7). Introduction to MIDI and computer music. https://cecm.indiana.edu/361/midi.html

Checkoway, B., & Richards-Schuster, K. (2003). Youth participation in community evaluation research. *American Journal of Evaluation, 24*(1), 21–33. https://doi.org/10.1177/109821400302400103

Chen, P., Weiss, F., Nicholson, H., & Girls Incorporated. (2010). Girls Study Girls Inc.: Engaging girls in evaluation through participatory action research. *American Journal of Community Psychology, 46*(1–2), 228–237. https://doi.org/10.1007/s10464-010-9328-7

Cheng, V., Davenport, T., Johnson, D., Vella, K., Mitchell, J., & Hickie, I. (2018). An app that incorporates gamification, mini-games, and social connection to improve men's mental health and well-being (MindMax): Participatory design process. *JMIR Mental Health*, *5*(4), Article e11068. http://mental.jmir.org/2018/4/e11068/

Children's Commissioner. (2017). *The case for a UNCRC general comment on children's rights and digital media*. Children's Commissioner for England.

Cibrian, F., Ley-Flores, J., Newbold, J., Singh, A., Bianchi-Berthouze, N., & Tentori, M. (2020). Interactive sonification to assist children with autism during motor therapeutic interventions. *Personal and Ubiquitous Computing*, *25*, 391–410. https://doi.org/10.1007/s00779-020-01479-z

Clifford, B. (2013). Research: The ubiquitous handmaiden of professionalism. In R. Bayne & G. Jinks (Eds.), *Applied psychology: Research, training and practice* (pp. 16–32). SAGE. https://doi.org/10.4135/9781526401526

Coad, J. (2007). Using art-based techniques in engaging children and young people in health care consultations and/or researchers. *Journal of Research in Nursing*, *12*(5), 487–497. https://doi.org/10.1177/1744987107081250

Coad, J., & Coad, N. (2008). Children and young people's preference of thematic design and colour for their hospital environment. *Journal of Child Health Care*, *12*(1), 33–48. https://doi.org/10.1177/1367493507085617

Coad, J., & Shaw, K. (2008). Is children's choice in health care rhetoric or reality? A scoping review. *Journal of Adolescent Nursing*, *64*(4), 318–327. https://doi.org/10.1111/j.1365-2648.2008.04801.x

Cook, A., & Krueger-Henney, P. (2017). Group work that examines systems of power with young people: Youth participatory action research. *The Journal for Specialists in Group Work*, *42*(2), 176–193. https://doi.org/10.1080/01933922.2017.1282570

Cooper, K., Gillmore, C., & Hogg, L. (2016). Experience-based co-design in an adult psychological therapies service. *Journal of Mental Health*, *25*(1), 36–40. https://doi.org/10.3109/09638237.2015.1101423

Coyne, I. (2006). Consultation with children in hospital: Children, parents' and nurses' perspectives. *Journal of Clinical Nursing*, *15*(1), 61–71. https://doi.org/10.1111/j.1365-2702.2005.01247.x

(2008). Children's participation in consultations and decision-making at health service level: A review of the literature. *International Journal of Nursing Studies*, *45*(11), 1682–1689. https://doi.org/10.1016/j.ijnurstu.2008.05.002

Coyne, I., Prizeman, G., Sheehan, A., Malone, H., & While, A. (2016). An e-health intervention to support the transition of young people with long-term illnesses to adult healthcare services: Design and early use. *Patient Education and Counselling*, *99*(9), 1496–1504. https://doi.org/10.1016/j.pec.2016.06.005

Crane, S., & Broome, M. (2017). Understanding ethical issues of research participation from the perspective of participating children and adolescents: A systematic review. *Worldwide Evidence Based Nursing*, *14*(3), 200–209. https://doi.org/10.1111/wvn.12209

Curtis, K., Liabo, K., Roberts, H., & Roberts, H. (2004). Consulted but not heard: A qualitative study of young people's views of their local health service. *Health Expectations*, *7*(2), 149–156. https://doi.org/10.1111/j.1369-7625.2004.00265.x

Daniels, S., & Willard, V. (2023). Social media interactions after diagnosis: Social experiences of adolescents and young adults (AYA) with cancer. *Journal of Psychosocial Oncology*, *42*(3), 1–14. https://doi.org/10.1080/07347332.2023.2249876

Davis, S. R., Peters, D., Calvo, R., Sawyer, S., Foster, J., & Smith, L. (2018). "Kiss my asthma": Using participatory design approach to develop a self-management app with young people with asthma. *Journal of Asthma*, *55*(9), 1018–1027. https://doi.org/10.1080/02770903.2017.1388391

Dennis, S., Gaulocher, S., Caripiano, R., & Brown, D. (2009). Participatory photo mapping (PPM): Exploring an integrated method for health and place research with young people. *Health & Place*, *15*, 466–473. https://doi.org/10.1016/j.healthplace.2008.08.004

Department of Health. (2003). *Getting the right start: National Service Framework for Children*. Department of Health. www.doh.gov.uk/nsf/children/gettingtherightstart

DeSmet, A., Van Ryckeghem, D., Compernolle, S., Baranowski, T., Thompson, D., Crombez, G., Poels, K., Van Lippevelde, W., Bastiaensens, S., Van Cleemput, K., Vandebosch, H., & De Bourdeaudhuij, I. (2014). A meta-analysis of serious digital games for healthy lifestyle promotion. *Preventive Medicine*, *69*, 95–107. https://doi.org/10.1016/j.ypmed.2014.08.026

De Winter, M., Baerveldt, C., & Kooistra, J. (1999). Enabling children: Participation as a new perspective on child-health promotion. *Child: Care, Health, and Development*, *25*(1), 15–25. https://doi.org/10.1046/j.1365-2214.1999.00073.x

De Winter, M., & Noom, M. (2003). Someone who treats you as an ordinary human being . . . homeless youth examine the quality of professional care. *British Journal of Social Work*, *33*(3), 325–337. https://doi.org/10.1093/bjsw/33.3.325

Dolan, P., Brady, B., O'Regan, C., Brumovska, T., Canavan, J., & Forkan, C. (2010). *Big Brothers Big Sisters (BBBS) of Ireland: Evaluation study. Report 1: randomised control trial and implementation report.* UNESCO Child and Family Research Centre, National University of Ireland Galway.

Dong, Y., & Peng, C. (2013). Principled missing data methods for researchers. *SpringerPlus*, *2*, Article 222. https://doi.org/10.1186/2193-1801-2-222

Dunn, V., & Mellor, T. (2017). Creative, participatory projects with young people: Reflections over five years. *Research for All*, *1*(2), 284–299. https://doi.org/10.18546/RFA.01.2.05

Epstein, I., Stevens, B., McKeever, P., & Baruchel, S. (2006). Photo elicitation interview (PEI): Using photos to elicit children's perspectives. *International Journal of Qualitative Methods*, *5*(3), 1–11. https://doi.org/10.1177/160940690600500301

Esau, D., Ho, P., Blair, G., Duffy, D., O'Hara, N., Kapoor, V., & Ajiko, M. (2016). Engaging youth in rural Uganda in articulating health priorities through photovoice. *Global Health Promotion*, *24*(3), 59–67. https://doi.org/10.1177/1757975915614167

Evans, R. (2017). Critical reflections on participatory dissemination: Co-producing researcher messages with young people. In R. Evans, L. Holt, & T. Skelton (Eds.), *Geographies of children and young people: Vol. 2. Methodological approaches* (pp. 1–30). Springer. https://doi.org/10.1007/978-981-4585-89-7_27-1

Fallon, S., Smith, J., Morgan, S., Stoner, M., & Austin, C. (2008). 'Pizza, patients and points of view': Involving young people in the design of a post registration module entitled the adolescent with cancer. *Nurse Education in Practice*, *8*(2), 140–147. https://doi.org/10.1016/j.nepr.2007.07.005

Farthing, R. (2012). Why youth participation? Some justifications and critiques of youth participation using New Labour's youth policies as a case study. *Youth & Policy*, *109*, 71–97.

Fenge, L., Hodges, C., & Cutts, W. (2011). Seen but seldom heard: Creative participatory methods in a study of youth and risk. *International Journal of Qualitative Methods*, *10*(4), 418–430. https://doi.org/10.1177/160940691101000408

Firth, J., Torous, J., & Yung, A. (2016). Ecological momentary assessment and beyond: The rising interest in e-mental health research. Journal of Psychiatric Research, *80*, 3–4. https://doi.org/10.1016/j.jpsychires.2016.05.002

Fisher, J., & Jensen, T. (2013). From participatory design to co-creation: Using social media to engage youth. *ACIS 2013: Information systems: Transforming the Future: Proceedings of the 24th Australasian Conference on Information Systems*, pp. 1–10.

Flicker, S. (2008). Who benefits from community-based participatory research? A case study of the positive youth project. *Health Education & Behaviour*, *35* (1), 70–86. https://doi.org/10.1177/1090198105285927

Flicker, S., & Guta, A. (2008). Ethical approaches to adolescent participation in sexual health research. *Journal of Adolescent Health*, *42*(1), 3–10. https://doi.org/10.1016/j.jadohealth.2007.07.017

Flicker, S., Maley, O., Ridgley, A., Biscope, S., Lombardo, C., & Skinner, H. (2008). e-PAR: Using technology and participatory action research to engage youth in health promotion. *Action Research*, *6*(3), 285–303. https://doi.org/10.1177/1476750307083711

Foster-Fishman, P., Nowell, B., Deacon, Z., Nievar, M., & McCann, P. (2005). Using methods that matter: The impact of reflection, dialogue and voice. *American Journal of Community Psychology*, *36*(3–4), 275–291. https://doi.org/10.1007/s10464-005-8626-y

Fountain, S., Hale, R., Spencer, N., Morgan, J., James, L., & Stewart, K. (2021). A 10-year systematic review of photovoice projects with youth in the United States. *Health Promotion Practice*, *22*(6), 767–777. https://doi.org/10.1177/15248399211019978

Fox, M., Mediratta, K., Ruglis, J., Stoudt, B., Shah, S., & Fine, M. (2010). Critical youth engagement: Participatory action research and organizing. In L. Sherrod, J. Torney-Puta, & C. Flanagan (Eds.), *Handbook of research and policy on civic engagement with youth* (pp. 621–649). Wiley Press. https://doi.org/10.1002/9780470767603.ch23

Fox, R. (2013). Resisting participation: Critiquing participatory research methodologies with young people. *Journal of Youth Studies, 16*(8), 986–999. https://doi.org/10.1080/13676261.2013.815698

Freire, K., Pope, R., Jeffrey, K., Andrews, K., Nott, M., & Bowman, T. (2022). Engaging with children and adolescents: A systematic review of participatory methods and approaches in research informing the development of health resources and interventions. *Adolescent Research Review, 7*, 335–354. https://doi.org/10.1007/s40894-022-00181-w

Gal, T. (2017). An ecological model of child and youth participation. *Children and Youth Services, 79*, 57–64. https://doi.org/10.1016/j.childyouth.2017.05.029

Geppert, A. (2023). *Design for equivalence: Mutual learning and participant gains in participatory design process* [Dissertation]. Illinois Institute of Technology.

Gibbs, L., Kornbluh, M. K., Bell, S., & Ozer, E. (2020). Using technology to scale up youth-led participatory action research: A systematic review. *Journal of Adolescent Health, 67*(2), S14–S23. https://doi.org/10.1016/j.adohealth.2019.10.019

Gkintoni, E., Vantaraki, F., Skoulidi, C., Anatassopoulos, P., & Vantarakis, A. (2024). Promoting physical and mental health among children and adolescents via gamification: A conceptual systematic review. *Behavioural Science, 14*(2), Article 102. https://doi.org/10.3390/bs14020102

Goessling, K. (2020). Youth participatory action research, trauma and the arts: Designing youthspaces for equity and healing. *International Journal of Qualitative Studies in Education, 33*(1), 12–31. https://doi.org/10.1080/09518398.2019.1678783

Goodhart, F. W., Hsu, J., Baek, J. H., Coleman, A. L., Maresca, F. M., & Miller, M. B. (2006). A view through a different lens: Photovoice as a tool for student advocacy. *Journal of American College Health, 55*(1), 53–56. https://doi.org/10.3200/JACH.55.1.53-56

Gordon, E., Elwood, S., & Mitchell, K. (2016). Critical spatial learning: participatory mapping, spatial histories, and youth civic engagement. *Children's Geographies, 14*(5), 1–15. https://doi.org/10.1080/14733285.2015.1136736

Grady, C., Wiener, L., Abdoler, E., Trauernicht, E., Zadeh, S., Diekema, D., Wilfond, B., & Wendler, D. (2014). Assent in research: The voices of adolescence. *Journal of Adolescent Health, 54*(5), 515–520. https://doi.org/10.1016/j.jadohealth.2014.02.005

Green, E., & Kloos, B. (2009). Facilitating youth participation in a context of forced migration: A photovoice project in Northern Uganda. *Journal of Refugee Studies, 22*(4), 460–482. https://doi.org/10.1092/jrs/fep026

Greer, S., Ramo, D., Chang, Y., Fu, M., Moskowitz, J., & Haritatos J. (2019). Use of chatbot "Vivibot" to deliver positive psychology skills and promote well-being among young people after cancer treatment: Randomized controlled feasibility trial. *JMIR Mhealth and Uhealth, 7*(10), e15018. https://doi.org/10.2196/15018

Gregorious, S. (2017). Combining multiple qualitative methods in research on young disabled people in the Global South. In R. Evans, L. Holt, & T. Skelton (Eds.), *Geographies of children and young people: Vol. 2. Methodological approaches* (pp. 285–302). Springer. https://doi.org/10.1007/978-981-287-020-9_10

Hagen, P., Collin, P., Metcalf, A., Nicholas, M., Rahilly, K., & Swainston, N. (2012). *Participatory design of evidence-based online youth mental health promotion, prevention, early intervention and treatment.* Young and Well Cooperative Research Centre.

Halström, I., & Elander, G. (2004). Decision-making during hospitalization: Parents' and children's involvement. *Journal of Clinical Nursing, 13*(3), 367–375. https://doi.org/10.1046/j.1365-2702.2003.00877.x

Hampshire, K., Porter, G., Owusu, S., Mariwah, S., Abane, A., Robson, E., Munthali, A., Mashiri, M., Maponya, G., & Bourdillon, M. (2012). Taking the long view: Temporal considerations in the ethics of children's research activity and knowledge production. *Children's Geographies, 10*(2), 219–232. https://doi.org/10.1080/14733285.2012.667921

Harper, G., & Carver, L. (1999). "Out of the mainstream": Youth as partners in collaborative research: Exploring the benefits and challenges. *Health Education & Behaviour, 26*(2), 250–265. https://www.jstor.org/stable/45055036

Harragan, A. (2021). The 'do-ers' and the 'do nothings': (Non)Participation in community, recreation and place amongst young people in Manchester, UK. In L. Moran, K. Reilly, & B. Brady (Eds.), *Narrating childhood with children and young people: Diverse contexts, methods and stories of everyday life* (pp. 133–162). Palgrave Macmillan. https://doi.org/10.1007/978-3-030-55647-1_6

Hart, R. (1992). *Children's participation from tokenism to citizenship.* UNICEF International Child Development Centre.

Healy, K. (2021). Diversifying inclusive research with young people. In T. Wulf-Andersen, R. Folleso, & T. Olsen (Eds.), *Involving methods in youth research: Reflections on participation and power* (pp. 261–266). Palgrave Macmillan. https://doi.org/10.1007/978-3-030-75941-4_11

Hermann, T. (2002). *Sonification for exploratory data analysis* [Unpublished doctoral dissertation]. Technischen Fakultat der Universitat Biefeld.

Hermann, T., Hunt, A., & Neuhoff, J. (2011). *The sonification handbook.* COST.

Hermann, T., & Ritter, H. (1999). *Listen to your data: Model-based sonification for data analysis.* International Symposium on Intelligent Multimedia and Distance Education.

Hill, J. (2013). Using participatory and visual methods to address power and identity in research with young people. *Graduate Journal of Social Sciences, 10* (2), 132–151. https://hdl.handle.net/10547/622331

Hodges, H. R., Gillespie, S., Cherubni, F. D. S., Ibrahim, S. A., Gibson, H., Ali Daad, A. M., Davis, S. L., Abdi, S. M., Senesathith, V., Food, Culture, and Health Study Data Collection Team, & Ferguson, G. M. (2023). Ethical applications of digital community-based research with Black immigrant and refugee youth and families. *American Psychologist*, *79*(1), 9–23. https://doi.org/10.1037/amp0001191

Holland, S., Renold, E., Ross, N., & Hillman, A. (2010). Power, agency and participatory agendas: A critical exploration of young people's engagement in participative qualitative research. *Childhood*, *17*(3), 360–375. https://doi.org/10.1177/0907568210369310

Holmarsdottir, H. (2024). The digital divide: Understanding vulnerability and risk in children and young people's everyday digital lives. In H. Holmarsdottir, I. Seland, C. Hyggen, & M. Roth (Eds.), *Understanding the everyday digital lives of children and young people* (pp. 57–82). Palgrave Macmillan. https://doi.org/10.1007/978-3-031-46929-9

Information Commissioner's Office. (2022). *Age-appropriate design: A code of practice for online services*. Information Commissioner's Office.

Israel, B. A., Parker, E. A., Rowe, Z., Salvatore, A., Minkler, M., López, J., Butz, A., Mosley, A., Coates, L., Lambert, G., Potito, P. A., Brenner, B., Rivera, M., Romero, H., Thompson, B., Coronado, G., & Halstead, S. (2005). Community-based participatory research: Lessons learned from the Centers for Children's Environmental Health and Disease Prevention Research. *Environmental Health Perspectives*, *113*(10), 1463–1471. https://doi.org/10.1289/ehp.7675

Ito-Jaeger, S., Perez, E., Curran, T., & Crawford, P. (2022) What's up with everyone? A qualitative study on young people's perceptions of cocreated online animations to promote mental health literacy. *Health Expectations*, *25* (4), 1633–1642. https://doi.org/10.1111/hex.13507

James, C., Davis, K., Flores, A., Francis, J., Pettingil, L., Rundle, M., & Gardner, H. (2009). *Young people, ethics and the new digital media: A synthesis from the Gooplay Project*. Massachusetts Institute of Technology.

Jull, J., Giles, A., & Graham, D. (2017). Community-based participatory research and integrated knowledge translation: Advancing the co-creation of knowledge. *Implementation Science*, *12*(150). https://doi.org/10.1186/s13012-017-0696-3

Kennan, D., & Dolan, P. (2017). Justifying children and young people's involvement in social research: Assessing harm and benefit. *Irish Journal of Sociology*, 25(3), 297–314. https://doi.org/10.1177/0791603517711860

King, P., Cormac, D., Edwards, R., Harris, R., & Paine, S. (2022). Co-design for indigenous and other children and young people from priority social groups: A systematic review. *SSM Population Health*, *18*, Article 101077. https://doi.org/10.1016/j.ssmph.2022.101077

King's Fund. (2013). *Experience-based co-design toolkit*. https://www.pointofcarefoundation.org.uk/resource/experience-based-co-design-ebcd-toolkit/step-by-step-guide/1-experience-based-co-design/

Kirby, P., & Bryson, S. (2002). *Measuring the magic? Evaluating and researching young people's participation in public decision making*. Carnegie Young People Initiative.

Kirby, P., Lanyon, C., Cronin, K., & Sinclair, R. (2003). *Building a culture of participation: Involving children and young people in policy, service planning, delivery and evaluation* [Research Report]. Department for Education and Skills.

Kohfeldt, D., & Langhout, R. (2012). The Five Shys method: A tool for developing problem definitions in collaboration with children. *Journal of Community & Applied Social Psychology*, *22*(4), 316–329. https://doi.org/10.1002/casp.1114

Kornbluh, M., Watling, J., & Ozer, E. (2016). Scaling-up youth-led social justice efforts through an online school-based social network. *American Journal Community Psychology*, *57*(3–4), 266–279. https://doi.org/10.1002/ajcp.12042

Kovačič, T., Forkan, C., Dolan, P., & Rodriguez, L. (2021). *Enabling an inclusive and equitable quality education for all*. UNESCO Child and Family Research Centre, National University of Ireland, Galway.

Krane, V., Klevan, T., & Sommer, M. (2021). Youth involvement in research: Participation, contribution and dynamic processes. In T. Wulf-Andersen, R. Folleso, & T. Olsen (Eds.), *Involving methods in youth research: Reflections on participation and power* (pp. 46–72). Palgrave Macmillan. https://doi.org/10.1007/978-3-030-75941-4_3

Laaksonen, S. (2018). *Survey methodology and missing data: Tools and techniques for practitioners*. Routledge.

Labusch, A., Eickelmann, B., Casamassina, G., Drossel, K., Gudmundsdottir, G., Kazani, A., Misfund, L., Symeonaki, M., & Teidla-Kunitsón, G. (2024). Children's and young people's ICT experiences in school education: Participatory research design to engage children and young people as experts in research. In H. Holmarsdottir, I. Seland, C. Hyggen, & M. Roth (Eds.), *Understanding the everyday digital lives of children and young people* (pp. 143–165). Palgrave Macmillan. https://doi.org/10.1007/978-3-031-46929-9

Lamb, A., & Johnson, L. (2007). An information skills workout: Wikis and collaborative writing. *Teacher Librarian*, *34*(5), 57–59. https://hdl.handle.net/1805/8702

Larkin, M., Boden, Z., & Newton, E. (2015). On the brink of genuinely collaborative care: Experience-based co-design in mental health. *Qualitative Health Research*, *25*(1), 1463–1476. https://doi.org/10.1177/1049732315576494

Larsson, I., Staland-Nyman, C., Svedberg, P., Nygren, J., & Carlsson, I.-M. (2018). Children and young people's participation in developing interventions in health and well-being: A scoping review. *BMC Health Services Research*, *18*, Article 507. https://doi.org/10.1186/s12913-018-3219-2

Leask, C., Sandlund, M., Skelton, D., Altenburg, T., Cardon, G., Chinapaw, M., De Bourdeaudhjui, I., Verloigne, M., & Chastin, S. (2019). Framework, principles and recommendations for utilising participatory methodologies in the co-creation and evaluation of public health interventions. *Research Involvement and Engagement*, *5*, Article 2. https://doi.org/10.1186/s40900-018-0136-9

Leeman, R., DeMartini, K., Gueorguieva, R., Nogueira, C., Corbin, W., Neighbors, C., & O'Malley, S. (2016). Randomized controlled trial of a very brief, multi component web-based alcohol intervention for undergraduates with a focus on protective behavioural strategies. *Journal of Consulting and Clinical Psychology*, *84*(11), 1008–1015. https://doi.org/10.1037/ccp0000132.

Lenzi, S., & Ciuccarelli, P. (2020). Intentionality and design in the data sonification of social issues. *Big Data & Society*, *7*(2), 1–8. https://doi.org/10.1177/2053951720944603

Lightfoot, J., & Sloper, P. (2002). *Having a say in health: Guidelines for involving young patients in health service development.* Social Policy Research Unit, University of York.

(2003). Having a say in health: Involving young people with chronic illness or physical disability in local health services development. *Children & Society*, *17*(4), 277–290. https://doi.org/10.1002/CHI.748

Little, R. J. A. (1988). A test of missing completely at random for multivariate data with missing values. *Journal of the American Statistical Association*, *83* (404), 1198–1202. https://10.1080/01621459.1988.10478722

Livingood, W., Monticalvo, D., Bernhardt, J., Wells, K., Harris, T., Kee, K., Hayes, J., George, D., & Woodhouse, L. (2017). Engaging adolescents through participatory and qualitative research methods to develop a digital communication intervention to reduce adolescent obesity. *Health Education & Behaviour*, *44*(4), 570–580. https://doi.org/10.1177/1090198116677216

Lohmeyer, B. (2019). 'Keen as fuck': Youth participation in qualitative research as 'parallel projects'. *Qualitative Research*, *20*(1), 39–55. https://doi.org/10.1177/1468794118816627

Lundy, L. (2007). 'Voice' is not enough: Conceptualising Article 12 of the United Nations Convention on the Rights of the Child. *British Educational Research Journal*, *33*(6), 927–942. https://doi.org/10.1080/01411920701657033

(2018). In defence of tokenism? Implementing children's right to participate in collective decision-making. *Childhood*, *25*(3), 340–354. https://doi.org/10.1177/0907568218777292

Lupton, D. (2021). Young people's use of digital health technologies in the global north: Narrative review. *Journal of Medical Internet Research*, *23*(1), e18286. https://doi.org/10.2196/18286

Maftei, A., & Merlici, I. (2023). How should children and adolescents use digital devices in a healthy manner, and how should parents employ digital control? A mapping review of the literature. *International Journal of Social and Educational Innovation*, *10*(19), 134–165.

Maglajlic, R., & RTK PAR UNICEF BiH Team. (2004). Right to Know, UNICEF BiH – Developing a commination strategy for the prevention of HIV/AIDS among young people through participatory action research. *Childcare in Practice*, *10*(2), 127–139. https://doi.org/10.1080/1357527041000001693358

Mallan, K., & Singh, P. (2010). The challenges of participatory research with 'tech-savvy' youth. *Journal of Youth Studies*, *13*(2), 255–272. https://doi.org/10.1080/13676260903295059

Malloy, J., Partidge, S., Kemper, J., Braakhuis, A., & Roy, R. (2023). Co-design of digital health interventions with young people: A scoping review. *Digital Health*, *9*. https://doi.org/10.1177/20552076231219117

Martel, R., Darragh, M., Lawrence, A., Shepherd, M., Wihongi, T., & Goodyear-Smith, F. (2019). YouthCHAT as a primary care e-screening tool for mental health issues among Te Tai Tokerau youth: Protocol for a co-design study. *JMIR Research Protocols*, *8*(1), e12108.

Martin, P., Alberti, C., Gottot, S., Bourmaud, A., & Rochebrochard, E. (2023). Young people's proposals for a web-based intervention for sexual health promotion: A French qualitative study. *BMC Public Health*, *23*, Article 1389. https://doi.org/10.1186/s12889-023-16257-8

McCurdie, S., Taneva, S., Casselam, M., Young, M., McDaniel, C., Ho, W., & Cafazzo, J. (2012). mHealth consumer apps: The case of user-centred design. *Bioemed Instrumentation & Technology*, 46–56. https://doi.org/10.2345/0899-8205-46.s2.49

McMorrow, S., & Smith, S. (2016). Photovoice as a participatory assessment approach for examining disparities in obesity for African American teen girls. *The International Journal of Health, Wellness and Society*, *6*(3), 77–85. https://doi.org/10.1177/1524839921106571

Merves, M., Rodgers, C., Silver, E., Sclafane, J., & Bauman, L. (2015). Engaging and sustaining adolescents in community-based participatory research. *Family and Community Health*, *38*(1), 22–32. https://doi.org/10.1097/FCH.0000000000000057

Mitra, D., & McCormick, P. (2017). Ethical dilemmas of youth participatory action research in a democratic setting. *International Journal of Inclusive Education*, *21*(3), 248–258. https://doi.org/10.1080/13603116.2016.1260835

Moran, L., Reilly, K., & Brady, B. (2021). Introduction. In L. Moran, K. Reilly, & B. Brady (Eds.), *Narrating childhood with children and young people: Diverse contexts, methods and stories of everyday life* (pp. 1–34). Palgrave Macmillan.

Morrow, V. (2001). Using qualitative methods to elicit young people's perspectives on their environments: Some ideas for community health initiatives. *Health Education Research*, *16*(3), 255–268. https://doi.org/10.1093/her/16.3.255

Moskowitz, J. T., Carrico, A. W., Duncan, L. G., Cohn, M. A., Cheung, E. O., Batchelder, A., Martinez, L., Segawa, E., Acree, M., & Folkman, S. (2017). Randomized controlled trial of a positive affect intervention for people newly diagnosed with HIV. *Journal of Consulting and Clinical Psychology*, *85*(5), 409–423. https://doi.org/10.1037/ccp0000188

Moyer, M. (2023). *Engaging technologies of the self with youth: A critical contemplative pedagogy action research project* [Doctoral dissertation]. Miami University. https://etd.ohiolink.edu/apexprod/rws_olink/r/1501/10?clear=10&p10_accession_num=miami1689338623782483

Nagai, H., Nakazawa, E., & Akabayashi, A. (2022). The creation of the Belmont Report and its effect on ethical principles: A historical study. *Monash*

Bioethical Review, 40(2), 157–170. https://doi.org/10.1007/s40592-022-00165-5

The National Commission for the Protection of Human Subjects of Biomedical and Behavioural Research. (1978). *The Belmont Report: Ethical principles and guidelines for the protection of human subjects of research*. DHEW. https://videocast.nih.gov/pdf/ohrp_belmont_report.pdf

Neuhoff, J. (2019). *Is sonification doomed to fail?* The 25th International Conference on Auditory Display (ICAD, 2019). Northumbria University.

NSPCC. (2018). *Gillick competency and Fraser guidelines*. NSPCC Knowledge and Information Services. https://learning.nspcc.org.uk/research-resources/resources.

Ohno, T. (1987). *Toyota production system*. Productivity Press. (Originally published in 1978 in Japanese)

Olesen, E. S. B. (2019). Overcoming diagnostic uncertainty: Clinicians, patients and institutional work in practice. *Scandinavian Journal of Disability Research, 21*(1), 186–196. https://doi.org/10.16993/sjdr.638

Olesen, E. (2021). Self-filming as a method in youth research. In T. Wulf-Andersen, R. Folleso, & T. Olsen (Eds.), *Involving methods in youth research. Reflections on participation and power* (pp. 72–94). Palgrave Macmillan. https://doi.org/10.1007/978-3-030-75941-4_4

Oliveira, C., Pinto, R., Saraiva, B., Tebar, W., Delfino, L., Franco, M., Silva, C., & Christofaro, D. (2019). Effects of video games on children and adolescents: A systematic review and meta-analysis. *Scandinavian Journal of Medicine and Science Sports, 30*(1), 4–12. https://doi.org/10.1111/sms.13539

Oppong-Odiseng, A., & Heycock, E. (1997). Adolescent health services – through their eyes. *Adolescent Health Services, 77*(2), 115–119. https://doi.org/10.1136/adc.77.2.115

O'Reilly, M., & Parker, N. (2014). *Doing mental health research with adolescents and children*. SAGE.

Oridota, O., Shetty, A., Elaiho, C. R., Phelps, L., Cheng, S., & Vangeepuram, N. (2023). Perspectives from diverse stakeholders in a youth community-based participatory research project. *Evaluation and Program Planning, 99*, Article 102305. https://doi.org/10.1016/j.evalprogplan.2023.102305

Ortiz-Pena, M., Navarro-Oliva, E., Echeverria-Cerda, F., Guzman-Facundo, F., Pacheco-Perez, L., & Rodriguez-Puente, L. (2019). Social support perceived through Facebook, family and friends and alcohol consumption in adolescents. *Health and Addictions, 19*(2), 103–110. https://doi.org/10.4018/ijcbpl.2012010103

Ospina-Pinillos, L., Davenport, T. A., Ricci, C. S., Milton, A. C., Scott, E. A., & Hickie, I. B. (2018). Developing a mental health eClinic to improve access to and quality of mental health care for young people: Using participatory design as research methodologies. *Journal of Medical Internet Research, 20*(5), e188. http://www.jmir.org/2018/5/e188/

Østergaard, J. (2021). Photo-talk and music-talk among young people (formerly) in care. In T. Wulf-Andersen, R. Folleso, & T. Olsen (Eds.), *Involving methods in youth research: Reflections on participation and power* (pp. 125–154). Palgrave Macmillan. https://doi.org/10.1007/978-3-030-75941-4_6

Ozer, E. (2016). Youth-led participatory action research: Developmental and equity perspectives. *Advances in Child Development and Behaviour, 50*, 189–207. https://doi.org/10.1016/bs.acdb.2015.11.006

(2017). Youth-led participatory action research: Overview and potential for enhancing adolescent development. *Child Development Perspectives, 11*(3), 173–177. https://doi.org/10.1111/cdep.12228

Ozer, E., Afifi, R., Gibbs, L., & Mathur, R. (2018). Youth engagement and participation: Field-building across research and practice. *Journal of Adolescent Health, 63*(6), 671–672. https://doi.org/10.1016/j.jadohealth.2018.09.011.

Ozer, E., & Douglas, L. (2013). The impact of participatory research on urban teens: An experimental evaluation. *American Journal of Community Psychology, 51*(1–2). 66–75. https://doi.org/10.1007/s10464-012-9546-2

(2015). Assessing the key processes of youth-led participatory research: Psychometric analysis and application of an observational rating scale. *Youth & Society, 47*(1), 29–50. https://doi.org/10.1177/0044118X12468011

Ozer, E., & Piatt, A. (2017). *Adolescent participation in research: Innovation, rationale and next steps*. UNICEF–Innocenti Research Brief.

Ozer, E., Ritterman, L., & Wanis, M. (2010). Participatory action research (PAR) in middle school: Opportunities, constraints and key processes. *American Journal of Community Psychology, 46*(1), 152–166. https://doi.org/10.1007/s1046-010-9335-8

Ozer, E., & Wright, D. (2012). Beyond school spirit: The effects of youth-led participatory action research in two urban high schools. *Journal of Research on Adolescence, 22*(2), 267–283. https://doi.org/10.1111/j.1532-7795.2012.00780.x

Palmer, V., Weavell, W., Callander, R., Piper, D., Richard, L., Maher, L., Boyd, H., Herman, H., Furler, J., Gunn, J., Iedema, R., & Robert, G. (2019). The participatory Zeitgeist: An explanatory theoretical model of change in an era of coproduction and codesign in healthcare improvement. *Medical Humanities, 45*(3), 247–257. https://doi.org/10.1136/medhum-2017-011398

Patchen, L., Ellis, L, Xuyen, T., Ott, C., Chang, K., Araya, B., Atreyapurapu, S., Alyusu, A., & Gaines Lanzi, R. (2020). Engaging African American youth in development if a serious mobile game for sexual health education: Mixed methods study. *JMIR Serious Games, 8*(1), e16254. https://doi.org/10.2196/16254.

Patton, G. C., Sawyer, S. M., Santelli, J. S., Ross, D. A., Afifi, R., Allen, N. B., Arora, M., Azzopardi, P., Baldwin, W., Bonell, C., Kakuma, R., Kennedy, E., Mahon, J., McGovern, T., Mokdad, A. H., Patel, V., Petroni, S., Reavley, N., Taiwo, K., Waldfogel, J., . . . Viner, R. M. (2016). Our future: A Lancet commission on adolescent health and wellbeing. *Lancet, 387* (10036), 2423–2478. https://doi.org/101016/A0140-6736(16)00579-1

Pauletto, S., & Walus, B. (2018). *Reflecting on the role of sound in an immersive multimedia intervention for health communication.* https://eprints.whiterose.ac.uk/139210/

Percy-Smith, B. (2007). "You think you know?... You have no idea": Youth participation in health policy development. *Health Education Research*, *22*(6), 879–894. https://doi.org/10.1093/her/cym032

Petrie, S., Fiorelli, L., & O'Donnell, K. (2006). 'If we help you what will change?': Participatory research with young people. *Journal of Social Welfare and Family Law*, *28*(1), 31–45. https://doi.org/101080/09649060600762332

Ponto, H. (2017). *Young people's everyday lives in the city: Living and experiencing daily places.* University of Helsinki: Department of Geosciences and Geography. http://hdl.handle.net/10138/199511

Powers, J., & Tiffany, J. (2006). Engaging youth in participatory research and evaluation. *Journal of Public Health Management Practice*, S79–S87. https://doi.org/10.1097/00124784-200611001-00015

Primack, B., Carroll, M., McNamara, M., Klem, M., King, B., Rich, M., Chan, C., & Nayak, S. (2012). Role of video games in improving health-related outcomes. *American Journal of Preventive Medicine*, *42*(6), 630–638. https://doi.org/10.1016/j.amepre.2012.02.023

Prout, A. (2002). Researching children as social actors: An introduction to the children 5–16 programme. *Children & Society*, *16*(2), 67–76. https://doi.org/10.1002/CHI.710

Purdy, N., & Spears, B. (2020). Co-participatory approaches to research with children and young people. *Pastoral Care in Education*, *38*(3), 187–190. https://doi.org/10.1080/02643944.2020.1788816

Reilly, K., & Hughes, T. (2021). Exploring childhood in Ireland: Narrating the places and spaces of everyday life. In L. Moran, K. Reilly, & B. Brady (Eds.), *Narrating childhood with children and young people: Diverse contexts, methods and stories of everyday life* (pp. 189–212). Palgrave Macmillan. https://doi.org/10.1007/978-3-030-55647-1_8

Rodriguez, L. (2016). *Understanding adolescent adjustment to maternal cancer: A study of personal experiences and psychosocial factors that promote adjustment* [Doctoral dissertation]. National University of Ireland, Galway.

Rodriguez, L., & Brown, T. (2009). From voice to agency: Guiding principles for participatory action research with youth. *New Directions for Youth Development*, *2009*(123), 19–34. https://doi.org/10.1002/yd.312

Rodriguez, L., Dolan, P., & Brady, B. (2018). *Exploring the impact of mentoring relationships in adolescent empathy: A mixed methods approach.* UNESCO Child and Family Research Centre, National University of Ireland, Galway.

Rogers, A., D'Angelo, L., & Futterman, D. (1994). Guidelines for adolescent participation in research: Current realities and possible solutions. *IRN: Ethics & Human Research*, *16*(4), 1–6. https://doi.org/10.2307/3563665

Sartain, S., Clarke, C., & Heyman, R. (2000). Hearing the voice of children with chronic illness. *Journal of Advanced Nursing*, *32*(4), 913–921.

Sawyer, S., & Patton, G. (2018). Health and well-being in adolescence: A dynamic profile. In J. Lansford & P. Banati (Eds.), *Handbook of adolescent development research and its impact on global policy* (pp. 27–45). Oxford University Press. https://doi.org/10.1093/oso/9780190847128.003.0002

Shaffer, R. (1983). *Beyond the dispensary*. AMREF (The African Medical and Research Foundation).

Sharpe, L., Coates, J., & Mason, C. (2021). Participatory research with young people with special educational needs and disabilities: A reflective account. *Qualitative Research in Sport, Exercise and Health*, *14*(3), 460–473. https://doi.org/10.1080/2159676x.2021.1952297

Schelbe, L., Chanmugam, A., Moses, T., Saltzburg, S., Williams, L., & Letendre, J. (2014). Youth participation in qualitative research: Challenges and possibilities. *Qualitative Social Work*, *14*(4), 504–521. https://doi.org/10.1177/1473325014556792

Schjellerup, H. (2021). Broken routines and space for breathing: Using photos as a participatory and collaborative research strategy. In T. Wulf-Andersen, R. Folleso, & T. Olsen (Eds.), *Involving methods in youth research. Reflections on participation and power* (pp. 95–124). Palgrave Macmillan. https://doi.org/10.1007/978-3-030-75941-4_5

Seland, I. (2024). Intersecting knowledge on young people's well-being and use of digital technology across contexts: A scoping review synthesis. In H. Holmarsdottir, I. Seland, C. Hyggen, & M. Roth (Eds.), *Understanding the everyday digital lives of children and young people* (pp. 433–464). Palgrave Macmillan. https://doi.org/10.1007/978-3-031-46929-9

Shamrova, D., & Cummings, C. (2017). Participatory action research (PAR) with children and youth: An integrative review of methodology and PAR outcomes for participants, organizations, and communities. *Children and Youth Services Review*, *81*, 400–412. https://doi.org/10.1016/j.childyouth.2017.08.022

Shier, H. (2001). Pathways to participation: Openings, opportunities and obligations. *Children & Society*, *15*(2), 107–117. https://doi.org/10.1002/CHI.617

Shortt, N., & Ross, C. (2021). Children's perceptions of environment and health in two Scottish neighbourhoods. *Social Science & Medicine*, *283*, 1–11. https://doi.org/10.1016/j.socscimed.2021.114186

Simons, D., De Bourdeaudhuij, I., Clarys, P., De Cocker, K., Vandelanotte, C., & Deforche, B. (2018). A smartphone app to promote an active lifestyle in lower-educated working young adults: Development, usability, acceptability and feasibility study. *JMIR Mhealth and Uhealth*, *6*(2), e44. https://doi.org/10.2196/mhealth.8287

Sinclair, R. (2004). Participation in practice: Making it meaningful, effective, and sustainable. *Children & Society*, *18*(2), 106–118. https://doi.org/10.10002/CHI.817

Sloper, P., & Lightfoot, J. (2003). Involving disabled and chronically ill children and young people in health service development. *Child: Care, Health & Development*, *29*(1), 15–20. https://doi.org/10.1046/j.1365-2214.2003.00315.x.

Society for Adolescent Medicine. (2003). Guideline for adolescent health research. A position paper of the Society for Adolescent Medicine. *Journal of Adolescent Health*, *33*(5), 396–409. https://doi.org/10.1016/j.jadohealth.2003.06.009

Sommer, M., Ibitoye, M., Likindikoki, S., & Parker, R. (2021). Participatory methodologies with adolescents: A research approach used to explore structural factors affecting alcohol use and related unsafe sex in Tanzania. *The Journal of Primary Prevention*, *42*(4), 363–384. https://doi.org/10.1007/s10935-020-00586-0

Stafford, A., Laybourn, A., & Hill, M. (2003). 'Having a say': Children and young people talk about consultation. *Children & Society*, *17*(5), 361–373. https://doi.org/10.1002/CHI.758

Stephens, M., Keiller, E., Conneely, M., Heritage, P., Steffen, M., & Bird, V. (2023). A systematic scoping review of photovoice within mental health research involving adolescents. *International Journal of Adolescence and Youth*, *28*(1), 2244043. https://doi.org/10.1080/02673843.2023.2244043

Supper, A. (2014). Sublime frequencies: The construction of sublime listening experiences in the sonification of scientific data. *Social Studies of Science*, *44*(1), 34–58. https://doi.org/10.1177/0306312713496875

Szabó, T., & Laihonen, P. (2024). Building participatory video projects for multilingual schoolscapes. *International Journal of Multilingualism*. https://doi.org/10.1080/14790718.2024.2312890

Teixeira, S., Augsberger, A., Richards-Schuster, K., & Martinez, L. (2021). Participatory research approaches with youth: Ethics, engagement and meaningful action. *American Journal of Community Psychology*, *68*(1–2), 142–153. https://doi.org/10.1002/ajcp.12501

Terry, L., & Cardwell, V. (2016). *Refreshing perspectives: Exploring the application of peer research with populations facing severe and multiple disadvantage*. Revolving Doors Agency.

The British Psychological Society. (2021). *Ethics guidelines for internet-mediated research* [Report]. The British Psychological Society.

Tsang, V., Fletcher, S., Thompson, C., & Smith, S. (2020). A novel way to engage youth in research: Evaluation of a participatory health research project by the international children's advisory network youth council. *International Journal of Adolescence and Youth*, *25*(1), 676–686. https://doi.org/10.1080/02673843.2020.1716817

Ugras, T., Rizvanoglu, K., & Gulsecen, S. (2022). New co-design techniques for digital game narrative design. *International Journal of Child-Computer Interaction*, *31*(1), Article 100441. https://doi.org/10.1016/j.ijcci.2021.100441

UNESCO. (2022). *Youth as researchers: Exploring the impact of COVID-19 on youth* [Global Policy Brief]. United Nations Educational, Scientific and Cultural Organization.

United Nations. (2023). *Sonification: A tool for research, outreach, and inclusion in space sciences*. United Nations Office for Outer Space Affairs.

Valdez, E., Valdez, L., & Garcia, D. (2021). Using participatory methods to enhance youth engagement in substance use research. *Health Promotion Practice*, *22*(6), 747–749. https://doi.org/10.1177/1524839921990005

Väljamäe, A., Steffert, T., Holland, S., Marimon, X., Benitez, R., Mealla, S., Oliveira, A., & Jordà, S. (2013). *A review of real-time EEG sonification research*. International Conference on Auditory Display 2013.

Van Staa, J. S., Latour, J., & Trappenburg, M. (2009). Exciting but exhausting: Experiences with participatory research with chronically ill adolescents. *Health Expectations*, *13*(1), 95–107. https://doi.org/10.111/j.1369-7625.2009.00574.x

Vyas, K., Louie-Poon, S., & Meherali, S. (2022). Development of an adolescent advisory group to inform sexual and reproductive health research for first- and second-generation immigrant adolescents in Canada: A community-based participatory action research study. *Frontiers in Reproductive Health*, *4*. https://doi.org/10.3389/frph.2022.930314

Walker, B., & Nees, M. (2011). Theory of sonification. In T. Hermann, A. Hunt, & J. Neuhoff (Eds.), *The sonification handbook* (pp. 9–40). COST.

Waller, A., Franklin, V., Pagliari, C., & Greene, S. (2006). Participatory design of a text message scheduling system to support young people with diabetes. *Health Informatics Journal*, *12*(4), 307–321. https://doi.org/10.1177/1460458206070023

Walus, B., Pauletto, S., & Mason-Jones, A. (2015). *Evaluating the use of sonification and music to support the communication of alcohol health risk to young people: Initial results*. The 21st International Conference on Auditory Display.

(2016). Sonification and music as support to the communication of alcohol-related health risk to young people. *Journal of Multimodal User Interfaces*, *10*, 235–246. https://doi.org/10.1007/s12193-016-0220-0

Wang, C. (1999). Photovoice: A participatory action research strategy applied to women's health. *Journal of Women's Health*, *8*(2), 185–192. https://doi.org/10.1089/jwh.1999.8.185

(2006). Youth participation in photovoice as a strategy for community change. *Journal of Community Practice*, *14*(1–2), 147–161. https://doi.org/10.1300/J125v14n01_09

Wang, C., & Redwood-Jones, Y. (2001). Photovoice ethics: Perspectives from Flint Photovoice. *Health Education & Behaviour*, *28*(5), 560–572. https://doi.org/10.1177/109019810102800504

Watson, D., Abbott, D., & Townsley, R. (2006). Listen to me, too! Lessons from involving children with complex healthcare needs in research about multi-agency services. *Child: Care, Health and Development*, *33*(1), 90–95. https://doi.org/10.111/j.1365-2214.2006.00670.x

Whitehouse, S., Lam, P., Balka, E., Mclellan, S., Deevska, M., Penn, D., Issenman, R., & Paone, M. (2013). Co-creation with TickiT: Designing and evaluating a clinical eHealth platform for youth. *JMIR Research Protocols*, *2*(2), 1–14. http://www.researchprotocols.org/2013/2/e42/

Whittaker, R., Merry, S., Dorey, E., & Maddison, R. (2012). A development and evaluation process from mHealth interventions: Examples from New Zealand. *Journal of Health Communication: International Perspectives*, *17*(1), 11–21. https://doi.org/10.1080/10810730.2011.649103

Whittington, E. (2019). Co-producing and navigating consent in participatory research with young people. *Journal of Children's Services*, *14*(3), 205–216. https://doi.org/10.1108/JCS-02-2019-0007

Wilson, N., Dasho, S., Martin, A., Wallerstein, N., Wang, C., & Minkler, M. (2007). Engaging young adolescents in social action through photovoice. *Journal of Early Adolescence*, *27*(2), 241–261. https://doi.org/10.1177/0272431606294834

Winton, A. (2007). Using 'participatory' methods with young people in contexts of violence: Reflections from Guatemala. *Bulletin of Latin American Research*, *26*(4), 497–515. https://www.jstor.org/stable/27733966

Wong, N., Zimmerman, M., & Parker, E. (2010). A typology of youth participation and empowerment for child and adolescent health promotion. *American Journal of Community Psychology*, *46*(1–2), 100–114. https://doi.org/10.1007/s10464-010-9330-0

World Health Organization. (2011). *mHealth: New horizons for health through mobile technologies: Second global survey on eHealth.* World Health Organization.

World Medical Association. (2008). *Declaration of Helsinki: Ethical principles for medical research involving human subjects.* https://www.wma.net/wp-content/uploads/2018/07/DoH-Oct2008.pdf.

Wrede-Jänti, M., Aapola-Kari, S., & Lahtinen, J. (2021). This is where we love to hang out! Interactive maps as a method of gathering information on the everyday lives of Finnish young people in longitudinal qualitative study. In T. Wulf-Andersen, R. Folleso, & T. Olsen (Eds.), *Involving methods in youth research: Reflections on participation and power* (pp. 241–260). Palgrave Macmillan. https://doi.org/10.1007/978-3-030-75941-4_10

Wridt, P. (2018). Young people's participation in program design research, monitoring and evaluation. In J. Lansford & P. Banati (Eds.), *Handbook of adolescent development research and its impact on global policy* (pp. 432–453). Oxford University Press. https://doi.org/10.1093/oso/9780190847128.003.0022

Wulf-Andersen, T., Folleso, R., & Olsen, T. (2021a). Involving methods in youth research: Reflections on participation and power. In T. Wulf-Andersen, R. Folleso, & T. Olsen (Eds.), *Involving methods in youth research: Reflections on participation and power* (pp. 1–16). Palgrave Macmillan. https://doi.org/10.1007/978-3-030-75941-4

(2021b). Power and reflexivity: Positions and positioning in involving research with young people. In T. Wulf-Andersen, R. Folleso, & T. Olsen (Eds.), *Involving methods in youth research: Reflections on participation and power* (pp. 17–46). Palgrave Macmillan. https://doi.org/10.1007/978-3-030-75941-4

Yamaguchi, S., Bentayeb, N., Holtom, A., Molnar, P., Constantinnescu, T., Tisdall, E., Tuong, J., Iyer, S., & Ruiz-Casares, M. (2023). Participation of children and youth in mental health policymaking: A scoping review. *Administration and Policy in Mental Health*, *50*(1), 58–83. https://doi.org/10.1007/s10488-022-01223-0

Yi-Frazier, J., Cochrane, K., Mitrovich, C., Pascual, M., Buscaino, E., Eaton, L., Panlasigui, N., Clopp, B., & Malik, F. (2015). Using Instagram as a modified application of photovoice for storytelling and sharing in adolescents with Type 1 diabetes. *Qualitative Health Research*, *25*(10), 1372–7382. https://doi.org/10.1177/1049732315583282

Young, B., Dixon-Woods, M., Windridge, K., & Heney, D. (2003). Managing communication with young people who have a potentially life threatening chronic illness: Qualitative study of patients and parents. *BMJ*, *326*(7384), Article 305. https://doi.org/10.11.36/bmj.326.7384.305

Young, E. (2021). *A participatory design method for qualitative data sonification* [Doctoral dissertation]. University of Lancaster.

Zeldin, S., Camino, L., & Mook, C. (2006). The adoption of innovation in youth organisations: Creating the conditions for youth-adult partnerships. *Journal of Community Psychology*, *33*(1), 121–135. https://doi.org/10.1002/jcop.20044

Zeldin, S., Petrokubi, J., & MacNeil, C. (2008). Youth-adult partnerships in decision making: Disseminating and implementing an innovative idea into established organizations and communities. *American Journal of Community Psychology*, *41*(3-4), 262–277. https://doi.org.10.1007/s10464-0089158-z

Zhang, L. (2023). The relationship between social media use and collective identity among the HIV/AIDS-affected adolescents: From the online social support perspective. *Vulnerable Children and Youth Studies*, *18*(3), 359–366. https://doi.org.10.1080/17450128.2023.2182932

Index

www.ingramcontent.com/pod-product-compliance
Ingram Content Group UK Ltd.
Pitfield, Milton Keynes, MK11 3LW, UK
UKHW020510100325
455776UK00024BA/606

9 781009 450478